Syrian Foreign Policy

Examining Syrian foreign policy during the Ba'th years from 1963 to 1989, this book traces the alliances of the Levantine country from a historical perspective and in the context of recent political developments.

Syrian Foreign Policy analyses the pivotal alliances of Damascus using a theoretical framework based on neoclassical realism, an approach which incorporates domestic factors such as the role of ideology within a realist perspective. Covering Syria's relations with Egypt, Iraq, Jordan, Saudi Arabia, Iran and the Soviet Union, it asks the question: what led to the formation of each alliance and what has caused either its break up or its continuation? Belcastro seeks to answer this question but also reflects on the country's foreign policy today and its broader implications for Syria and the whole region.

Making use of case studies to build upon a strong theoretical analysis, this book will be useful to students and scholars of Middle Eastern politics, as well as politics and International Relations more generally.

Francesco Belcastro is a Lecturer in International Relations at the University of Derby and a Fellow at the Centre for Syrian Studies, University of St Andrews.

Routledge/St. Andrews Syrian Studies Series
Edited by Professor Raymond Hinnebusch
Centre for Syrian Studies, University of St Andrews

Editorial Board:
David Lesch, *Trinity University, Texas*
Yezid Sayigh, *Carnegie Research Centre, Beirut*
Christopher Phillips, *Queen Mary University, London*
Eberhard Kienle, *Institut Francaise Proche Oriente (IFPO)*

This series aims to be the major venue for the dissemination of research on modern Syria. Although it will not neglect Syria's past, the focus is on the current conflict. It showcases work that locates cutting edge empirical research within innovative theoretical frameworks from all disciplines on, for example, social movements, civil wars, intervention, identity conflicts, failed states, post-war reconstruction, authoritarian resilience, and non-state governance.

The Muslim Brotherhood in Syria
The Democratic Option of Islamism
Naomí Ramírez Díaz

The Syrian Uprising
Domestic Factors and Early Trajectory
Edited by Raymond Hinnebusch and Omar Imady

State and Tribes in Syria
Informal Alliances and Conflict Patterns
Haian Dukhan

Syrian Foreign Policy
The Alliances of a Regional Power
Francesco Belcastro

For more information about this series, please visit: www.routledge.com/middle eaststudies/series/RSASSS

Syrian Foreign Policy
The Alliances of a Regional Power

Francesco Belcastro

LONDON AND NEW YORK

First published 2019
by Routledge
2 Park Square, Milton Park, Abingdon, Oxon OX14 4RN

and by Routledge
605 Third Avenue, New York, NY 10017

First issued in paperback 2020

Routledge is an imprint of the Taylor & Francis Group, an informa business

© 2019 Francesco Belcastro

The right of Francesco Belcastro to be identified as author of this work has
been asserted by him in accordance with sections 77 and 78 of the
Copyright, Designs and Patents Act 1988.

All rights reserved. No part of this book may be reprinted or reproduced or
utilised in any form or by any electronic, mechanical, or other means, now
known or hereafter invented, including photocopying and recording, or in
any information storage or retrieval system, without permission in writing
from the publishers.

Trademark notice: Product or corporate names may be trademarks or
registered trademarks, and are used only for identification and explanation
without intent to infringe.

British Library Cataloguing-in-Publication Data
A catalogue record for this book is available from the British Library

Library of Congress Cataloging-in-Publication Data
Names: Belcastro, Francesco, author.
Title: Syrian foreign policy : the alliances of a regional power /
Francesco Belcastro.
Description: Milton Park, Abingdon, Oxon ; New York, NY : Routledge,
2019. | Series: Routledge/St. Andrews Syrian studies series | Includes
bibliographical references and index.
Identifiers: LCCN 2019002226 (print) | LCCN 2019004463 (ebook) |
ISBN 9780429060779 (Ebook) | ISBN 9780429595189 (Adobe Reader) |
ISBN 9780429593895 (ePub) | ISBN 9780429592607 (Mobipocket
Encrypted) | ISBN 9780367183172 | ISBN 9780367183172(hardback) |
ISBN 9780429060779(ebook)
Subjects: LCSH: Syria–Foreign relations–20th century. | Syria–Foreign
relations–Middle East. | Middle East–Foreign relations–Syria.
Classification: LCC DS95.5 (ebook) | LCC DS95.5 .B45 2019 (print) |
DDC 327.5691–dc23
LC record available at https://lccn.loc.gov/2019002226

ISBN 13: 978-0-367-72982-0 (pbk)
ISBN 13: 978-0-367-18317-2 (hbk)

Typeset in Times New Roman
by Wearset Ltd, Boldon, Tyne and Wear

To Nada, and to Syria

Contents

Foreword		ix
Acknowledgements		x

PART I
Foreign policy and alliances   1

1	Introduction	3
2	The alliances of an authoritarian regime	13
3	Alternative explanations	32

PART II
The alliances of Syria   45

4	The foreign policy of Syria	47
5	Syria and Egypt	59
6	Syria and Jordan	71
7	Syria and Iraq	81
8	Syria and Iran	91
9	Syria and Saudi Arabia	103
10	Syria and the USSR	114

viii *Contents*

PART III
Alliances and beyond 127

11 Alliances and beyond 129

12 Conclusion 150

Bibliography 155
Index 166

Foreword

The study of alliances is one of the key concerns of realist analysis and Stephen Walt (1987) famously made a study of Middle East and North Africa alliances the main evidence for his claim that realist rules hold even in regions where shared identity might be thought to nullify them. Others have followed in his footsteps, seeking to trace out the interaction between the threats and interests fore-fronted by realism and ideational variables, including Rubin (2014), Haas (2012), Ryan (2009) and Gause (2003). Francesco Belcastro's volume, which deploys neoclassical realism to understand the impact of ideology on the effectiveness of power balancing through alliance making, is a valuable contribution to this on-going debate. The book is also valuable in that it makes the only systematic theoretically framed survey of Syria's alliances, looking at six pivotal alliances over a period of several decades. As such, the book is a welcome contribution to studies of Syria and its international relations and foreign policy. It therefore constitutes an important addition to the Routledge/St Andrews Series on Modern Syria.

Raymond Hinnebusch
St Andrews, January 2019

Acknowledgements

I would like to thank my family for their love and support, especially my mum Donatella and dad Claudio, my sister Ilaria, my nonni that are no longer with us and my nonna that still is, my aunts, uncles and cousins, particularly my Auntie Giovanna and my Uncle Enrico, the academics of the family. And my wife Nada, to whom this book is dedicated. You are the sweetest.

This book is largely based on my PhD dissertation. In St Andrews, I was lucky to work under the supervision of two great scholars. I owe a lot to both, at a professional as well as personal level. My first supervisor Professor Ray Hinnebusch provided guidance, support and feedback. Ray is a great academic and a true gentleman. Professor Nick Rengger was a constant source of encouragement and guidance. Nick was the kindest, most generous and brightest person I have ever met, and I miss him greatly.

I would also like to thank my colleagues and friends in St Andrews. Their friendship made my PhD years so enjoyable. I am so grateful; I would not hate you even if you were to become sad, boring, wannabe hipsters.

I am indebted to the many scholars that contributed to the project at different stages, and I regret not being able to mention them all. Louise Fawcett and Ryan Beasley were excellent examiners and their invaluable feedback made this book much better. The advice and encouragement I received at different stages from Adham Saouli, Jasmine Gani, Marwa Daoudy, Antonio Di Biagio Nicola Morfini, Roddy Brett, Fiona McCallum, Baris Cayli, Chris Philipps, Haian Dukhan, Edward Burke, Samir Al-Taqi, Özlem Tür, the 'Syrian gang', Clara Eroukhmanoff, Alex Nunn and many other colleagues and friends helped me cross the finish line. My Head of School and Head of Discipline at Derby, Phil Hodgson and Charlotte Hargreaves, respectively, helped me greatly by reducing my teaching load to allow me to complete the project.

The team at Routledge/Taylor & Francis as well at the copy-editors at Wearset have been incredibly supportive and patient. I would also like to thank the anonymous reviewers for their thorough work.

Finally, I would like to thank my friend Samhar, who is largely responsible for my falling in love with Syria, Lina for marrying him and inviting me to the wedding and Osama, Mudar and the guys for adopting me while I was there.

Part I
Foreign policy and alliances

1 Introduction

The topic of this book

The topic of this book is the alliances of Syria during the years between 1963 and 1989. Syria, the self-proclaimed 'beating heart of the Arab nation', played a pivotal role in regional politics. The alliances of Damascus have often been considered paradoxical and hard to explain. Allied to revolutionary Iran and at odds with Ba'thist Iraq, hostile or friendly towards the Gulf monarchies, on the brink of war with Turkey or Israel: the tale of Syria's regional relations is rich and complex. The country therefore provides a stern test for any theoretical explanation of alliances. Syrian politics has been dominated since the early 1960s by the Ba'th party, the purest expression of Pan-Arab ideology. The Ba'th, more than any other political force, incarnated the strive towards Arab unity as well as a strong anti-imperialist stance. How did this ideological orientation shape the alliances of Syria? Did the policy-makers in the country pursue a more narrowly defined national interest, or did they act according to the predicaments of Pan-Arabism? In order to answer this question, the book will look at the development of Syria's key alliances. It will show how, despite the continuity in Ba'th rule, the foreign policy of Syria changed dramatically throughout the years of this study. This readjustment was clearly shaped by changes at an external level, but it also coincided with the new leadership of Hafez Al-Assad. Under the new presidency Syria abandoned its stance of unlimited revisionism in favour of more limited regional goals. This foreign policy was more in tune with the geopolitical reality of the region, as it was based the power gap between Syria and its regional rivals.

This book is also a study of alliances more generally, albeit building on the Syrian case: how they are formed and why they endure or collapse. Alliances are a central component of a state's foreign policy. They are the cornerstone of every grand strategy, the most visible sign of continuity or rupture when a new regime comes to power. Furthermore, alliances shape history. To think of their relevance in world politics, one can try to imagine how different things could have been without the World War II alliance that defeated Nazi Germany and its allies, or how crucial the Israeli–American alliance has been to Middle East politics. This book focuses specifically on the alliances of one authoritarian regime,

4 *Foreign policy and alliances*

the Syrian Arab Republic. How did leaders in Damascus choose their allies? Were their choices driven by systemic or domestic considerations?

The argument

The question I seek to answer in this book is rather straightforward: what factors drove the Syrian state to form or break its alliances? Most of the explanations of Syrian (and more broadly Middle Eastern) alliances provided by the literature are based on structural realist or constructivist approaches. According to the former, alliances are mainly a reaction to a growth in power or threat by regional or international actors. For proponents of the latter, ideology, identity and perceptions (and in the case of Syria its Pan-Arabism) shape foreign policy and alliances. Both explanations, however, capture only partially the complex nature of Syrian alliances. Syrian foreign policy and alliances were clearly shaped by the difficult geopolitical environment in which the Syrian state found itself from its foundation. Surrounded by bigger and often hostile neighbours, Damascus often had to 'balance against threats'. Ideology, however, also played an important role. During most of the 1960s, Syria had been the maverick of Arab politics, a bastion of radical Pan-Arab ideology. Syrian policy-makers had shown a high degree of hostility towards other Arab powers, accused them of a lack of commitment towards the Pan-Arab cause. This changed sharply in the following decades, when Syrian foreign policy lost its ideological nature.

An approach based on neoclassical realism will allow a focus on the interaction of international and domestic factors and its effect on the alliances of Syria. This research maintains that the alliance choices of Syria have to be analysed within the broader context of a reshaping of the country's foreign policy. Syria's regional goal changed from unlimited to limited revisionism, leading to an adjustment in its alliance pattern. This change was a result of both systemic and domestic factors. The regional dynamics and unfavourable balance of power in the Middle East system shaped the alliance choices of Syria. This unfavourable balance of power was worsened by the 1967 rout at the hands of Israel. Despite this resounding defeat, Syrian foreign policy did not immediately adjust to the new situation on the ground. On the contrary, the Jadid regime in power during the last years of the decade pushed Syria towards more radical positions. Significant changes to Syrian foreign policy and alliances only took place in 1970 when the new regime led by Hafez Al-Assad took power.

Methodology and contribution

This book builds a model of alliances in order to explain the choices of the Syrian Arab Republic during the years between 1963 and 1989. A model differs from a theory as it does not seek to find 'laws' that apply to all cases but has the (rather less ambitious) goal to explain more specific phenomenon or phenomena. The model built by this analysis seeks to explain how an authoritarian regime chooses its allies. It recognises that alliance formation is a multi-layered and complex phenomenon. It therefore seeks to 'simplify' its different dimensions and provide a linear yet comprehensive explanation of the alliance process.

The model of the book is based on the neoclassical realist paradigm. The study is based in neoclassical realism inasmuch as it seeks to re-introduce some of the topics and analytical features of classical realism that had been left out from the realist mainstream with the positivist and structural turn. Neoclassical realism has been chosen because it allows the author to incorporate a domestic factor within a realist (and structural) based analysis. Classical and neoclassical realism are theories of foreign policy as well as theories of International Relations: a model based on these theories is therefore a better fit for a study that seeks to analyse outcomes at a state rather than systemic level.

This research is qualitative and based on the use of a limited number of case studies: one state and its key relationships. The analysis is divided in two parts: the first provides an overview of the foreign policy of the country to illustrate the change from unlimited to limited revisionism. The second part focuses on Syria's key relationships. For each alliance, the book provides a historical analysis in order to explain the formation, strengthening or termination of the alliance itself. The use of qualitative analysis and a small number of case studies presents both advantages and disadvantages. The use of quantitative analysis and statistical methods might have offered a broader, more comprehensive analysis of the issue. A mixed approach, using both quantitative and qualitative analysis, might have therefore been preferable for a study that aimed to create a theory of alliance formation in the mould of the balance of power. A qualitative approach has been chosen because of the specific focus of this study. This book focuses on the interaction between systemic and domestic factors. The complexity of this interaction would have been harder to capture in a quantitative analysis. The focus on a small set of alliances will allow an analysis of the details of the 'complex' relationship between systemic and domestic dimensions.

The six case studies of this book are Syria's relationships with Egypt, Iraq, Jordan, Saudi Arabia (also referred to as the KSA), Iran and the Soviet Union (referred to throughout this volume also as the USSR). This is by no means a comprehensive list of all the alliances of Syria. These case studies have been chosen because of their relevance based on two criteria.[1] The first is the presence of an alliance or a temporary alignment between the country and Syria during the period of this study. Countries such as Israel or Turkey, that had no relations or only hostile ones with Damascus during the years of this study, have been excluded. The second factor is the country's influence in the Levant sub-region during the period of this study. Countries such as Algeria have entertained positive relations with Syria, but because of their distance and relative lack of involvement in the Levant region, their influence remained largely symbolic. An extra-regional power such as the USSR has therefore been included because of its important role in regional politics.

The dates of the study have been chosen because of their relevance in Syrian and Middle Eastern politics. In 1963 the Ba'th party took power for the first time in the country. The Ba'th has ruled the country continuously since the 1963 coup

6 *Foreign policy and alliances*

d'état. The year 1989 is an important date for the Middle East as it is for world politics. During the Cold War the competition between the two superpowers had strongly influenced regional politics. In the aftermath of the collapse of the USSR, the Syrian regime had to readjust its foreign policy to a unipolar Middle East. This systemic change will represent the cutting off point for this study, although Chapter 11 of this volume will include a discussion of the alliances of Syria after 1989.

This research relies mostly on secondary sources. These include the main works on the modern history and politics of the Middle East and the Levant. The rich literature on the politics and external relations of Syria, as well as on other Middle Eastern countries, is also widely used. These secondary sources are in some sections complemented with newspaper and magazine articles from the period covered by this study.

This book seeks to contribute to two separate literatures. The first is the study of the alliances of Syria, and more broadly to the field of International Relations of the Middle East. The foreign policy of Damascus during these years is central to the politics of the Levant and the broader region. This book is also part of a broader literature (discussed later in this chapter, p. 8) that brings together International Relations theory and Middle Eastern studies. Several of these works, although different in terms of theoretical framework and scope of the analysis, seek to bring together structural and 'domestic/ideological' factors. This book contributes to this growing literature by putting forward a framework to understand the interaction between these two levels within the context of Middle Eastern politics. The second contribution is to the literature on alliances and particularly the neoclassical realist research paradigm. Most neoclassical realist works have so far focused on great powers and democratic regimes. The study of a regional power and an authoritarian regime will contribute significantly to this research agenda.

Key terms specified

Alliance

The term alliance has been used in different ways in the literature,[2] it is therefore useful to define what alliance means in this study. This research adopts the definition given by Stephen Walt:

> ... a formal or informal relationship of security cooperation between two or more sovereign states. This definition assumes some level of commitment and an exchange of benefits for both parties; severing the relationship or failing to honour the agreement would presumably cost something....[3]

Walt's definition has been chosen because it includes both 'long-term commitments' and short-term alignments. Furthermore, this definition emphasises the mutual exchange aspect of alliances.

Introduction 7

Ideology

Ideology is a concept that is frequently used in International Relations and more generally in social sciences. However, even a quick survey of the literature shows a certain degree of inconsistency in the use of the term. Ideology commonly indicates a certain set of beliefs or concepts (connected among them) that shapes how individuals or societies seek to organise their social interactions. Another important aspect of ideology is highlighted by Sartori, who defines ideology as 'A typically dogmatic, i.e. rigid and impermeable, approach to politics'.[4] Sartori's definition reflects the dichotomy between pragmatic and ideological approaches to politics. The former is more flexible and reactive to changing external circumstance, the latter guided by the set of principles that constitute the ideology. This dichotomy will be central to the study of alliances carried out by this study.

System

The International Relations literature offers different interpretations of what a system is. Robert Gilpin's seminal: *War and Change in World Politics*[5] provides the most articulated discussion of system and its influence on state's behaviour. In his study Gilpin adopts the definition of system given by Mundell and Swoboda:[6] 'A system is an aggregation of diverse entities united by regular interaction according to a form of control'. A state system is therefore composed of several actors (the states), that regularly 'deal' with each other, and whose behaviour is shaped by the system itself. Being part of one specific system rather than another therefore influences how states conduct their foreign policy, and particularly how they form alliances.

Region

This book deals with regions and regional powers. What constitutes a region? Buzan and Wæver provide a definition of region that will be adopted in this analysis:[7]

> Regions, almost however defined, must be composed of geographically clustered sets of such units–states–and these clusters must be embedded in a larger system, which has a structure of its own. Regions have analytical, and even ontological, standing, but they do not have actor quality.

Regions are subsystems within the broader world system: as such they have their own patters of interaction and their own distribution of power. They are not, however, isolated from the world system. In some cases (such as the region of this study, the Middle East) external actors play an important role in regional politics.

8 *Foreign policy and alliances*

Relevant literature

This study draws on several bodies of research. The first is the extensive literature on alliances present in both International Relations and foreign policy analysis. Attempts to bring together International Relations theories and Middle Eastern studies remain relatively rare.[8] One exception is represented by the *International Society and the Middle East: English School Theory at the Regional Level*[9] volume, edited by Barry Buzan and Ana Gonzalez Perez. This book contains a series of excellent chapters applying the key tenets of the English school to the region. Among the works on alliances that use the Middle East region as their case studies are Stephen Walt's structural realist *The Origins of Alliances*[10] and Michael Barnett's constructivist *Dialogues in Arab Politics.*[11] These two works are analysed in detail in Chapter 3 of this volume. Gause's work[12] focuses on threat perception and alliances in the Gulf region. Gause's main finding is that states prioritise aggressive intentions over aggregate power when deciding whether to balance. Looking at the case of Syria, Gause concludes that the alliance with Iran was mainly motivated by Iraq's aggressive intentions (rather than by Iraq's aggregate power). Michael Haas in *The Clash of Ideologies*[13] analyses the role of ideology in alliance formation. Haas also discusses the Syrian–Iranian alliance, concluding that despite ideological differences, systemic dynamics (such as the regional ideological multipolarity) pushed the two countries to align. Salloukh on the other hand focuses on the relation between regime autonomy and foreign policy in the Middle East region and analyses the competing theoretical approaches that have been applied to the region.[14] Paul Noble's influential work puts forward the idea of an 'Arab system' rather than a Middle East system.[15] Stephen David argues that in the Third World leaders balance against domestic threats rather than external ones.[16] His 'Omnibalancing Theory' seeks to correct the balance of threat by adding domestic threat. Weeks' work focuses on whether certain kinds of authoritarian regimes are more likely to go to war than others.[17] The author concludes that authoritarian regimes change significantly in terms of their war prowess according to aspects such as leader-domestic actor relations, kind of leader and domestic audience (particularly whether they are military or civilians). Hansen seeks to show how the systemic shift from bipolarity to unipolarity altered the dynamics of Middle Eastern politics.[18] Hansen's attempt is partially successful: while in cases such as the Yemen's reunification the effects of the end of bipolarity are clear, cases such as the Iraq wars present more complexity that make mono-causal explanations hard and rather unconvincing.

A growing literature of studies analysing the foreign policy of Levantine countries has developed. Lynch in *State Interests and Public Sphere* analyses how the foreign policy of Jordan is changed by an expansion of the public sphere.[19] His focus on the public sphere dimension allows the author to focus on how identities (and consequently foreign policies) are formed and changed. Lynch sees an area of potential interaction between rationalist and constructivist approaches. Like Lynch's work, Ryan's *Inter-Arab Alliances: Regime Security and Jordanian Foreign Policy* provides a theory-based analysis of the foreign policy of the Kingdom.[20] Ryan's main argument is 'that states align ... according to relatively narrow interests of regime security'. While maintaining that states do not have a 'national interest' as such, Ryan does focus on the interaction between the domestic and international. Furthermore, Ryan's work contains two chapters that focus specifically on Syrian–Jordanian relations. Laurie A. Brand's *Jordan's Inter-Arab Relations: The Political Economy of Alliance Making* represents one of the most comprehensive applications of political economy to the study of alliances.[21] Brand's work is particularly relevant to this study as the author underlines how Jordan's foreign policy was often formulated with domestic 'financial' considerations in mind. Brand's argument shares several aspects with this book's analysis of how Syrian foreign policy and particularly some of its alliances served 'domestic' purposes. Salloukh's remains one of the few studies that focuses on Lebanese foreign policy.[22] Salloukh analyses the interaction between domestic and international factors in the case of Lebanon, 'a polarised, regionally contested, and internationally entangled state.'[23] Fred Lawson's *Why Syria Goes to War: Thirty Years of Confrontation*[24] explains Syria's shifts from a more aggressive to more conciliatory stance with changes at domestic levels. Syria's involvement in external conflict is explained with changes at domestic level, and particularly in the economic model adopted by the country.

This book draws on the research tradition of political realism. Realism can be defined as a school of thought in only a very broad sense. Robert Gilpin defined it as a 'philosophical disposition'[25] given the limited number of assumptions shared by realists. Realism's fundamental assumptions have been listed by Randall Schweller and David Priess:[26]

> Assumption One: humans do not face one another primarily as individuals but as members of groups that command their loyalty.

> Assumption Two: international affairs take place in a state of anarchy.

> Assumption Three: the nature of international interaction is essentially conflictual.

> Assumption Four: power is the fundamental feature of international politics.

The concept of state goals used in this research is present in the work of classical realists, and particularly Arnold Wolfers.[27] Unlike structural/neorealism, classical realism differentiates states according to their foreign policy. Alliances in the work of classical realist authors are therefore shaped by the goals that states are pursuing: revisionist states will seek allies to challenge the balance in the system, status quo powers will look for other states willing to defend it. State goals were later recovered and used by neoclassical realist authors such as Randall Schweller.[28] Neoclassical realism seeks to bring together systemic elements (typical of structural realist analysis) and domestic elements. The work of

10 *Foreign policy and alliances*

authors such as Lobell *et al.* builds on the relation between external and internal dimensions, and how this interaction influences foreign policy outcomes.[29] This research draws on neoclassical realist scholarship inasmuch as it integrates a domestic variable (leadership ideological orientation) within a systemic framework.

Several works on the politics and international relations of the Middle East have informed this study. A prime example is the work of authors such as Hinnebusch[30] and Etheshami,[31] whose work greatly contributed to the theorisation of the Middle East system and its key features. Furthermore, this study is indebted to a rich body of literature that does not deal with alliances but explains the Arab state and the Syrian one and is therefore particularly relevant to the integration of the domestic dimension. These works include those by Ayubi[32] and Saouli[33] on the Arab state or Hinnebusch[34] and Perthes[35] on Syrian politics. Philipps' work provides an excellent analysis of the events that led to the 2011 uprising in Syria, that are discussed in Chapter 11.[36]

The development of a rich literature on regions and regional politics represents an important contribution to the International Relations literature: the increased relevance of regional interactions and the discipline's growing attention to regions as the main level of analysis. As Mark Beeson notes: 'One of the most widely noted and counter-intuitive features of the contemporary "global" era is that it has distinctively regional flavour'.[37] An example of this branch of literature is the work of Louise Fawcett on regionalism and alliances.[38] Scholars have analysed different aspects of this complex phenomenon: from the structural relevance of regions in the United States dominated world that emerged after the Cold War[39] to the role of regional institutions[40] or economic areas. Regions are clearly very relevant phenomena and, as Rick Fawn stresses, the subject of concurrent theories explaining their relevance and functions.[41] Particularly relevant to this analysis is the work by Buzan and Wæver on regional security, that provides the definition of region used by this study.[42]

The structure of this book

This booked is composed of three parts. The first comprises Chapters 1 to 3. Chapter 2 develops the model of alliances used by this research. Chapter 3 analyses two alternative explanations of the alliances of Syria, based respectively on structural realism and constructivism. Part II examines the foreign policy and alliances of Syria. Chapter 4 provides a brief overlook of the foreign policy of Syria. Chapters 5 through 10 each analyse one relationship between Syria and another country. Chapter 5 deals with the relationship with Egypt, Chapter 6 with Jordan and Chapter 7 with Iraq. Chapters 8, 9 and 10 deal with Iran, Saudi Arabia and the Soviet Union respectively. The third part is composed of Chapters 11 and 12. Chapter 11 sums up the analysis carried out in the previous chapters and looks at the alliances of Syria after 1989. Chapter 12 draws some final conclusions.

Notes

1 Lebanon has been excluded from the analysis because its political fragmentation and particularly its relationship with Syria made it difficult to classify its relationship as an alliance.
2 For instance, Glenn H. Snyder in *Alliance Politics* (Ithaca: Cornell University Press, 1997) includes in his analysis only 'formal' agreement, differentiating between alignments and alliances.
3 Stephen Walt, *The Origin of Alliances* (Ithaca: Cornell University Press,1987), 1.
4 Giovanni Sartori, "Politics, Ideology, and Belief Systems," *American Journal of Political Science* 63 (June 1969): 358–415.
5 Robert G. Gilpin, *War and Change in World Politics* (Cambridge: Cambridge University Press, 1981).
6 Robert Mundell and Alexander Swoboda, *Monetary Problems of the International Economy* (Chicago: University of Chicago Press, 1969), 393.
7 Barry Buzan and Ole Wæver, *Regions and Powers: The Structure of International Security* (Cambridge: Cambridge University Press, 2003).
8 Fred Lawson, "International Relations Theory and the Middle East," in *International Relations of the Middle East* (4th edition), ed. Louise Fawcett (Oxford: Oxford University Press, 2016).
9 Barry Buzan and Ana Gonzalez Perez, *International Society and the Middle East: English School Theory at the Regional Level* (Basingstoke: Palgrave Macmillan, 2009).
10 Walt, *The Origins of Alliances*.
11 Michael Barnett, *Dialogues in Inter-Arab Politics: Negotiations in Regional Order* (New York: Columbia University Press, 1998).
12 Gregory Gause III, "Balancing What? Threat Perception and Alliance Choice in the Gulf," *Security Studies* 13, 2 (2003): 273–305.
13 Michael Haas, *The Clash of Ideologies: Middle Eastern Politics and American Security* (Oxford: Oxford University Press, 2012).
14 Regime autonomy in regional foreign policy choices in the Middle East, see Bassel Salloukh, "Regime Autonomy in Regional Foreign Policy Choices in the Middle East: A Theoretical Exploration," in *Persistent Permeability?: Regionalism, Localism, and Globalization in the Middle East*, ed. Bassel Salloukh (London: Routledge, 2004), 81–103.
15 Paul Noble, "From Arab System to Middle Eastern System? Regional Pressures and Constraints," in *The Foreign Policies of Arab States: The Challenge of Globalization*, eds. Bahgat Korany and Ali E. Hillal Dessouki (Cairo: American University Press, 2008), 67–166.
16 Stephen David, "Explaining Third World Alignment," *World Politics* 43, 2 (January 1991): 233–256.
17 Jessica Weeks, *Dictators at War and Peace* (Ithaca: Cornell University Press, 2014).
18 Birthe Hansen, *Unipolarity in the Middle East* (New York: St. Martin's, 2001).
19 Marc Lynch, *State Interests in Public Spheres: The International Politics of Jordan's Identity* (New York: Columbia University Press, 1999).
20 Ryan R. Curtis, *Inter-Arab Alliances: Regime Security and Jordanian Foreign Policy* (Gainesville: University of Florida Press, 2009).
21 Laurie A. Brand, *Jordan's Inter-Arab Relations: The Political Economy of Alliance Making* (New York: Columbia University Press, 1994).
22 Bassel Salloukh, "The Art of the Impossible: The Foreign Policy of Lebanon," in *The Foreign Policies of Arab States: The Challenge of Globalization*, eds. Bahgat Korany and Ali E. Hillal Dessouki (Cairo: American University in Cairo Press, 2009), 283–317.
23 Ibid., 283.

12 Foreign policy and alliances

24 Fred Lawson, *Why Syria Goes to War: Thirty Years of Confrontation* (Ithaca: Cornell University Press, 1996).
25 Robert G. Gilpin, "The Richness of the Tradition of Political Realism," *International Organization* 38, 2 (Spring 1984): 287–304, 289.
26 Randall Schweller and David Priess, "A Tale of Two Realisms: Expanding the Institutions Debate," *Mershon International Studies Review* 41, 1 (May 1997): 7.
27 Arnold Wolfers, *Discord and Collaboration: Essays in International Politics* (Baltimore: Johns Hopkins University Press,1962).
28 Randall Schweller, "Unanswered Threats: A Neoclassical Realist Theory of Underbalancing," *International Security* 29, 2 (Fall 2004); Randall Schweller, "New Realist Research on Alliances: Refining, not Refuting, Waltz's Balancing Proposition," *American Political Science Review* 91, 4 (December 1997).
29 Steven Lobell, Norrin M. Ripsman and Jeffrey W. Taliaferro, eds., *Neoclassical Realism, the State, and Foreign Policy* (Cambridge: Cambridge University Press, 2009).
30 Raymond Hinnebusch, *The International Politics of the Middle East* (Manchester: Manchester University Press, 2003).
31 Anoushiravan Ehteshami and Raymond Hinnebusch, *The Syrian–Iranian Alliance: Middle Powers in a Penetrated Regional System* (Manchester: Manchester University Press, 1997).
32 Nazih Ayubi, *Over-stating the Arab State: Politics and Society in the Middle East* (London: I.B. Tauris, 2001).
33 Adham Saouli, *The Arab State: Dilemmas of Late Formation* (London: Routledge, 2012).
34 Raymond Hinnebusch, *Syria: Revolution from Above* (London: Routledge, 2001).
35 Volker Perthes, *The Political Economy of Syria under Assad* (London: I.B. Tauris, 1995).
36 Christopher Philipps, *The Battle for Syria: International Rivalry in the Middle East* (Yale: Yale University Press, 2016).
37 Mark Beeson, "Rethinking Regionalism: Europe and East Asia in Comparative Historical Perspective," *Journal of European Public Policy* 12 (2005): 969.
38 Louise Fawcett, "Alliances, Cooperation and Regionalism in the Middle East," in *International Relations of the Middle East*, ed. Louise Fawcett (Oxford, Oxford University Press, 2005).
39 Peter Katzestein, *A World of Regions: Asia and Europe in the American Imperium* (Ithaca: Cornell University Press, 2005).
40 See for example Louise Fawcett, "Exploring Regional Domains: A Comparative History of Regionalism," *International Affairs* 80 (2004).
41 Rick Fawn, "Regions and Their Studies: Where from, What for and Where to?," *Review of International Studies* 35 (2009): 5–34.
42 Buzan and Wæver, *Regions and Powers*.

2 The alliances of an authoritarian regime

This chapter builds a model that explains alliances: why they are formed and why they endure or are broken. A model is more limited (and surely less ambitious) than a theory. It does not seek to find laws that apply to a category of phenomena under all circumstances. A model seeks to explain a more specific set of relations or incidences, and as such it needs to be complemented with specific information regarding the case or cases analysed. The model built by this research analyses the alliance choices of an authoritarian regime, the Syrian Arab Republic. The model is based on the concept of state goals. State goals represent a state's attitude towards the regional system. They therefore indicate whether a state supports the (regional or international) system or seeks to challenge it, in other words, whether it is a status quo or revisionist power. The use of state goals allows a focus on the interaction between international and domestic factors. Whether a state is a status quo or a revisionist power depends first on external and systemic factors such as its strength and position within the system. Domestic factors will also affect a state's goals and consequently its alliances.

The model

State goals

How do states choose their allies? When do they form or break alliances? The model in this study explains the alliance process using the concept of state goals. A state goal is a unit-level factor that represents a state's attitude towards the global or regional system. As Noble points out, systemic variables on their own can explain policy outcomes (such as alliances) only to a certain extent.[1] In the words of the Canadian scholar: 'there is an important intervening variable that must be added: the positional characteristics (a mixed of systemic and unit-level factor) of the state whose policy is being analysed'.[2] Unit-level adds another dimension to structural 'threat-reaction'-like alliance formation process, rather than replacing it completely. The use of unit-level variables is an important feature of the work of classical realists such as Wolfers[3] and Morgenthau.[4] These authors differentiated among states according to their attitude towards the

14 *Foreign policy and alliances*

system, using categories such as revisionist and status quo powers. Classical realism's concept of states goals has traditionally been criticised because of its reliance on intuition. State goals could potentially be infinite, and particularly difficult to define and rank. This study addresses this limitation by using what Renning and Ringsmose described as updated classical approach. This approach:

> ... will be classical because it is attuned to the subject matter of politics, and it will be updated because it draws on Max Weber's method of ideal types (Weber, 1949). These ideal types are feats of imagination, combining interpretive and scientific conceptions of knowledge, which emphasize certain aspects of reality, and the purpose of using them, of matching ideals with reality, is to understand concrete instances or cases of reality.[5]

The use of 'ideal-types' allows one to divide states into a finite number of categories according to their state goals. A similar argument is put forward by Randall Schweller with his 'balance of interests' theory.[6] States in his analysis are classified according to their satisfaction with the system. On one end of the scale there are unlimited revisionists (that Schweller defines as 'wolves'); states that seek to challenge the system at any cost. At the other end, there are status quo defenders (called 'lions'); powers that are happy with the system and willing to defend it against potential challengers.

Three ideal-types of regional states are included in this analysis: status quo power, limited revisionist and unlimited revisionist.[7] These categories are present, albeit with different names and definitions, in the work of most classical realists. Status quo powers are states that are content with the regional system and their position within it, and therefore seek to defend this balance. As Schweller suggests: 'The primary goal of these states is consistent with contemporary realism's assumption of actors as defensive positionalists and security-maximizers'.[8] Unlimited revisionists on the other hand are states that are highly dissatisfied with the regional system. These states tend to be status quo powers' nemesis, for they seek to subvert the same regional balance that status quo powers seek to defend. Their emergence is often associated with what Robert Gilpin defines as systemic wars.[9] Limited revisionists have an 'intermediate' stance towards the regional system. They are not satisfied with their position in the system, but they seek to achieve only moderate change. This can be because they are relatively small powers that cannot aim at regional domination or because their claims can potentially be accommodated within the existing system.

System and state goals

What factors determine state goals? In line with realist tradition, the first dimension of goal formation in this model is external and structural. In the work of all realist scholars, whether classic, structural or neoclassical, the system represents the first determinant of state behaviour and alliances. The system where a state is

The alliances of an authoritarian regime 15

located, the distribution of power and a state's relative position will be the first factors shaping state goals. A strong power that benefits from the balance of the system will most likely be a defender of the status quo. A rising state that sees its power growing in comparison with other regional states on the other hand will seek to improve its position within the system.[10] The systemic component included in this model is the distribution of power. This concept refers to how military, economic, technical and other capabilities are distributed in a system. The distribution of power shapes relations among regional actors and particularly alliances. Changes in the distribution of power are, in structural analysis, the main 'engine' behind the alliance formation process. Systems are classified based on their power distribution as unipolar, bipolar and multipolar.

Unipolarity is the concentration of an overwhelming amount of military, economic and other resources in one state. Unipolar regions are systems in which the hierarchy is uncontested: countries might potentially be unhappy with the regional system, but do not have the resources to challenge it. What can alter this situation is the emergence of another pole within the region[11] or the 'entrance' of a new actor in the regional system, an external power that did not previously play a key role in the region, but can now constitute a pole, on its own or aligned with another regional actor. As unipolar systems are characterised by a lower level of conflict, the drive towards alliance formation is less strong than in other systems.

A system is commonly defined as bipolar when two poles have a comparable share of military, economic and cultural resources, whilst being significantly superior to any other actor. A bipolar system sees a contested hierarchy. The distribution of power per se pushes the two poles to collide. The regional hierarchy is a result of this tension; the rules of the system are rules of competition. Bipolarity itself drives states towards alliance formation; both because there is higher systemic pressure towards it and because of the costs of neutrality.

A system is defined as multipolar when three or more poles have a comparable level of military, economic and cultural power, whilst being significantly superior to any other actor. A multipolar region is characterised by the interaction between several actors having similar, or at least comparable, power and prestige and therefore capacity to shape the system. The rules of the system are decided by the interaction of three or more actors rather than 'imposed' by one power.

Changes in the distribution of power are in structural analysis the main factors driving changes in foreign policy and alliances. Changes create incentives or threats that drive states to form (or break) alliances. For instance, the rise of a new regional power will push other states to form a coalition to keep the system in balance. The emergence of a new potential hegemon could turn what was previously a revisionist power into a defender of the status quo. Because the power relations between actors in any system are not fixed, and can always change, there is always at least the potential for a realignment of alliances.[12] Different factors can lead to changes in state goals, from diverging rates of growth among actors in the system to military or technological improvements.[13] In some case

16 *Foreign policy and alliances*

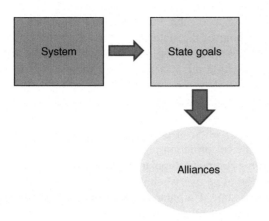

Figure 2.1 Structure and state goals.

the entry in the system of a new actor that was previously marginal but is now seeking to play a more central role can also lead to a structural change.

The distribution of power on its own can explain structural phenomena such as the formation or breaking of coalitions of states, or whether systemic wars are more likely to occur. When looking at state goals, however, the distribution of power has to be complemented with the state's specific position within the system itself. What is the state's relative strength compared with the other regional actors? Is the power of the state growing or diminishing compared with the other powers in the system? For instance, in a bipolar system a state's goals and its alliance patterns will change significantly based on whether the state is the strongest pole of power, a second pole seeking to challenge the first or a smaller state.

Ideological orientation

Whilst structural changes are a key factor shaping state behaviour, this model maintains that the systemic level is not the only determinant of state goals. Non-structural factors can, under some circumstances, modify state behaviour. Intervening factors at different levels can be used to explain variations from structural analysis, but this study focuses specifically on the domestic dimension. The domestic variable used here is leadership's ideological orientation. A leadership's ideological orientation refers to the instances where leaders will formulate their policies (and in the context of this study, pursue different alliances) not on the basis of external constraints and incentives, but rather on the basis of their ideological beliefs or preferences.

Several unit-level variables have been used by neoclassical realist scholars. Ripsman, Taliaferro and Lobell[14] divide the factors used by different realist scholars into four categories:[15] 'images and perceptions of state leaders, strategic

The alliances of an authoritarian regime 17

culture, state- society relations, and domestic institutional arrangements'. The first category refers to how the preferences, ideology or personalities of the foreign policy executive (FPE) affect foreign policy outcomes. Strategic culture refers to the role of beliefs, ideologies or culture at state or society level. State society relations is a broad category that incorporates all those variables that relate to 'the character of interactions between the central institutions of the state and various economic and/or societal groups'.[16] The fourth category, domestic institutions, refers to how state institutions, norms and processes influence foreign policy outcomes.

The choice of an appropriate intervening variable is central to both the analysis' explanatory power and its theoretical consistency. The selection of a domestic variable can follow a deductive or inductive process.[17] The process has to consider both the phenomenon or phenomena that the study seeks to explain and the specific features of the case analysed. In the case of this model, what domestic factors influence state goals and consequently its alliances? The case analysed by the study should also guide the selection of the domestic variable. It is in fact reasonable to expect that this interaction will change on the basis of the state/states that the researcher is seeking to analyse. While in a presidential system the potential repercussions of electoral results might influence foreign policy choices, leaders in authoritarian regimes might be more concerned with their relations with some key actors rather than broader public opinion. The choice of leadership ideology in this model is inductive and stems from the features of the subject of this study.[18] The role of trans-national ideologies is extremely prominent in the Middle East region. It is therefore reasonable to expect that ideology will shape state behaviour and alliance preferences of regional leaders. Syria was, during the heyday of Pan-Arabism, the self-styled beating heart of the Arab nation. The Ba'thist regime in power from 1963 up to the modern day represented, together with its Iraqi counterpart, the purest expression of Pan-Arab ideology. This research therefore incorporates leaders' ideological orientation in order to analyse how this affected the foreign policy and alliances of Damascus.

Leadership ideology falls within the first category of Ripsman *et al.*; the image and perception of state leaders. The focus of the domestic analysis therefore is on the FPE, the individuals that 'sit at the helm of the state.'[19] The FPE includes those policy-makers that oversee states' foreign policy. Who these individuals are and what their relationship with other domestic actors is can vary significantly among different regimes. Regardless of how it is composed, the FPE is the central actor in most neoclassical realist-based models, as it represents the point of interaction between international and domestic levels. The FPE is typically concerned with both international and domestic considerations. Its main function is to formulate the state's external foreign policy, but it is composed of individuals that are also domestic political actors.

'Ideological' leaderships will pursue goals dictated by their political beliefs, sometimes disregarding material elements such as their states' capabilities or their national interest.[20] A Marxist regime committed to 'exporting the revolution'

18 *Foreign policy and alliances*

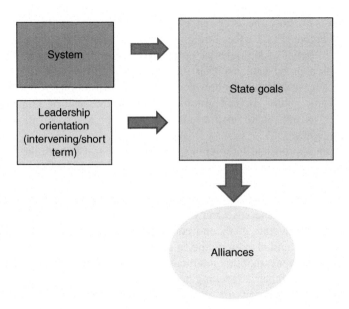

Figure 2.2 Ideology.

will not formulate foreign policies based on a narrow concept of state interest, but will rather seek to put into place policies it sees as beneficial to this goal. A political leader with strong beliefs (for instance one that is ardently religious) could follow the goal of imposing its ideological views on its neighbours rather than pursuing more narrowly defined state goals. A more pragmatic leadership on the other hand will seek to select and implement the policies that it sees as best suited to the country's national interest. Ideological and pragmatic regimes will therefore react differently to external constraints and incentives. The foreign policy selected by more pragmatic regimes will closely resemble the prediction of realist analysis; policy-makers will seek to implement the foreign policy they see as more beneficial to their states. Ideological leaders on the other hand will 'elaborate' external changes through the prism of their broader goals.

Structural and domestic dimensions

Systemic and domestic factors both influence a state's attitude towards the system; how do the two interact? What determines whether policy-makers will follow the threats and incentives from the system or their own ideological preferences when the two clash? In this model (as in most realist analysis) the system determines what could be defined as 'expected behaviour'. The distribution of power and a state's position within the system will therefore initially determine its state goals. Divergences from these expected alliances depend on the leadership's ideological orientation. Domestic intervening variables have been defined by Lobell an 'imperfect transmission belt' between the incentives and constraints coming from the external dimension and the policies that the state implements.[21]

Leadership ideology therefore explains variations from 'expected structural' behaviour. For instance, a state led by highly ideological leaders seeking to impose their view over the system can be an unlimited revisionist regardless of its relative strength. On the other hand, a state that has the power to challenge the existing system and impose itself as a regional leader could fail to do so because of its leadership's ideological orientation. In the long-term, we can expect that state goals will tend to align themselves with the structure of the system. The system can 'punish' ideological foreign policies that do not consider the balance of power and therefore drive policy-makers to moderate their stance. 'Extreme' foreign policy can also lead to the replacement of the leadership with a less ideological one. In the short-term, however, the foreign policy chosen by ideology-driven FPE can vary significantly from the expected realist predictions.

State goals and alliances

Having analysed how the international and domestic dimension influence state goals, this section will analyse the relation between state goals and alliances. States have different goals and carry out different strategies to reach them. These goals and strategies will shape their alliance preferences. Policy-makers operate in the international or regional arena, seeking to achieve some goals or objectives, whether they entail defending or challenging the status quo, seeking to improve their position or defending what they already have. Alliances are functional to reaching these goals. This does not necessarily mean that states will seek allies that have the same goals, but rather those that are 'functional' to achieving their goals. Which ally provides the best guarantee against a growing threat or which is more likely to help a state pursue its long-term goals? Which would help the state to defend, challenge or subvert the current status quo? The ideal-types included in this study describe state's expected alliances based on their attitude toward the system.

'Status quo powers' are stability seekers. These states are happy with the balance in the system that they perceive as favouring them. Their goal is therefore to maintain, and when possible consolidate, the system as it is. In terms of alliances, status quo powers are typically 'balancer against'. These states will seek to balance the threat represented by a regional revisionist, particularly unlimited ones aiming at subverting the system. Status quo powers will therefore seek other status quo powers seeking to protect the existing status quo. But they will also seek to ally themselves with those states that can contribute to keep the system in balance as they are pivotal to regional stability. This often means luring limited revisionists away from unlimited revisionists. England's European policy from the sixteenth century onwards has been defined as the archetype of balancing and status quo policy. The country consistently aligned itself against the growing European power to keep the continent in balance.

20 *Foreign policy and alliances*

'Unlimited revisionists'' attitude towards the system places them at the opposite of status quo powers. The latter seek to defend the balance in the system, unlimited revisionists on the other hand seek to subvert a balance that they see as penalising them. Unlimited revisionists are typically growing powers that see the existing system as obsolete and (crucially) not beneficial to them. These states do not seek small changes within the system; they rather want to challenge the system altogether. Their foreign policy is often driven by ideological considerations; these states seek to reorder the system according to their principles and values (as well as placing themselves on top of the new system). These states are 'risk-takers' as they are extremely unsatisfied with their conditions in the system and they are willing to take great risks to improve their position.[22] In terms of alliances, unlimited revisionists will seek to gather the support they can to challenge the balance in the system. Unlimited revisionists will seek to win the support of other regional actors by promising them an improved position in the system. However, because their foreign policy is often extreme and uncompromising, unlimited revisionists will be at odds with those powers that they see as ideological rivals. Furthermore, as they aim to challenge the existing regional balance, they will not only look for allies to assist them in their quest to challenge the system, but also attempt to target the allies of the main status quo powers. Historical examples of unlimited revisionists are Hitler's Germany or Napoleon's France.[23] These powers did not seek to simply change the system in which they were located, but rather to turn it completely upside down (and place themselves at the top of the system itself).

'Limited revisionists' are unhappy with their position in the system, but they are more risk adverse than unlimited revisionists. They could be relatively smaller powers that do not have the same ambitions as unlimited revisionists. Their claims can be accommodated within the existing system, and therefore they do not seek to change the systemic balance altogether, but rather to improve their position within it. These states seek allies that might support their aspirations but are more 'moderate' and ready to compromise than unlimited revisionists. Limited revisionists often form alliances with unlimited revisionists to take advantage of their attempts to challenge the regional system. But they can also align themselves with status quo powers if these partnerships are functional to reaching their (limited) goals. Ultimately, these states seek allies that might favour the achievement of their objectives, whether by providing military and strategic support, adding diplomatic leverage or providing economic help. Pre-World War II Europe provides an example of limited revisionist in Fascist Italy.[24] Because of its (relatively) low military and economic capabilities, the country did not seek regional or world domination but rather an improvement of its position. The rising power of Nazi Germany provided Fascist Italy with an opportunity to bandwagon and seek to profit from its attempt to challenge the system.[25] Yet Italy's aspirations were not necessarily incompatible with the existing system and could have been accommodated by the status quo powers had Mussolini have chosen a different path.

The model and Syria

How did international and domestic factors shape Syria's foreign policy and alliances? Syria has often been described as 'revisionist', a state whose main goal was to challenge the regional status quo rather than defend it. Syria's geopolitical conditions and the dynamics of the Middle East region undoubtedly constrained the foreign policy options available to Syrian policy-makers. Syrian foreign policy, however, changed significantly during the years of this study. For most of the 1960s the country was 'the maverick' of Arab politics, a radical and often unpredictable regional player.[26] In the 1970s the foreign policy of the country became more moderate and less ideological. Damascus' alliance pattern changed accordingly. The alliance policy of Syria before 1970 was uncompromising towards all states accused of being pro-Western and not committed enough to the support of the Arab and Palestinian cause. In the following decade the alliance policy of the country became more flexible and characterised by openings towards regional powers previously regarded as ideological rivals. Using the ideal-types developed in the previous section, the foreign policy of the country changed from unlimited to limited revisionism. These changes, however, did not happen only because of systemic factors but also because of domestic changes, and particularly the end of the Jadid era and takeover of power by Hafez Al-Assad and his men.

System: Syria and the Middle East region

The system (or subsystem) where a state is located, the pattern of interaction among key actors and the position of a state within the system itself are key determinants of foreign policy. The regional dynamics of the Middle East have strongly shaped Syria's regional goals. In the previous section (p. 15) a multipolar region was defined as a system in which three or more poles have a comparable level of military, economic and cultural power, whilst being significantly superior to any other actor. The relationship among these poles of power is what defines the regional dynamics, the overall pattern of relations among regional actors: 'Regional powers define the polarity of any given RSC ... their capability looms large in their regions ...'.[27] The Middle East during the period analysed was characterised by the presence of several regional poles. Egypt, Turkey and Iran are undoubtedly poles of power because of their size and population[28] (as well as because of the role they historically played in the region). Iraq's size (over $400,000 \text{ km}^2$) and population (approximately 10 million inhabitants in 1970, and up to 17 million by 1989) combined with its resources (oil and gas) and central position in the region make it a pole of power.[29] Saudi Arabia's resources and consequent economic power, as well as its centrality in the Gulf, make it an important regional player. Israel's limited territory (around $20,000 \text{ km}^2$) and population (around 3 million inhabitants in 1970, up to 4.5 million by 1989) mean that it does not qualify it as a pole of power.[30] Nonetheless, Israel is – according to most indicators – the most developed country in the

22   *Foreign policy and alliances*

region and possesses what is by far the most modern and efficient army.[31] Israel is a case of a potential great power that lacks recognition by other members of the system to be fully become such.

It can also be argued that the Syrian Arab Republic itself constituted a pole of power, at least from the 1970s onwards. Syria's population and territory are smaller than all the previous states except Israel. The country does not have the military might and economic and technological strength of Israel, nor the resources of Iraq or Saudi Arabia. Furthermore, the country was in the first years of its history a weak and fragmented actor. Since 1970 though, Hafez Al-Assad progressively managed to bring the country and Syrian foreign policy under his control in the following decades. Syria's geopolitical centrality, projection of power in the neighbouring countries (particularly Lebanon) as well as the key role it played in the anti-Western and anti-Israeli coalition (particularly after Egypt's 'jump' into the Western camp) allows one to define the country as a regional pole of power.[32] The Middle East is therefore clearly a multipolar system: seven states have been defined as 'poles of power'.[33]

Relations among key actors were characterised by competition more than cooperation. The Middle East is a region of aspiring and failed hegemons. Louise Fawcett stresses how several actors (such as Egypt or Iraq) have historically had hegemonic aspirations, while some others that would have the potential (such as Israel or Iran) are prevented by factors such as their regional isolation, domestic structure and (in the case of Israel) external dependence.[34] Since the end of World War II, the region has seen plenty of conflict and instability. The main regional actors were often engaged in conflicts, directly or through their proxies. Some of these, such as the 1980–1988 Iraq–Iran war, were what Gilpin defines as hegemonic or unlimited wars, conflict during which the parties seek to overthrow the opponent rather than inflicting a tactical defeat.[35] Inter-state relations in the region were also often characterised by attempts to overthrow other states' regimes and by constant support of domestic opposition groups.

Within the region, Syria is both important and vulnerable. Its centrality and relative strength make the country particularly exposed to external threats. As Hinnebusch notes, Syria lacks both strategic defensive depth and borders that are easy to defend.[36] It is a relatively small country surrounded by bigger and often aggressive neighbours. Iraq, Turkey and particularly Israel all represented significant threats to Damascus during the period of this study. Israel showed itself to be willing and able to increase its territory at the expense of neighbours and Syria in particular. With the 1967 war, Syria lost the strategic Golan Heights to Israel, further worsening its geopolitical conditions vis-à-vis its neighbour. The 1973 war restored the shattered Arab pride and dramatically improved Al-Assad and Syria's status in the Arab arena but did little to improve Syria's geopolitical deficit. While Israel was perceived as a threat by different Arab powers, the sense of being locked in a confrontation with Tel Aviv was primarily felt by Syrian policy-makers.[37] Israel arguably represented the biggest threat to Syria during most of the period of this study, but certainly not the only one. Neighbouring Iraq had historical claims on Syria,

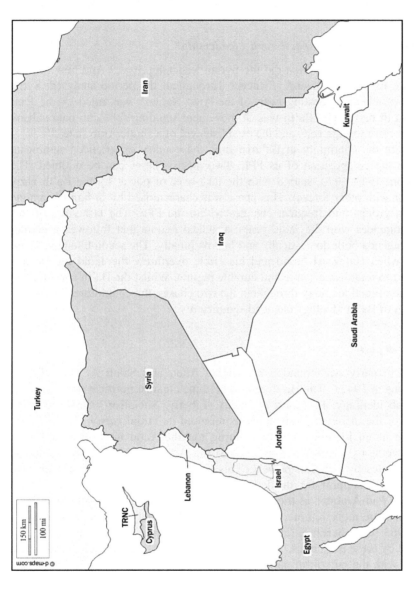

Map 2.1 Map of the Middle East (TRNC, Turkish Republic of Northern Cyprus).

24   *Foreign policy and alliances*

developed during the years of the Hashemite monarchy. These territorial ambitions remained a feature of Syrian–Iraqi relations during the Ba'thist years.[38] Turkey had openly threatened to intervene against the Syrian regime during the 1950s and the two countries had often been at odds over the vital issue of the waters of the Euphrates river.

Domestic: from ideological to realist leadership?

What ideological orientation did the Syrian leadership have? And how did this influence its state goals and alliances? Throughout the period analysed, Syria, the self-proclaimed 'beating heart of the Arab Nation', was ruled by the Pan-Arab Ba'th party. The Ba'th was 'a movement standing for Arab nationalism, freedom from foreign rule, and the establishment of a single Arab state'.[39]

Despite the continuity in Ba'thist rule, the country experienced significant shifts in the composition of its FPE. Two macro-phases can be outlined. The first, from 1963–1970, started with the take-over of power by the Ba'th party (together with other forces). This phase was characterised by in-fighting among different groups and frequent changes within the FPE. The last years of this phase coincides with the Jadid years: a radical regime that followed a revolutionary agenda both domestically and internationally. The second, longer, phase started when Hafez Al-Assad and his circle overthrew the Jadid regime and managed to establish a stable and durable regime. Whilst the Ba'th party represented the official ideology throughout the two phases, the commitment and interpretation of Ba'th ideology changed significantly.

The Ba'th party

The Ba'th party was founded by Michel Aflaq and Salah Al Din Bitar in Damascus in 1947.[40] The Ba'th represented the clearest political declination of Pan-Arab ideology. Its motto of 'Unity, Liberty, Socialism' shows how the merger of the different Arab states represented its initial *raison d'etre*.[41] Pan-Arabism as an ideology sought to bring together (and in its first and most radical versions unify in a single state) the Arabs that had been divided in several states by colonial powers. This focus on anti-Imperialism translated into a strong support for the Palestinian cause that became more and more central to Pan-Arabism as the possibility to unify all Arabs in a single political entity became more remote. The different leaders that controlled the country from 1963 were therefore (at least to a certain degree) committed to and constrained by these principles. This commitment to the Pan-Arab cause was often at odds with the pursuit of narrower national interest. In the case of Syria, the proximity to Israel made support of the Palestinian cause particularly dangerous.[42] Tel Aviv had shown willingness to punish the support of Palestinian resistance with military actions. Despite their allegiance to Ba'thism, the regimes that dominated Syria differed significantly in their foreign goal priorities. The first Ba'thist leaderships prioritised Pan-Arabism over the narrower

The alliances of an authoritarian regime 25

Syrian national interest. This policy was overturned in the aftermath of 1970, when Hafez Al-Assad and his circle took power of the country.

1963–1970: radical Ba'th regimes

The Ba'th party emerged as the dominant force in Syrian politics after years of domestic fighting. Its success appeared highly unlikely just a few years earlier, when the party was one of several actors in Syrian foreign policy and the charismatic attraction of Nasser led to the merger of Syria and Egypt.[43] The short-lived experience of the United Arab republic represented a key step in the Ba'th party's journey towards power.[44] In 1963 the party first rose to power through a coup d'état carried out together with Nasserites and other officers. In the unstable phase that followed, the executive powers were formally split between a 20-man committee (called the National Council of Revolutionary Command) and a government led by Ba'thist ideologue Salah Al-Din Bitar.[45] The National Council was composed of representatives of the different factions that had carried out the coup d'état: Ba'thists, Nasserites and Independents. Despite this complex system, the real power was held by a small number of officers, most of them Ba'thists or Nasserites. Within a few months the two groups were at odds over the crucial theme of the relationship with Egypt, while unity talks between Cairo, Damascus and Baghdad were taking place.[46] The Ba'th came out on top in the military showdown that followed due to its control of key positions within the army.[47] Having prevailed in the confrontation with their most dangerous rivals, the Ba'th officers proceeded to settle the score with the remaining 'independent' faction led by then Defence Minister Ziad Al-Hariri. The Ba'th party was in power on its own for the first time in Damascus.

By the time it had taken power in Damascus, the Syrian Ba'th had morphed into a different party from the one imagined by its founder Michel Aflaq. The Syrian Ba'th (like its Iraqi counterpart) had seen bitter infighting between different factions. The middle class-based 'civilian' leadership that had been the founding force behind the party had gradually been pushed aside by a younger generation of Ba'thists.[48] This faction, often referred to as Neo-Ba'th, was mainly rooted in the Syrian military. Most of its members were soldiers of lower-class background coming from Syria's numerous minorities. The first public face of the Ba'th regime was General Amin Al-Hafiz. This Sunni soldier from Aleppo was Prime Minister and Chief of Staff during the first Ba'thist years. Initially put in place to govern on behalf of Syria's emerging strong man, Salah Jadid, the general attempted to grow his own power by aligning himself with the civilian faction led by Michel Aflaq.[49] This led him to clash with the Military Committee dominated by Jadid himself. Another showdown followed, with Al-Hafiz and his allies on one side and Jadid and his on the other.

The February 1966 coup d'état that followed resulted in Salah Jadid and his circle assuming direct power. The government that was established was, in the words of Patrick Seale: 'The most radical that Syria had ever experienced'.[50] Salah Jadid assumed the (rather unambitious) role of 'Secretary of Ba'th Regional Command', leaving eye-catching jobs to other personalities. Three 'radical

26 *Foreign policy and alliances*

doctors' took the most visible positions: Nur Al-Din Al-Atassi (Head of State), Yusuf Zayin (Prime Minister) and Dr Ibrahim Maklus (Foreign Minister). The three had been voluntary medics in Boumedienne's forces in Algeria during the 1954–1962 war against the French. This experience had contributed to radicalisation of their opposition to colonial powers. This ideological inclination was shared by most of the men in power, including Salah Jadid. In the realm of foreign policy this translated into a strong opposition towards 'conservative' powers such as Saudi Arabia, seen as closely aligned to the imperialist cause. It also meant strong competition with states whose ideology was a different version of Pan-Arabism, be it Nasser's Egypt or post-1968 Ba'thist Iraq. The support of the Palestinian cause and the pursuit of a 'socialist revolution' became the priorities for the new Ba'thist regime.[51] The radical leftist policies put into place by the Jadid regime alienated significant sectors of Syrian society and threatened to undermine the recently established Ba'thist control of the country. It was, however, the Pro-Palestinian stance and particularly the decision to allow Palestinian guerrillas to operate from Syrian territory that created more problems to the regime in the short term. Syria had an important role in the growth of Palestinian militias from 1964 onwards. This was intended by Syrian policy-makers as a retaliation against the frequent border skirmishes that inevitably saw Israel punishing the vastly inferior Syrian army. The inability or unwillingness to restrain Palestinian militias was, however, one of the key factors that led to the Syrian–Israeli escalation.

The 1967 war was a watershed in regional politics. The defeat represented a turning point in Syrian domestic politics too. The dominant Jadid faction reacted to the defeat by doubling its efforts to reshape Syrian society. On the other hand, the Minister of Defence Hafez Al-Assad and his supporters favoured a 'national' approach centred on the reconstruction of the Syrian army and on the need to recover the Golan Heights. In foreign policy, Al-Assad favoured a less confrontational approach towards fellow Arab states.[52] The 1970 Black September crisis is the episode that best illustrates the different approaches to foreign policy and particularly to the Palestinian resistance. After months of tension, King Hussain of Jordan moved to crush Palestinian militias that were threatening his control over the Kingdom.[53] The Palestinians asked Syria to support them, and the then-Minister of Defence responded by providing weapons and diplomatic support. As the crisis worsened, Al-Assad sent a division of his army to support the Palestinian guerrillas.[54] However, when he was met with a robust Jordanian reaction (and with the threat of an Israeli or Western intervention) Al-Assad refused to commit his air force and decided to extract his troops. This half-hearted intervention confirms that Al-Assad, whilst not indifferent to the Palestinian cause, had grown to prioritise Syrian national interest. A few months later Al-Assad moved to oust Salah Jadid and his circle out of power.

1970 and the 'moderate' Ba'th regime

The 1970 coup d'état was another intra-Ba'th struggle, the results of several months of struggle between the two strong men of the country. Jadid and

Al-Assad were the last remaining members of the Military Committee that had taken over the party and the country. They were both Ba'thist and Alawites. To the outside world, differences in their political views were hardly discernible. The two men were, however, extremely different in terms of personality, and the men that governed the country with and for them were very different. Crucially, unlike his predecessor, Al-Assad was able to consolidate the power in his hands and gradually establish complete control over the country. The consolidation of power in the hands of the President represented a trade-off. The process of selection and implementation of policies became more effective and 'rational' according to Syria's geopolitical conditions by progressively becoming the exclusive realm of a man and his close circle.[55]

The man who was to rule the country for 30 years was born in the village of Qurdaha near Latakia on 6 October 1930. Originally peasants, his family had grown to the status of minor notables and were well known within the Alawi community of the area. Like many members of his long-discriminated sect, Hafez Al-Assad sought in the militancy of the Ba'th party and career in the Syrian army a way to overcome the limitations of his background.[56] When he took over power, Assad was able to impose his control over the country as he quickly moved to shape Syrian domestic and foreign policy. The Black September events clearly showed the difference in conception of foreign policy between Jadid and Al-Assad. The main difference was not one of political beliefs; by all accounts both Jadid and Al-Assad were committed Ba'thists, men of the Pan-Arab left and stanch supporters of the Palestinian cause. What clearly separated Al-Assad from Jadid and his circle was how these beliefs could be translated into foreign policy. Jadid and his group had a strong sense of 'mission': Syria as a centre of the Arab world could not limit its foreign policy to national goals.[57] Al-Assad had learnt the hard lesson of realpolitik from the 1967 defeat. Rhetoric commitment to the Pan-Arab cause was not going to solve Syria's foreign policy dilemmas and was instead alienating other Arab states that were potential allies. Without giving up its support for the Palestinian cause, Al-Assad also believed that, given the reality on the ground, Syria and the Arabs had to operate to change the balance of power in their favour rather than pursuing the unrealistic goal of eliminating Israel from the map. Jadid's foreign policy was one of ideology and principles; Al-Assad's was rooted in geopolitical realities.[58]

Differences between the two Ba'thist regimes were not limited to foreign policy but also extended to their different views of society. Observers of Middle Eastern politics have often underlined how the Al-Assad regime owed its longevity to the inclusion of social groups that had been hostile towards previous regimes. The 'Corrective' movement led by Al-Assad aimed at reversing some of the excesses of the previous era, and particularly those 'leftist' economic policies that had alienated big sections of Syrian society. This allowed the regime to open up to a broad coalition of forces that had previously been antagonised by the radical measures of the Jadid years. Sectors of the bourgeoise of main Syrian cities proved to be a great asset to the regime.[59] At the same time, the increase in

28 *Foreign policy and alliances*

the size and scope of the bureaucratic machine proved to be a further factor of strength for the regime.

The broadening of its social base, together with the political and diplomatic capital that Al-Assad obtained because of the much-improved performance in the 1973 war, allowed the Syrian leadership to strengthen its grip on the country.[60] In key sectors the policy process was based on the interaction between the centres of power: the President, the army and the party. However, the balance of forces between the three changed significantly. Throughout the first half of the 1970s the presidency was the most powerful of the three centres but could not 'effectively or safely govern without the army or the party. The army and the party are parallel structures. Both are sources of elite recruitment and political influence'.[61] This included Vice-President Khaddam and senior high-ranking generals such as Hikmat al-Shihabi and Mustafa Tlas.[62] These individuals were initially more than advisors to the President. Kissinger observed in the aftermath of the 1973 war how Al-Assad had to discuss his next steps in negotiations with the country's top leaders, in sharp contrast with the Egyptian President Sadat that was able to decide on his own without a need to consult.[63] Al-Assad's leadership in the field of foreign policy was consolidated throughout his first decade of leadership: by the 1980s foreign policy had become his exclusive realm. Within less than a decade Syria had become what Hinnebusch defines as a 'presidential monarchy',[64] a state where foreign policy (and therefore alliance choices) are the exclusive realm of the President and his close advisors.

System and ideology: Syria as a revisionist state

The dynamics of Middle Eastern politics and particularly Syria's placement within the system were in many ways 'extreme' and shaped Syria's state goals and alliances. The Middle East as a multipolar 'system of competition' constrains state behaviour more than comparatively less conflict-ridden regions. Within this system, Syria was a middle-sized power surrounded by bigger and often threatening neighbours. This geopolitical reality shaped Syrian foreign policy. Within the context of Middle East regional dynamics, Syria could not be a status quo power, for there was no favourable status quo to defend. The revisionism of Damascus depended mostly on the unfavourable geopolitical situations under which the state gained its independence. Syria did not, however, possess the resources to be an unlimited revisionist, a state seeking to alter completely the regional balance. Its power and size compared with other regional actors only allowed it to be a limited revisionist. Syria could operate to modify a system that it perceived as hostile and unfavourable, rather than subverting the regional balance altogether.

Despite this stringent systemic and geopolitical conditions, Syrian foreign policy in the pre-1970 phase does not appear to follow closely systemic logics. During years between 1963 and 1970 Syria was an unlimited revisionist seeking to subvert the systemic balance. The regime in Damascus was both uncompromising in its support of the Palestinian cause and hostile towards states it

The alliances of an authoritarian regime 29

considered as 'ideological rivals'. This is particularly evident in the aftermath of the1967 debacle. The defeat at the hands of Israel dramatically tilted the regional balance in favour of Tel Aviv. Rather than addressing the unfavourable balance of power that emerged from the 1967 war by balancing against the Israeli power, the Syria Ba'thist leadership increased its hostile rhetoric towards fellow Arab states. The Jadid regime proved to be implacably hostile to the Gulf monarchies even though these powers represented a potential source of support useful in addressing the gap with Israel. This policy was not reversed until the 1970 regime change that saw Hafez Al-Assad and his circle taking power. The new leadership imposed a significant change on Syria's overall foreign policy. The scaling down of Syria's goals meant that these were now more in tune with the constraints of Syrian geopolitical constraints.[65] The most evident sign of this change was a radical change in alliance policy. The next chapters will look at two alternative explanations of the alliances of Damascus.

Notes

1 Paul Noble, "Systemic Factors Do Matter: Reflection on the Use and Limitations of Systemic Analysis," in *Persistent Permeability: Regionalism, Localism and Globalization in the Middle East*, eds. Bassel Salloukh and Rex Brynen (Aldershot: Ashgate Publishing, 2004), 34.
2 Ibid., 34.
3 Arnold Wolfers, *Discord and Collaboration: Essays on International Politics* (Baltimore: Johns Hopkins Press, 1962).
4 Hans J. Morgenthau, *Politics Among Nations: The Struggle for Power and Peace* (New York: Knopf, 1948).
5 Sten Renning and Jens Ringsmose, "Why are Revisionist States Revisionist? Reviving Classical Realism as an Approach to Understanding International Change," *International Politics* 45 (2008): 32.
6 Randall Schweller, "Bandwagoning for Profit: Bringing the Revisionist State Back in," *International Security* 19, 1 (Summer 1994): 72–107.
7 These are not all of the 'typologies of states' but rather only those that are relevant to this analysis. Other ideal-types include hegemonic powers (in what some authors define as 'hierarchical regions') or small powers (what Schweller defines as 'lambs').
8 Schweller, "Bandwagoning for Profit," 101.
9 Robert G. Gilpin, *War and Change in World Politics* (Cambridge: Cambridge University Press, 1981).
10 The use of state goals seeks to incorporate purely structural 'balance of power'-like alliances. States are survival-seekers, and therefore tend to react to external threats by balancing against it. But states are not only survival-seekers, and therefore do not form alliances only as a reaction to changes in the balance of power or to react to growing threats.
11 In *War and Change in World Politics*, Gilpin shows how, given the different growth rates of different states and the problems of allocating and distributing the resources necessary to maintain its role, a hegemonic power is likely to face a challenger at some stage.
12 Gilpin, *War and Change*.
13 Ibid., Chapter III.
14 Norrin M. Ripsman, Jeffery W. Taliaferro and Steven E. Lobell, *Neoclassical Realist Theory of International Politics* (Oxford: Oxford University Press, 2016), ch. III.
15 Ibid., 58.

30 Foreign policy and alliances

16 Ibid., 71.
17 Ibid., 109.
18 Ibid., 121.
19 Ibid., 61.
20 It is important to stress how this statement is not in contrast with realist logic, only with structural realist logic. Structural realists see a state's policy choices as a direct product of incentives and constraints coming from the system. Classical realism on the other hand contains elements that could be defined as 'normative': leaders can decide to ignore systemic imperatives but in doing so they act against 'national interest'.
21 Steven E. Lobell, Norrin M. Ripsman and Jeffery W. Taliaferro, "Introduction," in *Neoclassical Realism, the State, and Foreign Policy*, eds. Steven E. Lobell, Norrin M. Ripsman and Jeffery W. Taliaferro (Cambridge: Cambridge University Press, 2009).
22 Schweller, "Bandwagoning for Profit."
23 Ibid., 112.
24 Randall Schweller, "Neorealism's Status-Quo Bias: What Security Dilemma?," *Security Studies* 5 (1996): 90–121.
25 Schweller, "Bandwagoning for Profit."
26 Raymond Hinnebusch, *Syria: Revolution from Above* (London: Routledge, 2001).
27 Barry Buzan and Ole Wæver, *Regions and Powers: The Structure of International Security* (Cambridge: Cambridge University Press, 2003), 37.
28 Egypt had a population of around 36 million inhabitants in 1970 and 55 million in 1989 in a territory of around one million km^2, and is the biggest Arab state as well as the biggest country in the region. Turkey's population exceeded 34 million inhabitants in 1970 and 53 million in 1989 while its territory extends for nearly 800,000 km^2. Furthermore the state enjoys a crucial geopolitical location that makes it a key factor in regional politics. Iran is a bigger territory than both of these states, at over 1.6 million km^2 and with a population of nearly 28 million inhabitants in 1970 and nearly 55 million in 1989. Data from "World Bank Open Data," The World Bank, accessed 9 September 2017, https://data.worldbank.org/.
29 The World Bank, "World Bank Open Data."
30 Ibid.
31 Israel has traditionally shown little restraint in using this military superiority in successive military confrontations with its neighbours.
32 Syria enjoyed prestige, in the sense this term as used by Robert G. Gilpin (*War and Change*); this prestige allowed the country to play a role in many ways more important than pure power would have allowed it to do.
33 While another classification based on different principles might result in a smaller number of 'poles', no criteria would result in less than three powers, the minimum requirement for a system to be considered multipolar.
34 Louise Fawcett, "Alliances and Regionalism in the Middle East," in *International Relations of the Middle East* (3rd edition), ed. Louise Fawcett (Oxford: Oxford University Press, 2013).
35 Gilpin, *War and Change*, 199.
36 Hinnebusch, *Syria*, 137.
37 Patrick Seale, *Assad of Syria: The Struggle for the Middle East* (London: I.B. Tauris, 1988), 185.
38 Hinnebusch, *Syria*.
39 John F. Devlin, "The Baath Party: Rise and Metamorphosis," *The American Historical Review* 96, 5 (December 1991): 1396.
40 Eberhard Kienle, *Ba'th vs Ba'th: The Conflict between Syria and Iraq 1968–1989* (London: I.B. Tauris, 1990), 3.
41 Devlin, "The Baath Party."
42 Hinnebusch, *Syria*, 141.

The alliances of an authoritarian regime 31

43 Kienle, *Ba'th vs Ba'th*, 12–13.
44 Seale, *Assad of Syria*.
45 Ibid., 79.
46 Malcolm H. Kerr, *The Arab Cold War: Gamal Abd Al-Nasir and his Rivals, 1958–1970* (3rd edition) (Oxford: Oxford University Press, 1971), 68–75.
47 Seale, *Assad of Syria*.
48 Devlin, "The Baath Party," 1403.
49 Kerr, *The Arab Cold War*, 119–120.
50 Seale, *Assad of Syria*, 104.
51 Hinnebusch, *Syria*, 45.
52 Seale, *Assad of Syria*, 151.
53 Avi Shlaim, *Lion of Jordan: The Life of King Hussein in War and Peace* (London: Penguin Books, 2017), 311.
54 Kerr, *The Arab Cold War*, 149.
55 Raymond Hinnebusch and Anoushiravan Ehteshami, "The Foreign Policy of Syria," in *The Foreign Policy of Middle Eastern States*, eds. Raymond Hinnebusch and Anoushiravan Ehteshami (Manchester: Lynne Rienner, 2003), 141–166.
56 Seale, *Assad of Syria*.
57 Ibid., 132–135.
58 Ibid., 169–175.
59 Hinnebusch, *Syria*, 61–62.
60 Batatu shows how this control remained based on the support of the Alawite community and of rural sectors of society, see Hanna Batatu, "Some Observations on the Social Roots of Syria's Ruling Military Group and the Causes for its Dominance," *Middle East Journal* 35, 3 (Summer 1981): 331–344.
61 Amos Perlmutter, "The Comparative Analysis of Military Regimes: Formations, Aspirations, and Achievements," *World Politics* 33, 1 (October 1980): 115.
62 Seale, *Assad of Syria*, ch. XII.
63 Mohammad Heikal, *The Road to Ramadan* (London: Collins, 1975).
64 Hinnebusch, *Syria*, 63.
65 Ibid., 146.

3 Alternative explanations

This chapter looks at two theoretical frameworks and their explanations of Syria's foreign policy and alliances. International Relations as a subject is characterised and enriched by the images provided by different theoretical approaches. A brief study of two different paradigms will complement and frame the model of this analysis. The two theories chosen are structural realism and constructivism. Selecting two frameworks to analyse a central topic such as alliances inevitably implies a degree of subjectivity, for many other works or approaches could have been included.[1] The two theories have been chosen because of their importance in the literature as well as because of their similarities with the argument of this book. These two frameworks represent central traditions within the field and have been applied to the foreign policy of Syria or to its alliances. Furthermore, both structural realism and constructivism are connected to the model of this analysis. Structural realism represents the starting point of any analysis based on neoclassical realism. The model in this book seeks to update and build on this theory rather than rejecting it completely. Constructivism is a broad theoretical approach that became central to the study of International Relations from the 1990s onwards. The branch of constructivism analysed in this study focuses on the role of ideology and how it shapes state behaviour. Ideological orientation is the domestic-level factor integrated in this analysis.

Structural realism has been the dominant realist paradigm since the publication in 1979 of the *Theory of International Politics* by Kenneth Waltz.[2] While its predominance within the realist tradition has been challenged by the emergence of neoclassical realism, structural realism remains an important paradigm in the study of alliances. In 1987 Waltz's most distinguished student, Stephen Walt, published *The Origins of Alliances*,[3] to date the most developed defensive realist theory of alliance formation. Walt applies his theory of alliance formation, the 'balance of threat', to the Middle East region between 1958 and 1979. His analysis seeks to evaluate whether balancing or bandwagoning are the most common reaction to threats. The constructivist paradigm refers here to the work of Michael Barnett[4] and Murhaf Jouejati.[5,6] This is not the only analysis of how ideology affects state behaviour: another notable example is Mark Haas' *Clash of Ideology*.[7] The constructivist/institutionalist framework has been chosen because of its focus on ideology. This research concentrates on the role of that Pan-Arabism has in shaping state foreign policy. Testing this concept is particularly interesting in the case of Syria, the self-proclaimed 'beating heart of the Arab nation'. The modern Syrian state was a product of colonial divisions, without any previous history as an independent entity. Its political identity was therefore often defined as belonging to the larger Arab nation rather than the 'national' state.

Structural realism

The structural realist framework, and more specifically the balance of threat, has several points in common with this study. The model of this book seeks to incorporate and build on the balance of threat-like alliance formation rather than rejecting it. In line with neoclassical realist research, this analysis maintains that balancing against power or threat is one of the causes that leads states to ally. Structural realism (or neorealism) imposed itself as one of the dominant paradigms in International Relations in the 1970s, as part of the wider positivist wave in the social sciences. Neorealism is primarily a theory of International Relations rather than a theory of foreign policy. It therefore focuses mainly on systemic outcomes rather than state behaviour (such as foreign policy or alliances). Several authors have, however, developed the work started by Kenneth Waltz, working towards making the structural realist paradigm more useful at foreign policy level. One of these authors is Stephen Walt, Kenneth Waltz's former PhD student at the University of California, Berkeley. In *The Origins of Alliances* Walt builds on the traditional 'balance of power' to create his theory of alliance formation: the balance of threat.[8] The central tenet of the balance of threat is that states will form alliances as a response to perceived dangers from other actors in the system. Differently from what happens in the traditional balance of power, an increase in the strength of one actor will not necessarily drive other states to balance against it. States will instead form alliances as a reaction against growing (perceived) dangers, that Walt measures by introducing four parameters of threat evaluation. These parameters are geographical proximity, offensive capabilities, offensive intentions and aggregate power. Aggregate power refers to a state's military and economic strength, population size as well as to its technological and industrial development.[9] A state that has great power is perceived as a bigger threat by regional actors. Geographical proximity refers to the idea that states are more threatened by actors nearby than by those situated far away. This has to do mainly with the idea of power projection: even powerful states struggle exerting their influence on regions that are located far away from their territory. It is therefore normal that states will feel more threatened by neighbouring countries than by countries situated far from them. Offensive power is 'the ability to threaten the sovereignty or territorial integrity at an acceptable cost'.[10] Offensive power therefore indicates how easily a state can 'translate' its power into military capabilities. The final parameter is aggressive intentions. With this parameter Walt introduces a more direct reference to 'threat perception': states will

34 Foreign policy and alliances

be more threatened by states that they consider more likely to attack them. This could be because they consider a particular state to be overall expansionist and aggressive, or because they feel that the state is particularly threatening towards them.

The addition of these variables makes the balance of threat much more relevant than the traditional balance of power at foreign policy level. The main aim of Walt's research is, however, still systemic, looking at whether balancing[11] is more common than bandwagoning.[12] Walt singles out the circumstances under which a state is more likely to balance or bandwagon. He finds that small states are more likely to bandwagon than bigger states, mainly because small states have got little to gain from joining a defensive coalition.[13] Furthermore, states are more likely to bandwagon when there is a lack of potential allies.[14] Finally, states are more likely to balance in peacetime or when the outcome of a conflict is unsure, while they are more likely to bandwagon in the last phases of a war when the outcome of the conflict is certain.[15]

Two other aspects included by Walt are particularly relevant to the foreign policy of Syria: the role of ideology and transnational penetration as factors influencing alliances.[16] In Walt's work, some ideologies will create 'solidarity' among states and therefore favour the formation of an alliance between them. Other ideologies can have the opposite effect, particularly: 'when the ideology calls for the members to form a centralised movement obeying a single authoritative leadership, the likelihood of conflict among the members in increased'.[17] The relevance of ideology will largely depend on the threats that the state faces. When a state is relatively secure, ideology will play an important role. When a state is under immediate treat, it will seek allies regardless of their ideology. Transnational penetration, defined as 'the manipulation of one state's domestic political system by another',[18] also affects the potential formation of alliances. Yet Walt outlines how this falls short of being a causal correlation, as 'widespread contacts between two states are ... as likely to be the result of common interests and a close alliance as they are to be the cause of them'.[19] Both ideology and transnational penetration are in Walt's analysis as secondary factors that affect the formation of alliances and are subordinated to structural factors.

The balance of threat and the alliances of Syria

What does the balance of threat say about the alliances of Syria? Given its geopolitical conditions, Syria should be an ideal candidate for balance against threat behaviour. The country has in fact constantly faced external threats from different neighbouring countries including Israel, Turkey and Iraq. Applying Walt's four parameters of threat evaluation, these states all represented (at different stages and in some cases at the same time) significant threats to Damascus. Accordingly, the foreign policy and particularly the alliances of Syria should follow quite closely a balance of threat logic. Walt applies the balance of threat to the Middle East region, including therefore Syria and includes in his study the alliances of the main Middle Eastern states and external actors involved in the system during 1955–1979.[20] In this way, he identifies 36 alliance commitments, 12 of which involve Damascus (in one case as a member of the United Arab Republic rather than on its own). Six of them refer to the period analysed by this study.[21] Walt divides the period of his study in two phases, the first going from 1955 to the 1967 war and the second from 1967 to the 1979 Camp David Accords.

According to Walt, the first phase was dominated by three developments. The first was the attempt by Nasser's Egypt to establish its control over the Arab world.[22] These attempts failed because of the formation of counter-coalitions of states threatened by Egypt's predominance. The second factor was the Arab–Israeli conflict and particularly the presence of Israel.[23] Opposition to Tel Aviv during those years is an aspect shared by all Arab states; these states, however, disagreed on how to deal with Israel. The third trend was the increase of a super-power's presence in the region.[24] Both the United States and the USSR strengthened their involvement in the region by building closer relations with regional actors. This increased involvement added a further dimension to regional relations.

These three structural changes deeply affected the foreign policy of Syria. The relationship with Egypt in particular was central to Damascus' foreign policy and alliances. Egypt was, during these years, both a potential threat and an ally against Israel. Walt focuses specifically on the year 1963, undoubtedly a crucial phase for the regional system. Walt interprets the signing of a Union Pact between Egypt, Iraq and Syria as an alliance, although a short-lived one. He maintains that the three parties 'establish a formal union in order to promote Pan-Arab ideal'.[25] Quite interestingly, Walt indicates this alliance as a reaction against the threat represented by Egypt itself, with Syria and Iraq bandwagoning and Egypt balancing (against a threat that Walt does not specify).[26] More convincing is the explanation given for the other 1963 alliance, the one between Syria and Iraq. Walt sees this alignment between the two Ba'th powers emerging as a reaction against the threat represented by Egypt. In particular it was 'Nasser's hostility towards the Ba'th'[27] that pushed the two countries towards forming a union.

Walt also focuses on the 1966–1967 relations between Syria and Egypt. He explains the alignment between the two Arab powers as a balancing act against the Israeli threat (with Jordan bandwagoning). According to Walt, this alignment was also one of the key factors leading to the Six Day War. The signing of a defensive pact between Nasser and the NeoBa'th in Syria was crucial to the start of the war. In Walt's interpretation, Nasser signed the agreement in the hope of controlling the radical Syrian regime. The Egyptian leader found himself engulfed in a confrontation with Israel, but also became more belligerent, mostly due to the support he obtained from the Soviet Union and fellow Arab states.[28] Walt sees this support as the final push towards the war.

Moving on to the 1967–1979 phase, Walt sees two main trends shaping regional politics (together with the involvement of superpowers in the region).

36   *Foreign policy and alliances*

The first is the presence of a new main regional threat. The 1967 war reduced the danger represented by Egypt and increased that of Israel. This initially led to more inter-Arab cooperation, but in the aftermath of the 1973 war the main Arab powers split over how to approach the topic of peace with Tel Aviv.[29] The second trend is the decline in the importance of Pan-Arabism as a factor shaping inter-Arab politics. Because ideology became gradually less relevant, 'material interests' became more important than competition over a central role in the Arab world.[30]

The threat represented by Israel is seen by Walt as the key factor behind the establishment of the 1973 war alliance. Walt identifies this as a tripartite alliance formed by Syria, Egypt and Saudi Arabia against the threat represented by Israel, with Jordan: 'bandwagoning with Israel by limiting its participation'.[31] The three countries joined forces (military ones for Syria and Egypt, financial and diplomatic for Saudi Arabia) to balance against the danger represented by another regional actor, in this case Israel. An important factor in the formation of this alliance was the improvement in inter-Arabs relations: 'With Nasser's death and Assad's ascendance in Syria, the last obstacles to effective re-alignment were removed'.[32] During the heydays of Pan-Arabism Nasser represented a threat to other Arab states, and his rivalry with the Syrian and Iraqi Ba'th had caused divisions in the Arab system. In the aftermath of the 1973 conflict the alliance collapsed, and the two Arab powers faced the negotiations separately. Walt sees the development of the peace process itself as the main factor that separated Syria and Egypt: 'the pressure of peace-making that drove them apart'.[33] This pressure led to a return to the pattern of competition that had characterised Syrian–Egyptian relations before the establishment of the 1973 war alliance.

Another three alliances involving Syria were, in Walt's view, established as a result of developments in Arab–Israeli relations: the 1975–1977 Syrian–Jordanian and 1978 Syrian–Iraqi alliances, and the Steadfastness Front. In the case of the Syrian–Jordanian alliance, it was the Sinai II agreement and the side-lining of both Jordan and Syria that led to a sudden improvement in the relationship.[34] The joint military exercise and military coordination between the two countries were a response to this isolation. Walt, however, indicates that Syria and Jordan were balancing against the threat represented (quite peculiarly) by the United States and Iraq.[35] According to Walt, the establishment of an alliance between the two states that were ideological rivals had also been made possible by the declining relevance of Pan-Arabism. The détente collapsed in the aftermath of the Camp David agreements because of King Hussein's unwillingness to openly condemn the Egyptian move, as well as his refusal to join the Steadfastness Front.

The Steadfastness Front was formed by the 'radical' powers opposed to Sadat's initiative: Syria, Libya, South Yemen, Algeria and the Palestine Liberation Organization. Walt dedicates little attention to this alliance, that he sees as largely symbolic and with the goal of pressuring Sadat into rejecting the peace process with Israel. Tel Aviv and Cairo are in this case indicated as the main threat that led to the formation of the alliance. More important in Walt's analysis, and certainly more central to Syrian's broader foreign policy, was the 1978 alignment with Iraq. This brief détente represents one of the most puzzling aspects of regional politics in the late 1970s. Walt sees the rapprochement between Baghdad and Damascus as a result of changes in regional policies, and particularly Egypt's new foreign policy. Egypt's defection to the pro-American camp and its path towards peace with Israel represented a threat to both Syria and Iraq. According to him the two countries were: '... united by their opposition to Egypt's actions, alarmed by Israel's invasion of southern Lebanon in March 1978, and concerned by the rise of Shi'ite fundamentalism during the Iranian revolution, the two Ba'ath states momentarily suspended their long-standing differences'.[36] The short-lived union was therefore a consequence of the rise of mutual threats and primarily the country's isolation after Egypt's defection. The alignment was short lived because it was 'undermined by the burden of past hostility and by each side's refusal to subordinate itself to the other'.[37]

The balance-of threat

The foreign policy of Syria during the years of this study confirms Walt's key tenet: states do ally as a reaction against threats (rather than against pure power). Several of Syria's alliances followed a balance against threat logic. The alliances with Jordan and Iraq (as well as the alliance with Iran, that Walt does not include in his analysis because of his timeframe) were all formed by isolated states that had to counter a growing external threat. In a system where conflict is a frequent occurrence, the balance of threat gives important insights into state alliance choices. The main limitation of Walt's analysis is that it captures only one side of alliance formation, the defensive one. Walt's analysis focuses essentially on the short-term and threat reaction dimension of alliances. As a structural realist, Walt is less concerned with long-term foreign policy trajectories. Some of Syria's alliances, such as those with Iraq and Iran,[38] were formed to counter external threats but collapsed (in the case of Iraq) or grew (in the case of Iran) despite the persistence of external threats.

Other alliances were not formed as a reaction against external threats. The complex alliance pattern of the 1960s shows how structural analysis has to be complemented with domestic-level considerations. The shifting alliances of Syria, Iraq and Egypt in fact depend as much on changes at regime level (that Walt partially registers with his aggressive intentions parameter) as they do on external factors. The 1973 war alliance can hardly be interpreted as purely defensive given the fact that its purpose was to wage war on Israel. Other alliances analysed in later chapters are particularly hard to explain according to the balance of threat. This is the case with the Saudi Syrian relationship, for the establishment of the alliance was not motivated by external threats but rather depended on the two countries' regional goals.

38 *Foreign policy and alliances*

Constructivism/institutionalism

The second theoretical approach analysed is the constructivist/institutional one. This framework is particularly relevant to this study. This book integrates a domestic parameter that has been defined as 'ideological orientation' within a realist analysis, and the study of aspects such as ideology has been one of the main contributions of constructivism. This school of International Relations emerged as a sociological theory in opposition to both neorealism and liberal institutionalism. Alexander Wendt's 'Anarchy is What States Make of It: The Social Construction of Power Politics'[39] represented the first elaboration of the new theoretical framework and of its research agenda. In the following decades the constructivist research agenda has grown significantly. Constructivists broadly focus on how images, identities and ideas shape relations among states. Fierke has noted how constructivism has occupied a 'middle ground between rationalist and post-structuralist approaches to [International Relations]'.[40] Significant distinctions have also emerged among constructivists. A key factor of disagreement among constructivist scholars is the rejection or (partial) acceptance of rationalist ontology.[41] Furthermore, constructivist scholars have differed in terms of the focus of their analysis, with factors such as identity, norms and ideology central to the work of different strands of constructivism.

The work of the authors analysed in this section concentrates on the role of ideology. Michael Barnett in 'Institutions, Roles, and Disorder: The Case of the Arab States System'[42] starts his analysis by questioning the contribution of the rationalist/realist approach in explaining the dynamics of the Arab state system. Realism's emphasis on 'national interest' ignores, in Barnett's view, the effect of Pan-Arabism in shaping and constraining policy-makers in Arab countries. Ideologies impose specific roles on states and therefore they are a key determinant of state behaviour. Roles 'can be understood as how the individual (or state) participates in society according to a particular identity and comes to modify behavior accordingly'.[43] In 'Dialogues in Arab Politics' Barnett applies this theoretical framework to the study of inter-Arab relations. The two ideologies that shaped the Arab states' behaviour were sovereignty and Pan-Arabism: 'Arab leaders were embedded in a structure defined by Arabism and sovereignty that shaped their identities, interests, presentation of self, survival-seeking strategies, and strategic interactions. It all begins with Arabism'.[44] Barnett therefore sees the interaction between Arab identity and state sovereignty as the factor determining inter-Arab politics.[45] Relations among Arab states were characterised by actors seeking to shape the norms of Pan-Arabism. Arab regimes battled over the meaning of Pan-Arabism, and over which policies (including alliance choices) were consistent with the ideology. The ability to influence and redefine Arab norms was in Barnett's view the field in which Arab leaders fought each other, rather than the material competition typical of realist analysis.

Murhaf Jouejati[46] seeks to use the concepts developed by Barnett in order to explain the diverging foreign policies of Egypt and Syria in the aftermath of the 1973 conflict.[47] Jouejati defines his approach as 'institutional', as it analyses the effects of sovereignty and Arabism (in Jouejati's work defined as informal institutions) on the foreign policy of Syria and Egypt. Jouejati argues that Syrian and Egyptian foreign policies were constrained by both sovereignty and Pan-Arabism, although in different ways. This 'discrepancy' explains the different foreign policies of Damascus and Cairo.[48] Sovereignty will influence/constrain states to act as a 'realist': states will choose foreign policy according to their perceived national interest. This 'selfish' orientation is at odds with Pan-Arabism. This other institution pushes states towards pursuing Arab unity and Arab interests over national ones.[49] This tension is present in all Arab states; whichever of the two institutions puts more constraints on policies will change from country to country. Essentially, in countries where the sense of national identity is stronger, sovereignty will have a greater influence on foreign policy. In countries where Arab nationalism predates and its stronger that national identities, Arabism will represent the dominating influence. Syria falls in the latter category, a state where Arab identity was stronger than 'national' one.[50]

Constructivism and the alliances of Syria

What does the constructivist/institutionalist framework tell us about the alliances of Syria? Barnett's and Jouejati's works provide several insights on the country's foreign policy. Arguably, no Arab state was as influenced by Pan-Arab ideology as the self-styled 'beating heart of the Arab nation'. Pan-Arabism should therefore influence the foreign policy and particularly the alliance choices of Syria. It is, however, important to note how Pan-Arabism as an institution did not exert a constant influence on states.[51] The meaning of Pan-Arabism changed throughout time. Accordingly, the constraints of Pan-Arabism on state behaviour also gradually changed. The failure of the unity projects in the early 1960s and the Arab military defeat of 1967 altered the core norms of the ideology. By the mid-1960s the idea of bringing together the Arabs in a single super-state was largely discredited. Arab leaders had largely accepted state sovereignty and the border division inherited by Western powers. With the sunset of unity projects, the defence of the Palestinian cause and opposition to Israel became the central tenet of Pan-Arabism.

With his emphasis on inter-Arab dialogues, Barnett provides a very interesting account of the dynamics at play between Syria, Iraq and Egypt throughout the 1960s. Barnett's analysis focuses on 1963 and the unity talks that took place during that year. When Pan-Arab forces took over power in both Syria and Iraq, they immediately expressed their interest in pursuing a union with Egypt. However, policy-makers in both Baghdad and Damascus sought an alignment with Egypt for domestic as well as ideological purposes.[52] For the Syrians, their commitment to union with Egypt and Iraq was an attempt to avoid being outbid in their support for Pan-Arabism by international and domestic rivals. The first Ba'th regimes lacked strong support and the unity talks with the two Arab powers (and particularly with the very popular Egyptian leader) were a way of showing their own commitment to Pan-Arabism. When the talks failed, Syria

40   Foreign policy and alliances

and Iraq not only continued with negotiations but engaged in a fierce propaganda war with the Egyptian leadership over the responsibility for the failure.

Particularly compelling is Barnett's account of inter-Arab relations leading to the 1967 war. Nasser engineered and led the Arab summits system to control and coerce radical Arab states, particularly Syria. Barnett underlines how the defensive pact between Egypt and Syria was a result of Pan-Arab competition between the two countries. The radical Syrian regime challenged Nasser's Pan-Arab credentials and succeeded in obtaining his support, even though the Egyptian leader had initially no intention to get involved in a war with Israel. Because of the pressure exercised by the norms of Pan-Arabism: 'Nasser was caught between the symbolic and the strategic, and he sacrificed the latter'.[53] The 1967 defeat was in a way a consequence of Pan-Arabism and of the competition created among Arab states. The defeat, however, also changed the meaning of Pan-Arabism and opened a new era in which state sovereignty was recognised by Arab leaders as an important factor in their relations.

The development of Syria's alliances in the 1970s show the relative decline of Pan-Arabism, but also how it played a bigger role in Syria than in other countries. The way that the 1973 war alliance was built, and the 1973 war was fought, confirms how inter-Arab politics had changed. By 1970 Arab states had completely accepted the concept of state sovereignty as the cornerstone of their relationships.[54] The recognition of this principle had significantly changed the dynamics of inter-Arab politics, essentially creating a new order. The 1973 war alliance was 'state-centric' rather than Pan-Arab. The aftermath of the 1973 war on the other hand would show that the relationship between 'statism' and Arabism was still different in Egypt and Syria, and this explains their diverging paths in the aftermath of the war. Jouejati maintains that Sadat was able to 'switch policy' (opt out of the Arab–Israeli conflict, sign a peace agreement with Israel and join the pro-Western camp) while Al-Assad was not because Egypt's role was different from Syria's. As Al-Assad was more constrained by the institution of Pan-Arabism, he could not abandon the Palestinian and Arab cause and strike a deal with Israel.[55]

Despite the relative decline of Pan-Arabism, the Iran–Iraq triangle represents a particularly puzzling case from the point of view of the constructivist/ institutionalist framework. Siding with Persian Iran as this state was engaged in a war against Arab Iraq in fact represented a clear violation of Pan-Arab norms. Jouejati attributes the failure of the Syrian–Iraqi détente to a mix of ideological and 'realist' considerations: 'In claiming Damascus and Baghdad as the centers of authentic Baath ideology, the ideological rivalry set off a geopolitical competition that spilled over in other areas …'.[56] The role of Arabism in this case is not one that drove the two countries to cooperate but rather one that pushed them towards inter-Ba'th competition. The start of the Iraq–Iran war was an added pressure to the Syrian leadership. As Jouejati acknowledges: 'that Syria acted in concert with a non-Arab state against a fellow Arab country may also be interpreted as anything but Arabist'.[57] It is national interest that explains Syria's support of Iran, and why Damascus aligned itself with Tehran and not Baghdad.

According to Jouejati, Al-Assad initially opted to pursue national interest (supporting Iran) against the prescriptions of Pan-Arabism (supporting Iraq). When (in 1986) Iran brought the war to Iraqi territory and threatened to overrun Iraqi defences altogether, the Syrian President was forced by the norms of Pan-Arabism to distance himself from the Iranian military initiative, clearly stating that he was against any occupation of Arab land and increasing the diplomatic efforts to constrain his Persian ally.[58]

Sunayama's book represents the only study that deals specifically with the Syrian–Saudi relations, and it does so using an approach based on constructivism.[59] Her work focuses on the interaction between the transnational identities of Islamism and Arabism and how they shaped the relationship between Riyadh and Damascus. Sunayama's core argument is that despite their differences, these transnational identities shared some common norms. It was precisely these shared norms that allowed the two countries to build an alliance (although an uneasy one). Interestingly, Sunayama also maintains that it was the existence of these shared identities that gave Syria great leverage over Saudi Arabia.[60] The author also recognises the importance of 'systemic' and 'structural' factors on the alliance. In fact, when looking at the details of the Syrian–Saudi relationship in different historical phases, the author's analysis takes into great consideration power-based factors. As Chapter 9 of this volume will show, Sunayama's analysis shares several features with the analysis of this book.

The constructivist/institutionalist framework

The works of constructivist/institutionalist authors give a nuanced and rich contribution to the understanding of the foreign policy of Syria. Pan-Arabism had undoubtedly played a central role in the region and particularly in Syria. An analysis that aims at incorporating it into the explanation of Damascus' foreign policy makes an important contribution to the study of this topic. Relations among key Arab powers were often shaped by the inter-Arab dialogues that are the core of Barnett's analysis. This dimension of inter-Arab politics is particularly evident in some phases of regional history. The Egypt–Syria–Iraq triangle in the early 1960s is also a tale of rivalry over the rules of Pan-Arabism.

Despite these insights, this framework struggles to explain some of Syria's key relations. In cases such as the Syrian–Egyptian alliance, while capturing some important aspects of the relationship, the 'realist' and state-centric aspect of the alliance clearly prevails over the Pan-Arab one. The Damascus–Baghdad–Tehran triangle is particularly puzzling for any analysis based on the concept of identity, for Damascus consistently supported the Islamic (and Persian) Iranian republic that emerged after the 1979 revolution against a fellow Ba'thist state. In this instance, Jouejati presents an interesting case for the role of Arab identity, yet not an entirely convincing one. Al-Assad's behaviour during the Iran–Iraq war aimed at pursuing his country's interests (i.e. supporting Iran while not burning bridges with the oil rich monarchies) rather than coming from the conflicting constraints of Pan-Arabism and sovereignty.

42 *Foreign policy and alliances*

Conclusion

This chapter presented two explanations of the foreign policy and alliance formation of Syria. Both structural realism and constructivism/institutionalism provide a useful and fascinating explanation of the foreign policy and alliances of Syria. The balance of threat captures well the 'defensive' aspect that is central to the foreign policy of a state whose geopolitical conditions are as complicated as Syria's. The 'institutional' perspective draws attention to the role of Pan-Arabism for Syria, the self-proclaimed 'beating heart of the Arab nation'.

The two approaches, however, provide only a partial explanation of Syria's alliances. The balance of threat elaborated by Walt captures one aspect of alliance formation, the reactive one, but fails to incorporate the fact that alliances are formed 'for' (in order to reach foreign policy goals) and not only 'against' (in order to counter a threat). The balance of threat does not account for the formation or the collapse of alliances such as the Syrian–Egyptian or the Syrian–Iranian one, based on goals and not only on threats. The goal of this research will be to integrate the two aspects of alliance formation, the threat aspect examined by Walt, and the 'goals' typical of classical realism. The constructivist/institutionalist analysis shows how Pan-Arabism influenced the foreign policy of Syria. The influence of inter-Arab dynamics is clear during the 1960s, when the relations among main Arab actors were dominated by competition over the norms of Pan-Arabism. In the case of Syria, this competition was based on the struggle for legitimacy and supremacy among domestic actors. The influence of Pan-Arab norms on Syrian foreign policy and alliances diminished significantly in the 1970s and 1980s.

The theoretical framework of this book seeks to develop further some of the insights offered by both structural realism and constructivism. It does not reject *tout court* the analyses offered by the works of Walt, Barnett and the other authors mentioned in this chapter. It rather seeks to provide a different way of thinking about the interaction between the main elements present in the previous analyses. While the model of this book is based on the realist paradigm, it seeks to incorporate a non-realist factor such as leadership ideology. Neoclassical realism is well placed to provide a 'meeting space' between realism and constructivism, as shown by the work of authors such as Jennifer Sterling-Folker.[61] In this research in particular ideology is used as a tool to refine a study of alliances that is largely based on a realist logic. The next chapter will focus on the foreign policy of Damascus in order to provide a frame to develop the study of its key alliances.

Notes

1 For instance, Fred Lawson's *Why Syria Goes to War: Thirty Years of Confrontation* (Ithaca: Cornell University Press, 1996) attempts to explain Damascus' foreign policy as an elite domestic survival strategy.
2 Kenneth N. Waltz, *Theory of International Politics* (New York: McGraw Hill, 1979).
3 Stephen M. Walt, *The Origins of Alliances* (Ithaca: Cornell University Press, 1987).

4 Michael Barnett, *Dialogues in Inter-Arab Politics: Negotiations in Regional Order* (New York: Columbia University Press, 1998); Michael Barnett, "Sovereignty, Nationalism, and, Regional Order in the Arab States System," *International Organization* 49, 3 (Summer 1995): 479–510.

5 Murhaf Jouejati, "Syrian Foreign Policy: An Institutional Perspective on Why Assad Did Not Emulate Sadat" (PhD diss., University of Utah, 1998).

6 And in the case of Saudi Arabia, to the work of Sonoko Sunayama, see *Syria and Saudi Arabia: Collaboration and Conflicts in the Oil Era* (London: I.B. Tauris, 2007).

7 Mark Haas, *The Clash of Ideologies: Middle Eastern Politics and American Security* (Oxford: Oxford University Press, 2012).

8 Walt's argument was then developed and completed in following works, including: "Testing Theories of Alliance Formation: The Case of Southwest Asia," *International Organization* 42, 2 (Spring 1988): 275–316; "Why Alliances Endure or Collapse," *Survival: Global Politics and Strategy* 39, 1 (1997): 156–179, changing some aspects of the argument.

9 Walt, *The Origins of Alliances*, 22.

10 Ibid., 24.

11 In "Bandwagoning for Profit: Bringing the Revisionist State Back in," *International Security* 19, 1 (Summer 1994): 72–107, Randall Schweller criticises the definition of bandwagoning in the work of Walt, suggesting that it is different from the 'traditional' use of balancing in International Relations, being closer to giving in to pressure. This is because, in Schweller's view, Walt mistakes the reason why states bandwagon, or at least does not account for the fact that states often bandwagon pursuing goals rather than countering threats.

12 Walt, *The Origins of Alliances*, 17.

13 Ibid., 29.

14 Ibid., 30.

15 Ibid., 31.

16 Ibid., 33–36.

17 Ibid., 35.

18 Ibid., 46.

19 Ibid., 48.

20 Ibid.

21 The 1963 Tripartite Agreement; 1963 Syria–Iraq; Syria–USSR; October War Coalition; Syria–Jordan 1975 Alliance; Steadfastness Front.

22 Walt, *The Origins of Alliances*, 103.

23 Ibid., 103.

24 Ibid., 103–104.

25 Ibid., 89.

26 Ibid., 150.

27 Ibid., 85.

28 Ibid., 101.

29 Ibid., 145.

30 Ibid., 146.

31 Ibid., 152.

32 Ibid., 120.

33 Ibid., 131.

34 Ibid., 144.

35 Ibid., 150–151.

36 Ibid., 136.

37 Ibid., 138.

38 The case of the Syrian–Iranian alliance is not included in Walt's analysis because of the timeframe of his study.

44 *Foreign policy and alliances*

39 Alexander Wendt, "Anarchy is What States Make of It: The Social Construction of Power Politics," *International Organization* 46, 2 (Spring 1992): 391–425.
40 Karin M. Fierke, "Constructivism," in *International Relations Theories: Discipline and Diversity*, eds. Tim Dunne, Steve Smith and Milja Kurki (Oxford: Oxford University Press, 2013), 193.
41 Ibid.
42 Michael Barnett, "Institutions, Roles, and Disorder: The Case of the Arab States System," *International Studies Quarterly* 37, 3 (September 1993): 271–296.
43 Ibid., 274.
44 Barnett, *Dialogues in Arab Politics*, 11.
45 Ibid., 33.
46 Jouejati, "Syrian Foreign Policy."
47 Jouejati's work is used here as it represents an excellent application to the case of Syria in main constructivist works such as Barnett's (not only the previously cited article but also in the seminal *Dialogues in Arab Politics*) and also the work of constructivist author Shebley Telhami, "Power and Legitimacy in Arab Alliances: The New Arabism," in *Ethnic Conflict and International Politics in the Middle East*, ed. Leonard Binder (Miami: University Press of Florida, 1999).
48 Barnett, *Dialogues in Arab Politics*, 94.
49 Ibid., 95.
50 Jouejati, "Syrian Foreign Policy," 96–103.
51 Barnett, *Dialogues in Arab Politics*.
52 Ibid., ch. V.
53 Ibid., 148.
54 Ibid., ch.VI.
55 See for example, Jouejati, "Syrian Foreign Policy."
56 Jouejati, "Syrian Foreign Policy." 178.
57 Ibid., 168.
58 Ibid., 183–187.
59 Sunayama, *Syria and Saudi Arabia*.
60 Ibid., 216.
61 See for example "Neoclassical Realism and Identity: Peril Despite Profit across the Taiwan Straits," in *Neoclassical Realism, the State, and Foreign Policy*, eds. Steven Lobell, Norrin M. Ripsman and Jeffrey Taliaferro (Cambridge: Cambridge University Press, 2009).

Part II
The alliances of Syria

4 The foreign policy of Syria

How did the alliance pattern of Syria change during the years of this study? The model of this book looks at alliances within the framework of state's broader foreign policy. This chapter will, therefore, provide an overview of the foreign policy of Syria to show how this changed over the period analysed by this study. The first section will look at the formation of the Syrian state and at the first years of independence. The struggle against European colonial powers resulted in the emergence of a 'reduced' Syrian state. The instability that characterised the first decades of Syrian politics was one of the factors that allowed the Ba'th party, until then a marginal force in the country, to gain power in 1963. The Ba'th years are the focus of this analysis. Despite the long domination by this Pan-Arab force, the leadership in charge of the country and particularly the foreign policy executive changed several times. Two main phases can be identified. The first are the 'ideological years' (1963–1970). The first Ba'th years were characterised by domestic instability and intra-Ba'th divisions. In 1966 the military wing of the Ba'th party managed to seize power in Damascus. The foreign policy implemented by Salah Jadid and his circle can be described as 'radical'. The strong rhetoric against all enemies and the unwillingness to restrain Palestinian militias operating from Syrian territory led to isolation in the Arab world, and (more immediately) were among the causes of the 1967 defeat at the hands of Israel. In the aftermath of the conflict the Ba'thist leadership found itself divided between a 'revolutionary' faction led by Salah Jadid and a more moderate one led by Defence Minister Hafez Al-Assad. The second phase of Syrian foreign policy under the Ba'th started when the latter faction emerged victorious after another showdown in 1970. Al-Assad imposed a less ideological domestic and foreign policy. Under the new leadership the foreign policy of Syria changed from unlimited to limited revisionism.

The establishment of the Syrian state

Any analysis of the foreign policy of Syria has to start from the process that led to the country's independence. The genesis of the Syrian state was in many ways a traumatic one, and clearly shaped the foreign policy of the country during the first decades after independence. Like most of its neighbours, the Syrian Arab

48 *The alliances of Syria*

Republic emerged as an independent state after a long and painful decolonisation process. A region called 'Syria' had existed for a very long time, although the exact territory that this name indicated had frequently changed.[1] The name Syria was initially used by the Greeks, and then adopted by the Romans to refer to one of their provinces. Throughout history the term Syria or the Arabic Bilad Al-Sham referred to a much larger territory, including the modern Jordan, Israel and Palestine, Lebanon and parts of what is today Iraq and Turkey.[2] The Ottomans took over control of the region in early sixteenth century after defeating the reigning Mamlucks. After their conquest the Ottomans maintained most of the administrative divisions established by the previous power. Syria and chiefly the two cities of Aleppo and Damascus held an important role under the Ottomans.[3] The two cities were in fact capitals of two 'walayahs', administrative regions of the Ottoman Empire. The Turkish rule lasted for nearly 400 years, interrupted only by a few periods of unrest.

The European powers became progressively more involved (and invasive) in the Ottoman Empire's internal affairs but did not assume direct control over Syria until the aftermath of World War I. In October 1914 the Ottoman Empire joined the conflict as an ally of Germany against main colonial powers Britain and France. Lord Asquith, then British Prime Minister, allegedly commented that: 'The Ottoman empire has committed suicide'.[4] On 5 July 1920 the French entered Damascus and expelled King Faisal, ending (at least temporarily) Arab dreams of an independent state. The region was divided into four entities that were to later provide the basis for independent states: Syria and Lebanon came under French control in acknowledgment of the country's long-term interests in the area.[5] Trans-Jordan and Palestine (where the first problems between Jewish immigrants and Arabs had started to manifest themselves) fell under British control. Britain also kept Iraq within its sphere of influence. The Hashemite King Faisal was given the throne of the latter country as 'compensation' for the loss of Damascus. It was only 26 years later, after a bloody and bitterly contested French mandate, that Syria emerged as an independent country. The defeat of France at the hands of the Germans in World War II had weakened its control over the mandate. The state that emerged was, however, the 'smaller' one consolidated in the early 1920s after negotiations between the British and the French. Syria also suffered the loss of the Hatay province, gained by Turkey after a (bitterly criticised) referendum in 1939.

Syria formally reached its independence in April 1946 after a long struggle against the occupiers. The outcome of this fight for independence was, however, a disappointment for most Syrians. As Hinnebusch notes:

> In the wake of the Arab revolt of 1917, Syrians expected the creation of an independent Arab state in historic Syria (Bilad Al-Sham) linked to the wider Arab federation. Instead, betraying their promises to the Arabs, the Western powers subjugated the Arab East, dismembered historic Syria into four mini-states, Syria, Jordan, Lebanon and Palestine, and sponsored the colonization and establishment of the State of Israel and Palestine.[6]

The process that led to the creation of an independent Syrian state shaped the 'national psyche' and the first years of the country as an independent entity, as well as the geopolitical conditions that still affect the country's foreign policy today. First, given the lack of Syrian national identity, Arabism imposed itself as the unifying ideology keeping together the Syrian state.[7] Given the heterogeneity of Syria's population and the presence of significant religious minorities, Arab identity was more 'inclusive' than any form of identity based on religion. Second, the country found itself in a complex geopolitical condition, caused not only by the closeness to a formidable and aggressive rival such as the state of Israel but also by the presence of Iraq and Turkey, and by its 'soft' borders which were particularly hard to defend.

The first leaders of the country had to face significant internal and external threats. One of these was the ambitions that several actors had over Syria. The most obvious pretenders to Damascus were the Hashemites of Trans-Jordan and (particularly) Iraq.[8] Another problem was the weak and fragmented ruling class that had inherited power from the French. These elites were extremely divided. Daniel Pipes describes how important sectors of Syrian society were not won over by the 'national project' and naturally looked at those external actors that seemed able to re-establish something more like Greater Syria.[9] In 1948 the Syrians had their baptism of fire and encountered what was going to become their long-term foe. The Arab defeat in the first Arab–Israeli war and the establishment of the state of Israel represented another source of domestic instability in Syria.

The 1948 defeat undermined the position of the elites that had led the country to its independence. President Shukri Al-Quwatli had been the most representative figure of those years. His deposition in 1949 at the hands of Husni Al-Zaim was the start of a long period of instability characterised by continuous coups, often sponsored by external powers aiming at exerting their control over the country. Al-Quwatli was back as head of state between 1955 and 1958, albeit as a largely ceremonial figure. His mandate ended when Syria joined Egypt in the United Arab Republic, a move seen as a solution to the country's chronic instability. Part of the Syrian elite swallowed this decision without being too enthusiastic about it. In the aftermath of the 1956 Suez crisis the popularity of Gamal Abdel Nasser was incredibly high, and no Syrian politician was strong enough to openly oppose the move.[10] The unfortunate Egyptian experience had a formative effect on the group that a few years later was going to take over the country and particularly on the man that about ten years later was going to become the master of Syria.[11] By the early 1960s the Ba'th had become an important force in the country. The party also played a role in the union with Egypt: 'The Baath surely helped to create the U.A.R. and as just surely contributed to wreck it'.[12] In September 1961 a coup d'état (by then a regular occurrence in Syrian politics) ended the union with Egypt and re-established Syrian independence. The putsch was supported by the Syrian bourgeoisie who were largely hostile to Nasser's policies. The change of regime did not, however, bring more stability to the country. In the two following years the separatist regime led by Nazim Al-Qudsi was

50   *The alliances of Syria*

threatened by several competing groups of conspirators. In March 1963 a group of officers of different political affiliations moved to oust the Qudsi regime. They were met with little resistance by the secessionist leadership and easily took over power. Ba'thists and Nasserites had together led this bloodless coup, but their alliance was not going to be a lasting one.

1963–1970: the radical Ba'th in power

1963–1966: leadership fragmentation and foreign policy

In 1963 the Ba'th party was, for the first time in Syrian history, in a real position of power. The task of dislodging the Al-Qudsi regime had been a rather simple one. The one of imposing its control over the country, however, proved to be extremely complex. The Ba'th was the largest party in a wide coalition of forces and had crucially solidified its control over key positions in the Syrian Army. The group in power was divided and the balance among different groups extremely delicate.[13] First, there was the military/civilian divide. Young officers had been the driving force behind the March 1963 putsch. However, their lack of experience and of control over the Syrian state forced them to share power with 'civilians', in some cases representatives of the Syrian middle and upper classes that had ruled the country in the aftermath of independence.[14]

The division between Ba'thist and Nasserites was more troublesome and had direct foreign policy implications. The most urgent and probably the trickiest issue for the regime was in fact the relationship with Nasser's Egypt. The conspirators had overthrown a 'separatist' regime that was largely responsible for the breakup of the United Arab Republic. Nasserites wanted to bring Syria back into the sphere of influence of the Egyptian *Ra'is*, whilst the Ba'thists were more sceptical regarding the relationship with Cairo. Their hostility stemmed from their negative experience of the United Arab Republic as well as from ideological differences. Despite this, Tripartite Union negotiations between Baghdad, Damascus and Cairo started immediately after the March 1963 coup in Syria. These negotiations had mainly domestic purposes in Syria and Iraq; both Ba'thist leaderships pursued them to strengthen their domestic position in their own country.[15] Despite the publication of a constitution for a Tripartite United Arab Republic, conflict between Nasserites and Ba'thists was brewing in Syria. Worried about Nasser's growing influence in the country, the Syrian Ba'thists launched another coup d'état that effectively excluded Nasserites from power and ended any discussion on the Tripartite Union. The two Ba'th regimes proceeded with their plans of union without Egypt. However, in late 1963 a coup d'état led by General Abd Al-Salam Arif ended the brief Ba'thist rule in Baghdad and subsequently the talks of union between Syria and Iraq.

The Arab world during those years was divided into two different camps. On one side the conservative monarchies of the Gulf and Jordan, on the other the progressive republics led by Egypt. The competition among the two factions was not only symbolic; Saudi Arabia, Egypt and their respective allies clashed in a

Yemeni civil war. In 1962 a group of officers of leftist inclinations took over power and proclaimed the establishment of a republic. Imam Muhammad al-Badr, sponsored by the Saudis, opposed this move and led the resistance against the 'progressive' forces.[16] Nasser saw the conflict through the lens of ideological competition and decided to intervene in favour of the republic. Soon Cairo and Riyadh found themselves facing each other in Yemen.

The other key issue for the newly-installed Ba'thist regime was the relationship with its belligerent neighbour to the south-west. Skirmishes in the demilitarised zones (DMZs) had been a feature of Syrian–Israeli relations since the 1949 armistice. From the late 1950s onwards, however, the Israeli government had ramped up its attempts to increase the DMZs and particularly the crucial area along the Sea of Galilee. The help provided by the Syrian regime to the new Palestinian militias established in the country was partially an attempt to counter Israeli military superiority.[17] It was also a way of showing its commitment to the Palestinian cause and to put pressure on fellow Arab states. The Syrian regime in fact used the Arab–Israeli conflict to outbid fellow Arab states and 'force Nasser to the left'.[18]

The forces that dominated Syria during years 1963–1966 were 'ideological' according to the definition used by this study, but most of all they were extremely fragmented, and its main actors were too engaged in domestic struggles to produce a coherent foreign policy. Foreign policy within this context was a stick to brandish against domestic opponents. This ideological nature was evident in the hostile rhetoric towards fellow Arab states accused of having abandoned the Pan-Arab (and the Palestinian) cause. It also manifested itself in Syria's role in the creation of Palestinian militias and the choice to allow them to use Syrian territory to train and later on to carry out actions against Israel. The 1966 coup d'état signalled the end of this fragmentation and the takeover of power by the Ba'th faction led by Salah Jadid.

1966–1970: the Jadid years

The regime that emerged out of the 1966 coup d'état was controlled exclusively by the military wing of the Ba'th party. The 1966 showdown had seen the young officers' faction getting rid of the old Ba'th civilian leadership associated with party founder Michel Aflaq. It was the radical faction led by Salah Jadid that took most of the key jobs. The previous regimes had been described as 'ideological'. The Jadid regime was undoubtedly both more ideologically coherent and more radical.[19] Perhaps unsurprisingly, the resulting foreign policy was one of 'extreme Pan-Arabism'. Fellow Arab states were subject to an increased wave of hostile propaganda. The main target were the Gulf monarchies and particularly Saudi Arabia. The Wahabi monarchy was the ideological nemesis of the radical Ba'thist regime, and the already negative relationship between the two Arab powers further worsened during the Jadid years. The relationship with Iraq was similarly complicated. The relationship with the Arif regime was predictably cold, given the fact that the General had excluded the Iraqi Ba'th from

52 *The alliances of Syria*

power. When the Ba'th regained power in 1968, however, the relationship between the two Arab powers did not improve. On the contrary the radical Ba'th regime in Syria perceived the fellow Ba'th state as an ideological rival for predominance in the Pan-Arab camp.[20]

The mark of any regime that wanted to prove its Pan-Arab credentials was, however, its commitment to the Palestinian cause and its opposition to Israel. The relationship between Tel Aviv and Damascus worsened further under Jadid. The new Syrian regime openly declared its goal of leading a war to free Palestine, despite the limited military power of its army.[21] Border clashes became a nearly daily occurrence, particularly around the Sea of Galilee. Unable to contain Israel's military superiority, the Syrian regime attempted to bring the matter to the United Nations Security Council in the summer of 1966.[22] When the Council failed to offer even a symbolic condemnation of Israel, the Syrian regime started facing Israel by directly responding to each violation. This policy led to a series of confrontations between the two air forces in late 1966 and early 1967, invariably resulting in losses for the weaker Syrian army.

The rising tension between Tel Aviv and Damascus forced Gamal Abdel Nasser to align itself with the Syrians. In November 1966 he signed a bilateral defence agreement with Syria in the hope of containing the radicals in Damascus. The bilateral agreement between the two Arab capitals was an Egyptian attempt to control the and moderate the radical Syrian regime. The Egyptian leadership, however, was unable to restrain the Syrians (and even less the Palestinian militias operating from Syrian territory). Each round of military action against Syria (or Jordan) increased the pressure on the Egyptian leader. Gamel Abdel Nasser was forced by his own reputation as Arab leader to follow the Syrians on the path of confrontation. The Jadid regime had promised to make Damascus the capital of 'Arab resistance'.[23] Unlike the Syrians, the Egyptian leadership had no real appetite for a military showdown with Israel. When Nasser asked the United Nations forces to leave the Sinai Peninsula and proceeded to close the Strait of Tiran to Israeli ships, the Egyptian President was still calculating that war with Tel Aviv could be avoided.[24] However different their intentions, the two regimes shared the same lack of military preparedness. When Israel mounted a surprise attack on Egyptian forces, it caught the main Arab power by surprise and destroyed the majority of Nasser's airforce in the space of half a day. Having easily disposed of the Egyptians, the Israeli army proceeded to attack Jordan and later Syria. The defeat for the Arabs was complete. The whole region woke up in a state of total shock in the aftermath of the conflict. Within a few days, Israel had changed the map of the region, and completely altered the regional balance of power.

The 1967 war left the Ba'thist regime in a precarious position. Jadid and his officers had never enjoyed a broad consensus over the country. The 1967 defeat, however, had left them completely isolated and vulnerable.[25] The 'ideological' policy put in place by the Jadid regime had been exposed. The violent rhetoric against internal and external enemies and the unwillingness to constrain Palestinian militias operating in the country had been among the main factors leading to the conflict. The geopolitical reality that emerged in the aftermath of the 1967 conflict was different, and undoubtedly much harder, than the previous one. Israel had taken over the Golan Heights and enjoyed a significant strategic advantage over Syria. It had easily destroyed the armies of Egypt and Jordan and taken over the Sinai Peninsula, the West Bank and Jerusalem. From a geopolitical point of view, the war had been an earthquake. The Syrian leadership, however, was strongly divided on how to react to this shock.[26] Jadid and the radicals favoured a strengthening of the 'revolution' at home and an intransigent foreign policy abroad. On the other hand, the group led by the young Defence Minister Hafez Al-Assad sought a completely different line. Al-Assad and his circle disagreed with the Jadid group on some key policy points. The main one was the unchecked support of the Palestinian cause. Al-Assad considered the Palestinian militias responsible for the 1967 defeat and wanted to exercise more control over them. The issue of the relationship with other Arab states was also crucial. Al-Assad saw the radical Pan-Arab approach of the Jadid regime as a cause of isolation and favoured a more pragmatic approach to regional politics. The Defence Minister considered alliances as a key factor in order to reduce the gap with Israel. He favoured closer cooperation with Baghdad but also wanted to tone down the hostile rhetoric against Saudi Arabia and the Gulf countries.[27] The 1970 coup d'état that saw the young Alawite officer take over power therefore represented a crucial shift in Syrian foreign policy. Despite the continuation of Ba'th rule, the era of unlimited revisionism was over.

1970–1989: limited revisionism

This regime change led to a complete re-adjustment of the country's goals and strategies. Syrian foreign policy became more 'realist' to the extent that it was more attuned to the country's real capabilities. The country inherited by Hafez Al-Assad was a weak actor heavily penetrated by external powers. Syria was a middleweight surrounded by regional heavyweights. The country was also penalised by its position as minor regional client of the USSR after Egypt (and arguably Iraq) which prevented it from obtaining state-of-the-art military technologies from the Soviets. Hafez Al-Assad inherited a weak army (as confirmed by the 1967 debacle) demoralised by the Israel Defence Force's clear superiority, and a public opinion frustrated by 20 years of Arab political and military failures. In 1971 the National Congress of the Ba'ath Party acknowledged the scaling down of Syria's foreign policy goals.[28] Syrian regional goals throughout the Al-Assad years can be classified as limited revisionism. Damascus aimed to alter the regional balance that it saw as favourable to Israel, its main threat and geopolitical rival. The changes sought were, however, limited and achievable within the system rather than 'revolutionary'. Al-Assad and his men acknowledged Israel's military superiority and its strong relationship with the United States. The goal of wiping Israel off the map was therefore completely unrealistic. A more realistic goal was to gain a limited military victory on the ground, regain the lost Golan Heights and force Israel to negotiate with the Arabs from a

54 *The alliances of Syria*

position of parity. This strategy was flexible and opened up the possibility of a scaling down of the rivalry if Israel was willing to accept Syrian demands.[29]

Central to this limited revisionist strategy was a resetting of Syria's regional relations that had been damaged during the previous decade. As the next chapters will show, the new Syrian regime moved quickly to mend fences with powers that could provide military, economic or military support such as the Kingdom of Saudi Arabia or Egypt. Israeli military superiority had convinced Syrian policy-makers that the only way to face the Zionist state was to 'Arabise' what risked becoming essentially a bilateral dispute. Therefore, Syrian policy-makers tried to control Israel's relations with other Arab states to avoid isolation, 'actively obstructing schemes to draw other Arab states into partial, separate settlements with Israel'.[30] Syria would have inevitably succumbed if it was left alone to face Israel. Within the Arab framework (and particularly along with Egypt) the country had better chances of contrasting Israel.[31] Within this zero-sum game, the recovery of the Golan Heights lost in 1967 had an important strategic, and even more symbolic, value.[32]

Al-Assad's first task, however, was rebuilding the Syrian army and turning it into a force able to threaten the mighty Israeli power. His first years in power were devoted to restructuring Syria's defences. The way to achieve this was to enhance cooperation with the Soviet Union. At risk of losing part of its autonomy, Al-Assad knew that the country needed the USSR's support to address external threats and particularly Israel. While the other Arab states could provide economic and diplomatic support, the Soviet Union (through re-armament and 'protection') represented the only guarantee for Syria in the short term.

The aftermath of the 1973 war

The relative success of the 1973 war and Al-Assad's conduct in the aftermath of the conflict gave the Syrian leader a new status within the Arab world.[33] Al-Assad invested this political capital on the strengthening of a set of alliances. The military alliance with the Soviet Union and the relationship with Saudi Arabia (and the other Gulf States) were central to Al-Assad's attempt to overcome (or at least limit) its strategic deficit vis-à-vis its regional competitors. Other 'temporary' alignments such as the ones with Jordan between 1975 and 1977 and Iraq in 1978 also helped the regime to overcome its isolation. Damascus' difficult geopolitical conditions required resources that the country did not have. Al-Assad was forced to pursue a proactive alliance policy to muster the resources and support he needed.[34] Sadat's defection was in this sense both a blessing and a curse. Egypt's withdrawal from the Arab–Israeli conflict increased the pressure on Al-Assad, but it also made Syria a valuable asset for the Soviet Union and a more important actor in regional politics. The Syrian regime was able to use its stance as the 'defender of the Arab cause' successfully vis-à-vis other Arab states. The leadership in Damascus considered 'Syrian' and 'Arab' interests as overlapping: what was in Syria's interest was inevitably in the interest of the wider Arab nation.[35] Al-Assad clearly used this centrality as an important card in inter-Arab relations, particularly in the aftermath of Egypt's peace agreement with Israel.

Despite the (relative) success obtained in 1973, the years following the October War were far from easy for the Syrian President. The relationship with Egypt and President Sadat, already strained by the Egyptians' war conduct[36] and Al-Assad's belief that he had been deceived, worsened further.[37] Al-Assad's attempt to keep the Arab front united confirms his intention to keep the dispute 'multilateral'. Sadat nonetheless proceeded on the path that would have led him to unilateral peace with Israel. In the spring of 1975 the Lebanese Civil War started. Al-Assad, who had initially intervened to restore order in the country and protect his strategic interests, found himself fighting a bloody war against the Palestinians.[38] This act that cost him much in terms of both domestic and international consensus. In the attempt to prevent Israeli involvement in Lebanon, Syria would later have had to 'suffer' the 1982 invasion led by Sharon, the siege of Beirut and the expulsion of the Palestine Liberation Organization from the country. Despite defeat on the battlefield, the Syrian President won the diplomatic war and was rewarded with the role of power-broker in Lebanon.[39]

Threats and consolidation

The Ba'thist regime also had to face a significant domestic threat. A mix of economic concerns and discontentment with Syria's treatment of the Palestinians in Lebanon fuelled the support for Islamist opposition. The discontent against the Syrian regime turned into violence with a series of targeted killings that started in 1977. The Syrian regime blamed this on external enemies and particularly Iraq. Lefevre shows how the regime in Baghdad was in fact the first sponsor of Syrian Islamists.[40] The opposition was able to gather significant internal and external support and increase the scale of its attacks. By 1980 their strategy had shifted from assassinations to urban uprisings in cities such as Aleppo, Hama, Idlib and Homs. The regime, pushed by Al-Assad's younger brother Rifat, reacted to these developments with full military force.[41] An all-out war on the opposition was launched in several rebellious cities and culminated with the infamous Hama massacre. The violent suppression of the uprising in the central city led to the end of the Islamist challenge. It was, however, not the end of instability for the regime. Hafez Al-Assad's health had gradually deteriorated, and a few months after Hama, the Syrian leader collapsed. Rifat Al-Assad, emboldened by his brother's health issues, moved to take power.[42] The Syrian leader, still recovering, was able to gather enough support to stop the coup d'état. Rifat was defeated and exiled.

The foreign policy of Syria shows a high degree of continuity throughout the 1980s, as the systemic goal of Damascus remained constant. The 1980s were characterised by the same constraints and the same grand strategy (with the partial substitution of Egypt with Iran).[43] Al-Assad's biggest foreign policy headache in this phase was caused by the Iran–Iraq war that had started in 1980. In the aftermath of Egypt's 'betrayal' Al-Assad had attempted a re-alignment with Saddam Hussein's Iraq, which had nonetheless failed. Left isolated and feeling

56 *The alliances of Syria*

threatened by both Israel and Iraq, the Syrian leader found an ally in the Islamic Republic of Iran. Now this new alliance was tested by the war waged by Saddam against the Persians. Al-Assad's support of his ally in a war against a fellow Arab state left him facing isolation and hostility within the Arab world. When Iran survived the Iraqi offensive and managed to counter-attack, the Syrian President's risky strategic calculation won him a precious long-term ally.

By the mid-1980s, Hafez Al-Assad had managed to concentrate domestic power in his own hands. Syria was also in a much better position vis-à-vis Israel; through cooperation with his superpower ally the Syrian President had limited the Israeli ability to strike, although without ever reaching the long-sought goal of 'strategic parity'. Al-Assad could not hope to regain the Golan Heights by military means.[44] The cooperation with the Soviet Union, however, had provided Syria with significant deterrent capability, thanks primarily to the missile defensive system provided by Moscow.[45] Evron emphasises how the Syrian–Israeli mutual deterrence on the military front changed the nature of the confrontation with Israel that moved more and more on other scenarios (such as the Lebanese one).[46] The Soviet Union's gradual retreat from the region, and finally its collapse, changed the appearance of regional politics and forced Al-Assad to reshape his own strategy.

Conclusion: foreign policy and alliances

This chapter has provided an overview of the foreign policy of Syria. The Syrian Arab Republic owes much of its ideological foreign policy and 'revisionism' to the decolonisation process that saw it emerging as an independent state. The country was not only cut off from part of its historical territory, but also started off in a difficult geopolitical situation. Surrounded by bigger and often threatening neighbours, Syria had no status quo to defend. The first years of Syrian history were characterised by a high degree of external penetration, with regional powers competing to extend their influence over the country. Weak domestic elites attempted to gain legitimacy by aligning themselves with external powers. Too weak and fragmented to resist in the tough world of Middle East politics, in 1958 the Syrian regime surrendered its independence to Nasser's Egypt. The United Arab Republic, however, lasted less than three years. The aftermath of the secession saw a return to the usual degree of domestic infighting.

In 1963 the Ba'th party, the purest expression of Pan-Arab ideology, came to power through a coup d'état. The party has remained the dominant force in Arab politics until today. Despite this continuity, the foreign policy of Syria changed significantly during the Ba'th years. Two main historical phases have been analysed in this chapter: the unlimited revisionist (1963–1970) and the limited revisionist (1970–1989) years. The 1963–1966 phase saw the Ba'th party in power for the first time in Syrian history. In terms of foreign policy, these years were dominated by the relationship with regional powerhouse Egypt in the aftermath of the collapse of the Union. In 1966 the faction led by Salah Jadid took over power and imposed a 'radical' foreign policy inspired by intransigent

Pan-Arabism. The violent rhetoric against other Arab states culpable of a 'lack of commitment' to the Arab cause drove Syria towards regional isolation. The free reign given to Palestinian militias in the attempt to turn Damascus into a 'revolutionary capital' led to its 1967 defeat. The Six-Day War dramatically changed the regional balance in favour of Israel. This systemic change, however, did not lead to a re-adjustment by the radical Ba'th regime in power in Damascus. In 1970 the Defence Minister moved to take over power, starting a new era in Syrian foreign policy. Al-Assad reshaped the goals of Syrian foreign policy. The confrontation with Israel was scaled down from a revolutionary war to free occupied Palestine to a dispute among states. In this context, finding allies to support Syria (rather than alienating other states with radical intransigence) became a priority of Syrian foreign policy. The next chapters will look at a set of key alliances to show how each of them was shaped by these changes.

Notes

1 Eugene Rogan, *The Arabs: A History* (London: Penguin Books, 2012).
2 This 'large' Syria is the one that many nationalists had in mind when fighting for independence, creating the tension between different nationalists, and described by Daniel Pipes in *Greater Syria: The History of an Ambition* (Oxford, Oxford University Press, 1990).
3 Rogan, *The Arabs*, 132.
4 Abdul Latif Tibawi, *A Modern History of Syria, including Lebanon and Palestine* (London: Macmillan-St. Martin Press, 1969), 209
5 Patrick Seale, *The Struggle for Arab Independence: Riad El-Solh and the Makers of the Modern Middle East* (Cambridge: Cambridge University Press, 2010), 129.
6 Raymond Hinnebusch, "Revisionist Dreams, Realist Strategies: The Foreign Policy of Syria," in *The Foreign Policy of Arab States: The Challenge of Change* (2nd edition), eds. Bahgat Korany and Ali E. Hillal Dessouki (London: Routledge, 1991), 374.
7 Raymond Hinnebusch, *Syria: Revolution from Above* (London: Routledge, 2001), 18.
8 Malcolm H. Kerr, *The Arab Cold War: Gamal Abd Al-Nasir and His Rivals, 1958–1970* (3rd edition) (Oxford, Oxford University Press, 1971), 2.
9 Pipes, *Greater Syria*.
10 Kerr, *The Arab Cold War*, 13.
11 Patrick Seale, *Assad of Syria: The Struggle for the Middle East* (London: I.B. Tauris, 1988).
12 Tibawi, *A Modern History of Syria*, 406.
13 Hinnebusch, *Syria*, 45.
14 Seale, *Assad of Syria*, 70–78.
15 Kerr, *The Arab Cold War*, 48–51.
16 Sonoko Sunayama, *Syria and Saudi Arabia: Collaboration and Conflicts in the Oil Era* (London: I.B. Tauris, 2007).
17 Seale, *Assad of Syria*.
18 Kerr, *The Arab Cold War*, 122.
19 Ibid., 104–107.
20 Eberhard Kienle, *Ba'th vs Ba'th: The Conflict between Syria and Iraq 1968–1989* (London: I.B. Tauris, 1990), 38–42.
21 Hinnebusch, *Syria*, 141.
22 Seale, *Assad of Syria*, 120.
23 Ibid., 121.
24 Kerr, *The Arab Cold War*, 127.

58   *The alliances of Syria*

25 Seale, *Assad of Syria*, 143.
26 Ibid., 145–147.
27 Hinnebusch, *Syria*, 143.
28 Alisdair Drysdale and Raymond Hinnebusch, *Syria and the Middle East Process* (New York: Council on Foreign Relations Press, 1991), 103.
29 Ibid.
30 Raymond Hinnebusch and Anoushiravan Ehteshami, "The Foreign Policy of Syria," in *The Foreign Policy of Middle Eastern States*, eds. Raymond Hinnebusch and Anoushiravan Ehteshami (Manchester: Lynne Rienner, 2003), 152.
31 On the other hand, and in recognition of the validity of this policy, Israel's policy-makers have traditionally tried to 'separate' the Arabs and deal with the different countries individually.
32 Hinnebusch, "Revisionist Dreams," 379.
33 Moshe Ma'oz, *Assad: The Sphinx of Damascus* (London: Weidenfeld and Nicolson, 1988), 94
34 Hinnebusch, *Syria*, 146.
35 Ibid., 136.
36 After a successful first day of military operations in the Sinai Peninsula, the Egyptians contented themselves with sitting back and defending their limited gains, allowing the Israelis to concentrate their effort on the (much more sensitive) Golan Heights front. This strategy was significantly different from the war plan that the Egyptians had shown to both the Soviets and the Syrians. When Sadat finally gave in to Arab pressure and launched an attack on the Sinai Peninsula on the 14 October, the Israeli army had regrouped and easily outmaneuvered the Egyptian forces, leaving Sadat to cry for the superpowers to intervene and prevent the Israeli forces from sweeping up the Egyptians.
37 Seale, *Assad of Syria*.
38 Adeed Dawisha, *Syria and the Lebanese Crisis* (London: Macmillan Press, 1980).
39 Seale, *Assad of Syria*, 418–420.
40 Raphael Lefevre, *Ashes of Hama: The Muslim Brotherhood in Syria* (London: Hurst and Co., 2013), 129.
41 Seale, *Assad of Syria*, 327.
42 Ibid., 437–438.
43 Hinnebusch, *Syria*, ch. VII.
44 The loss of Egypt had in any case severely reduced the possibility of Syria recovering the Golan Heights by military means, given the impossibility of carrying out a 'two front strategy' such as the one that had proven to be successful in 1973, and from Al-Assad's perspective could have borne even better results had Sadat followed the initial plan presented to the Syrians. In this regard 'changing' Egypt for Iran was going to be a significant loss for Syria; while Tehran was to prove a valid ally in the Lebanese scenario through its proxy Hezbollah, its geographical distance from Israel itself was a strategic con for Syria.
45 Aharon Levron, "Syria's Military Strength and Capability," *Middle East Review* 19 (Spring 1987): 5–15.
46 Yair Evron, *War and Intervention in Lebanon: The Syrian–Israeli Deterrence Dialogue* (Beckenham, Kent: Croom Helm, 1987).

5 Syria and Egypt

The first relationship analysed by this study is the Syrian–Egyptian one. Syria has had, throughout its history as an independent state, strong links with the biggest Arab power. Egypt was seen by policy-makers in Damascus as an indispensable ally, but also as a rival and a potential threat. Given this centrality in Syrian foreign policy, it is not surprising that the relationship between the two Arab powers was clearly influenced by Damascus' change from unlimited to limited revisionism. Throughout the heydays of Pan-Arabism the issue of how to deal with Cairo represented a controversial matter for Syrian elites. The failed experience of the United Arab Republic strongly influenced the different Ba'th leaderships that ruled the country from 1963 onwards. Nasser and the Ba'th party were ideological and political rivals in the regional arena. The Ba'thist regimes 'challenged' Egypt on the grounds of its commitment to Pan-Arabism and dragged Nasser towards an unwanted confrontation with Israel. The radical Jadid regime in particular was at odds with Nasser's Egypt over virtually all key regional issues. In the aftermath of the 1967 war, these differences stemmed from the Syrian unlimited revisionism and Egypt's more moderate approach.

As Syria shifted from unlimited to limited revisionism, its relationship with Egypt changed from conflict to cooperation. The Al-Assad regime, less concerned with ideological competition, valued Egypt's role as the only potential military partner against Israel. The two new leaders of Syria and Egypt planned and carried out the 1973 war. Despite this, the regional goals of policy-makers in Damascus and Cairo were different and ultimately contrasting. Egypt was transitioning towards a rapprochement with Israel and the United States, shifting from revisionism to status quo. The war was therefore a way to gain a seat at the peace table rather than an attempt to challenge the regional balance. The long-term trajectories of the two countries diverged. Egypt's path towards peace with Israel represented a significant blow to Syria's regional strategy and led to a long halt in the relationship between the two Arab powers.

Syria and Egypt before 1963

The histories of Syria and Egypt in the aftermath of World War II are heavily intertwined. The two countries both suffered defeat at the hands of Israel in the

60   *The alliances of Syria*

1948 war. In Egypt, the defeat shaped the conditions leading to the coup d'état against the ruling monarch King Farouk. In 1954 a young Colonel named Gamel Abdel Nasser took up power in Cairo. Nasser was able to cement his control over the country and with the 1956 Suez Crisis he established himself as the most popular leader in the Arab world. By the late 1950s the region was strongly polarised by the division between pro-Western forces led by Iraq and the emerging 'leftist' block led by Nasser's Egypt. Cairo and Baghdad competed to exert their influence over their smaller and divided neighbour Syria. The attempt to extend their control over Damascus was part of the broader competition between the leaders of the two main regional blocs. Iraq initially seemed to hold an advantage due to its connections with sections of the Syrian ruling class.[1] However, Nasser's growing status in the Arab world drove Syria towards alignment with Egypt. Pan-Arab sentiments in the 'Arab street' reached an unprecedented level in the aftermath of the Suez Crisis. Neither the weakened Syrian politicians nor the Egyptian leader Nasser could resist the popular pressure towards the union between the two countries that was finalised in 1958.[2] The United Arab Republic was the realisation of Pan-Arabism as a political project. Two main Arab countries had decided to overcome the borders imposed by colonial powers and join forces. In the aftermath of the establishment of the United Arab Republic the impetus towards unification of the Arab world seemed to be unstoppable, with populations in most Arab countries prompting their leaders to join the newly formed state.[3] Despite popular enthusiasm, the differences and divisions between the leaderships of Egypt and Syria were significant and would soon emerge and wreck the union between the two powers. Egypt (and Nasser's) predominance created resentment in Syria. In 1961 a coup d'état supported by the Syrian bourgeoisie hostile to Nasser's policies ended the experiment of the union and appointed Nazim Al-Qudsi as the new Syrian President.

This bitter conclusion poisoned the relation between the two countries in the following years. Other regional powers, concerned about Nasser's influence, undoubtedly rejoiced upon hearing the news of the split between the two countries and its bitter aftermath. The collapse of the United Arab Republic was a blow to the popularity of Gamel Abdel Nasser. The 'separatist' regime of Syria, and the Egyptian leadership in the aftermath of the split, engaged in a volley of mutual accusations in the attempt to blame the other side for the failure of the project.[4] The Al-Qudsi regime, however, paid the higher price for the split. Never particularly popular in the country, due also to its role in ending the Union with Egypt, the regime survived in a precarious position for less than two years. In March 1963 a new coup d'état carried out by a mixed group of Ba'thist, Nasserites and independent officers deposed the separatist regime.

1963–1970: Nasser and the Ba'th

The 1963 coup saw 'Pan-Arab' forces back at the helm of the country after the secessionist years. It was the first time that factions ideologically committed to Pan-Arabism were in power in Syria for a significant amount of time. The

1963–1970 phase in particular was dominated by what was in many ways the 'original' Pan-Arab force, the Ba'th party. Given its ideological commitment to Arab unity, the Ba'th party might have been expected to rekindle the United Arab Republic project. However, the relationship between the Ba'th party and Egypt's Nasser was more complex (and certainly more conflict-ridden) than the rhetoric commitment of both parties to Arab unity would have suggested. The Ba'th party (in Iraq as well as in Syria) and Nasser soon proved to be rivals for political and ideological supremacy within the Arab world. The Ba'thist regimes challenged Nasser's role as an Arab leader by testing its commitment to the Palestinian cause and its opposition to Israel. This rivalry emerged clearly in Syria in the aftermath of the 1963 coup d'état, when Ba'thist and Nasserites briefly shared power in Damascus.

Nasserite officials played an important role in the putsch that deposed the Al-Qudsi regime. This group openly supported the Egyptian President and sought to rebuild the project of political union that had suddenly been interrupted in 1961. The Nasserites initially obtained important roles in the newly formed government: Muhammed Al-Sufi became Defence Minister and Rashid Al Qutayni deputy Chief of Staff.[5] However, they were a minority compared with their Ba'thist colleagues and (crucially) the latter group occupied a set of key positions in the army. The two groups had taken up power together but were divided on several key issues and particularly on the links with Cairo. Several key figures among the Ba'thists had observed first-hand (whether from Cairo or from Damascus) the collapse of the United Arab Republic. They feared that a close relationship with Egypt could have ended up with the bigger party dominating Syria. Furthermore, the Ba'thist leadership doubted the Pan-Arab credentials of Nasser and of his Arab Socialist Union. Despite these differences, Union talks between Egypt, Syria and Iraq started shortly after the takeover of power by the Ba'th in Damascus and Baghdad. Within a few months the three Arab powers signed a tripartite agreement that should have paved the way for a new union. Predictably, given the differences between the parties involved, the talks unravelled shortly afterwards. The final nail in the coffin was provided by clashes between Ba'thists and Nasserites in Syria.[6]

Nasser's support within Syria made the Ba'th regime particularly vulnerable when dealing with the Egyptian President. The Movement of Arab Nationalists, the main pro-Nasser political force in Syria, coordinated the different groups that sought to bring the country back under Nasser's influence. Their ability to mobilise Syrian masses was particularly concerning for the Ba'th party, that accused Nasser of trying to undermine its legitimacy in the country.[7] A showdown between the two forces was inevitable. The Ba'th party emerged victorious and was able to impose its control over Syria. The defeat of the Nasserites negatively influenced the relationship between the two leaderships in the following years. The relationship between Cairo and Damascus throughout 1964 and 1965 oscillated between ideological warfare and attempted reconciliations. Egyptian–Syrian contrasts were, however, part of a more generic phase of instability and competition among Arab powers.[8] It was, however, one specific

62 *The alliances of Syria*

issue, the relationship with Israel and the Palestinians, that became the focal point in Syrian and Egyptian politics from the second half of the 1960s onwards.

1966–1970

The relationship between Cairo and Damascus had been embittered by the collapse of the United Arab Republic and the clashes between Ba'thist and Nasserites. The already-strained relations became more complicated when the 'radical Ba'th' regime led by Salah Jadid took over power in Damascus in March 1966. The immediate effect of the takeover was an increase in the volume and venom of Syrian attacks towards enemies and 'friends' alike, including Egypt and its President. On the Syrian–Israeli front, what was already a delicate situation worsened further. Israel was clearly determined to establish its superiority vis-à-vis the new Syrian regime. Frustrated with years of border humiliation, the Jadid regime attempted to respond with all the means in its power. The 'institutional' approach clearly failed when the United Nations Security Council refused to offer even a symbolic condemnation of Israeli violations in the demilitarised zones.[9] The attempts to challenge Israeli military superiority resulted in a series of small border skirmishes, all inevitably favouring Israel. Supporting the Palestinian militias and encouraging them to use Syrian territory to launch attacks appeared as the only option to retaliate against Israel. The relationship with the Palestinian militias was also seen by the Syrian regime as a central aspect of its 'revolutionary' mission. Jadid and his men saw the support of the Palestinian cause against the Israeli occupier as a duty for any Arab country and framed this within the context of anti-colonial struggles taking place at the time in different parts of the world.[10] From Cairo, Nasser and his generals observed with growing discomfort the mounting crisis. Nasser had created the Palestine Liberation Organization in 1964 mainly to organise and control Palestinian resistance. This attempt had, however, backfired, with several groups (such as Yassir Arafat's Fatah or George Habash's Popular Front for the Liberation of Palestine) soon challenging the leadership of pro-Egyptian Palestine Liberation Organization leader Ahmad Shuqairy.[11] Syria had been crucial in the development and growth of these militias given the large number of Palestinian refugees present in the country.

Faced with a growing escalation on the Syrian–Israeli border, Nasser signed a bilateral defence pact with the Syrians in November 1967. There are no indications that he did this in preparation for war. Most observers agree that the goal of the pact was to gain some degree of control over the crisis rather than leaving it to the Syrian regime. Israeli sources maintain that Tel Aviv consciously exploited inter-Arab divisions in the lead up to the war.[12] The air battle that took place over the Sea of Galilee (and resulted in the loss of six Syrian planes) in April 1967 was the tipping point. The Syrian regime had not found a way to contain Israel, but the 'ideological' pressure it had exercised on Nasser had forced the Egyptians to get directly involved. Unable to resist the domestic and international pressure, the Egyptian President asked the United Nations secretary to withdraw United Nations Emergency Force troops from the Sinai Peninsula and subsequently closed the Tiran Strait to Israeli ships. Even at this late stage, the Egyptian leader had only partially understood Israel's intentions and still believed there was a way out of the military escalation he got involved in.[13] In his autobiography, Moshe Dayan maintains that the Egyptian leader knew that his actions would have been interpreted as an act of war by Israel but counted on the restraining influence of the two superpowers to avoid a military escalation.[14] Israel finally broke the impasse with a surprise attack on the 5 June 1967. Despite the mounting tension, there was no sign that the Arabs were expecting an attack. Nasser's aviation force was all but destroyed on the ground by simultaneous Israeli attacks. Without air cover, the Egyptian army was an easy target. After easily disposing of Jordanian and Syrian air forces, Israel's army proceeded to take over East Jerusalem and the West Bank from Jordan, the Golan Heights from Syria and the Sinai Peninsula from Egypt.

The defeat and humiliation did little to bring the two Arab capitals together. If anything, the defeat exacerbated what was already a difficult partnership. Nasser had in fact good reasons to blame the Ba'thists for the 1967 war. The Syrians had put him in an indefensible position. Standing by would have irremediably damaged his reputation as an Arab leader but supporting the Syrians meant risking getting embroiled in a confrontation with Israel. Nasser had reluctantly chosen the latter, and as a result he had found himself on the receiving end of a brutal defeat. The Ba'thist regime on its part showed little sign of more ideological flexibility in the aftermath of the defeat. On the contrary, the Syrian propaganda machine relentlessly attacked fellow Arab states considered to be responsible for the defeat. Saudi Arabia was clearly considered the main offender by the Jadid regime, that saw the Gulf Kingdom as his ideological nemesis. Riyadh was the subject of most of the criticism.[15] Egypt however was not spared. The accusations of lack of commitment to the Arab cause were particularly damaging for Nasser in the aftermath of the 1967 defeat.

The differences between the leaderships of the two countries stemmed from disagreements over how to react to the Six Day War. The Syrians and the Palestine Liberation Organization, supported by Algeria and Iraq, saw an armed struggle until the liberation of the occupied territories as the only viable solution.[16] Nasser and the Jordanian King Hussein on the other hand were more open to diplomatic solutions, and particularly to the possibility of United Nations-sponsored initiatives aimed at addressing more broadly the Arab–Israeli conflict. It is important to note how the difference between Nasser and the Jadid regime was here not only 'tactical' but was firmly rooted in different ideological views. Whilst committed to the Palestinian cause, Nasser separated this issue with the (more urgent) matter of recovering the land lost in 1967. He was therefore more flexible to adopting a multi-step approach. The Ba'thist regime in Syria on the other hand did not see any real difference between the Golan Heights and occupied Palestine. Committed to a 'strict' interpretation of Pan-Arabism and not particularly concerned with Syrian national interest, the Syrian regime saw both as occupied Arab land that had to be freed.[17] The difference between the two

64 The alliances of Syria

approaches emerged clearly in the following months. Syria assumed a rejectionist position and boycotted the 1967 Arab summit in Khartoum. The distance between the two Arab powers grew even further when Egypt (together with Jordan) immediately accepted United Nations Resolution 242. Whilst the resolution called for Israel's withdrawal to pre-1967 lines, it also contained a recognition of Israel. The latter was not acceptable (not yet, at least) to Syria as it was not to the Palestinians. The fact that the disagreement between the two Arab powers was ideological and not only tactical is confirmed by the fact that the War of Attrition and particularly the rejection by both parties of the Rogers plan did not result in a rapprochement between the two parties. A realignment between the two powers could only happen if one of them re-adjusted its regional strategy. The change of regime in Syria was going to create exactly this.

1970: a new era in the Syrian–Egyptian relationship

As shown in the previous chapter, improvements in the relations with the Arab world were the key priority of Hafez Al-Assad when he took over power in 1970. Egypt was in this regard crucial, as it represented the main potential military ally in a conflict with Israel that Al-Assad considered inevitable.[18] The alliance with Egypt was a cornerstone of the regional system envisaged by the Syrian leader. This stemmed from power-based calculations rather than from ideological solidarity or pro-Egyptian sentiments. His counterpart, the new Egyptian President Anwar Sadat, was equally convinced of the necessity of a military alliance with Syria. What the Syrian leader could not know in 1970 is that Sadat had rather different ideas on the future of the regional system and Egypt's position in it. The two leaders differed over the purpose of the next conflict with Israel. Sadat saw it as a tool to obtain a seat at the peace table. Al-Assad as a way to change an unfavourable Arab–Israeli balance of power.

The new Syrian President could have not been suspected of Egyptian sympathies. Like all the Ba'thists of his generation, Hafez Al-Assad admired the Egyptian leader and the way Nasser had stood up to Western powers and Israel in 1956.[19] However, his personal experience had made him wary of Egyptian influence in Syrian politics. Al-Assad (together with Jadid) had been one of several Syrian officials posted in Egypt during the brief period of the United Arab Republic. From Cairo he had observed how (to his horror) the Egyptian leadership had considered Syria more like an Egyptian province than as an equal partner. Together with his fellow Ba'thist officials Al-Assad had encouraged the coup that ended the Union and had been rewarded for it with a brief stay in a Cairo military prison. Upon returning to Syria, he had learnt how dangerous the embrace of Egypt had been for the smaller partner in the coalition. Clearly not enamoured with his fellow Arab state, the new Syrian President, however, disagreed with his predecessors' view over the relationship with Egypt.[20] Unlike Jadid, Al-Assad was concerned with Syria's geopolitical position and particularly with the comparative advantage that Israel enjoyed over the country. To have any chance of surviving another military confrontation with Israel (let alone win back the Golan Heights), Damascus needed to work together with whoever was in power in Cairo. This pragmatic and 'realist' approach to the relationship with Cairo was immediately evident during Al-Assad's first months in power. Nasser's death somehow simplified the task of dealing with Egypt. Whilst the Egyptian leader's reputation had been damaged by the 1967 defeat, his name still had an aura in the Arab world that made him rather threatening to fellow Arab leaders. His successor Anwar Sadat did not possess the same charismatic personality and was therefore an apparently easier partner for the Syrian leader.

In 1970 the new leaders of Syria and Egypt, Hafez Al-Assad and Anwar Sadat, were facing similar challenges. Both oversaw countries (and military apparatus) disheartened by the burning defeat at the hands of Israel, both had lost strategic territory and faced pressure to recover it. The two countries shared the same enemy, needed each other to pursue their respective goals and therefore appeared to be natural allies. Heikal's account[21] shows how Egyptian and Syrian top generals spent the best part of 1972 and 1973 secretly planning the October War. The rapprochement between the Kingdom of Saudi Arabia and Egypt had been the initial driving force behind the formation of the axis. The two countries had been engulfed in the long and bloody Yemeni civil war, from which Egypt came out battered and in a dire financial status. The early 1970s saw a spectacular change in the relation between the two Arab powers, driven by Egypt's more compromising stance and facilitated by the death of Nasser and the start of the Sadat presidency. It was the new Egyptian leadership that in turn mediated to bring about a rapprochement between the Kingdom of Saudi Arabia and Syria. This successful attempt resulted in an economic and trade agreement signed by the two countries in 1972.[22] The formation of this Damascus-Riyadh-Cairo union was functional for the competition between the two 'border states' and Israel, but also represented a moment of relative stability in the usually tumultuous Arab state system. In the following years, observers would often recall this brief phase of cooperation between the three powers almost with a sense of nostalgia for the golden days of Arab unity.[23] In reality, the seeds of the division that were to follow were already planted and would start emerging during the 1973 war.

The 1973 conflict

Both Al-Assad and Sadat thought that another conflict with Israel was inevitable. Yet the 'nature' and the goals of the conflict were, in their minds, drastically different. The war conduct of Egypt and Syria reflected their long-term goals. The two armies attacked simultaneously at 14:00 on the 6 October 1973.[24] The military operation took Tsahal by surprise and the Arabs recorded significant initial gains. Quandt shows how, given the military superiority shown by Israel only six years later, an attack by the Arab forces was not contemplated as a possibility by either Tel Aviv or external observers.[25] On the Sinai front, the Egyptian army was able to gain significant ground, and within a few hours the Bar-Lev line (the first line of Israeli defences) had been cleared. The Syrians' gains had been important too, and by the morning of 7 October Al-Assad's

66 *The alliances of Syria*

troops were in control of a good portion of the Golan Heights, including the highly strategic and symbolic observation point at Jebel el-Sheikh. By the second day of war the Israelis had decided to give priority to the Syrian front, most likely in virtue of their lack of strategic depth on the Golan Heights. This could have given the Egyptians room to advance. Sadat, however, was happy with the 10 km strip conquered in the first two days and ordered his army to stay put and defend what had already been gained. The Soviet ambassador to Cairo, Vinogradov, told Mohamed Heikal in a private conversation on the night of the 9 October that:

> I have been in almost continuous session today with our military attachés ... they don't like the way things are developing. I don't see why your troops are not advancing.... This is not only the sensible thing for your army to do, but it would help take the pressure off the Syrians.[26]

The debate over whether the Egyptian army could have advanced further is fascinating but fundamentally misplaced: the Egyptians did not need to advance. Sadat did not want to win the Sinai Peninsula back by military means (not that he would have necessarily minded to) as he had already calculated that the way to win it back was diplomatic. The shock caused by the first days of war was enough to start a peace process. Seen from this perspective, the attack launched by Egyptian forces on the 14 October is more puzzling. Heikal claims that Sadat gave in to Syrian requests and to Arab pressure, others say that Sadat feared a Syrian capitulation that might have ruined his plans.[27] In any case, the Egyptian offensive was not only late, but also unconvincing and half-hearted.[28]

The Syrians on the other hand fought a war to obtain a military victory. Al-Assad was thrilled by the initial results of the war, then puzzled and finally angered by the Egyptians' failure to advance. Syrian war conduct confirms that Al-Assad had no clue about Sadat's real goals.[29] By the 8 October the Syrians had to withstand growing Israeli pressure. This increased in the following days as the stalemate on the Sinai front allowed Israel to concentrate its forces on the Golan front. After nearly a week of contained but constant gaining, the Israelis were stopped on their way to Damascus by the joint effort of the Syrian forces supported by fresh reinforcements sent by Iraq and Jordan. As Tsahal's initiative gained momentum the Egyptian President increased his cry for a ceasefire, directed at both superpowers; Hafez Al-Assad was in no hurry to reach an armistice and tried to convince Sadat not to do so.[30]

The aftermath of the 1973 war

After the first days of Arab success, the Israeli army was able to counter-attack and eventually regain the upper-hand. The outcome of the war was welcomed as a big success throughout the Arab world. The reality on the ground was very different for the Egyptians. After the failure of the offensive on 14 October, Sadat was at the mercy of the Israelis; his 'open letter' to President Nixon on 16

October was by all means a request for ceasefire. When Resolution 338 was approved by the United Nations Security Council, Egypt was fast to accept it, despite the lack of any direct reference to an Israeli withdrawal.[31] Sadat probably had no alternative, as his Third Army had been outmanoeuvred and the Israelis were about to reach the port of Suez and the core of the country. On the other front, Al-Assad's defences were holding well on the Golan Heights. Helped by Iraqi and Jordanian reinforcements, the Syrian President was planning a counter-attack to regain some of the ground lost in the previous days of fighting. Sadat was facing an immediate threat to his country's survival as his defences were exposed to an Israeli attack. The Syrian President had the luxury of being able to wait, as his defences were not facing immediate collapse. If Al-Assad's military situation was better, in terms of the respective 'grand strategies', the war was a success for Sadat and a defeat for Al-Assad. Hinnebusch maintains that the ceasefire had left Syria in a much stronger position from a tactical point of view, but it was Egypt that was in a stronger diplomatic position since it was Cairo and not Damascus that the Israeli and American leadership wanted to engage with in a negotiation process.[32]

The differences caused by the diverging goals of Syria and Egypt had emerged already during the conflict and were to grow bigger immediately after. The rift opened wider during the aftermath of the war, characterised by Kissinger's diplomatic initiative and Sadat's willingness to disengage.[33] Al-Assad did not attend the December 1973 Geneva Conference (Sadat did) and, despite his personal grievances against the Egyptian President, tried to prevent his counterpart from unilaterally pursuing peace with Israel. By the beginning of 1974, Al-Assad had most likely comprehended Sadat's intentions, although he was not fully aware of the contact that the Egyptian counter-parts had had with the Americans. Al-Assad attempted to present a united front despite what he undoubtedly perceived as Sadat's betrayal, and aimed to increase the pressure on the Egyptian leader to prevent him from reaching peace with Israel. In terms of negotiating strength, Al-Assad obviously knew that separating from Egypt would have meant Damascus losing all the diplomatic advantage that it had gained with its good military performance in 1973.

Despite the triumphant tone assumed by its leaders and the public opinion in the aftermath of the war, Egypt's military performance had been rather modest.[34] Sadat had nonetheless reached his political goals. His 'shock diplomacy' had won him his long-term goal, the possibility to negotiate a peace agreement with Israel under the patronage of the United States. Seale claims that Sadat deceived Al-Assad and was in turn fooled by Henry Kissinger.[35] While it is likely that Sadat underestimated the Secretary of State's commitment to Israel, the Egyptian leader was taking a calculated risk in the hope of obtaining what he considered the two key goals of his foreign policy: the recovery of the Sinai Peninsula and a peace agreement with Israel. Kissinger's 'step-by-step' diplomacy provided the Egyptian President with the ideal conditions to pursue his goal. Sadat and Kissinger's diplomatic goals coincided nearly perfectly. Like the Egyptian President, the American Secretary of State needed an official

68   *The alliances of Syria*

framework of 'multilateral diplomacy' to keep all the key players happy, but was relying on bilateral (and secret) negotiations to reach the real agreements. William Quandt maintains that the Geneva Conference of 1973 served exactly the purpose of pleasing the Soviets by making them believe they were involved in the peace process, while carrying out a parallel diplomacy aimed to separate definitively the Soviet Union from its key ally in the region.[36] For both Sadat and Kissinger, the complicated disengagement agreement was the first practical step necessary towards the achievement of a political goal.

The pursuit of longer-term political goals explains Sadat's relative malleability in the disengagement negotiations, in stark contrast with Al-Assad's stubborn resistance against American pressure during the first diplomatic rounds with Henry Kissinger.[37] As Sadat envisaged warmer relations with the United States and a comprehensive peace agreement with Israel, the matter of military disengagement looked rather secondary to him. On the other end Al-Assad saw the 1973 conflict as one step in the long-term confrontation of Israel and was determined to get the best possible deal after the good display by his military forces. Al-Assad was at this stage ready to negotiate a comprehensive settlement, one that included a solution to the Palestinians' plight. This would have meant recovering the Golan Heights and overcoming the 'state of war' with Israel but would not have completely changed the nature of the relations with a state that would have remained an enemy. The Egyptian President grew increasingly annoyed at the Syrian's attempt to slow down the path he had chosen for his country. By early 1975 Al-Assad had started to realise that he had 'lost' Egypt but was determined to impose the highest possible price on Sadat for his defection. The two-year period that followed proved to be extremely negative for Al-Assad, who was outplayed by Sadat and Kissinger's diplomacy.[38]

The process of Egypt's detachment from Moscow culminated in March 1976 when Sadat abrogated the 'Treaty of Friendship' which the two countries had signed in 1971. This represented the last piece of the puzzle before Sadat's historical visit to Jerusalem and his speech to the Knesset on 20 November 1977. The Camp David Agreements reached the following year included two separate documents, *A Framework for Peace in the Middle East* and *A Framework for the Conclusion of a Peace Treaty between Egypt and Israel*. Although the two processes should have been carried out in parallel, the separation of the two issues allowed Sadat to free himself from the 'burden' of the Palestinian issue, a long-term goal of the Egyptian President. In the aftermath of 1977, the battle for the Middle East seemed to have one clear loser, Hafez Al-Assad. The Syrian President had lost his key ally and was left alone in his opposition to Israel. Israel and its patron, the United States, had managed to neutralise Egypt and take the biggest Arab country out of the equation. Anwar Sadat had reached his goal and moved Egypt from one side of the Middle East to the other. Sadat had won his peace agreement and was now free to pursue the 'new' Egyptian foreign policy in the American camp. This did not come without price: Egypt had to suffer long years of isolation from the Arab world in exchange for peace with Israel. Throughout most of the 1980s, the relationship between Syria and Egypt was virtually non-existent. When Egypt was readmitted into mainstream Arab politics, it was through its support of Iraq during the Iran–Iraq war. The relationship between Cairo and Damascus, however, never recovered the same centrality it had in the 1970s.

Conclusion: Syria and Egypt

The relationship between Syria and Egypt shows an interesting and complex interaction between structural and ideological elements. The regional balance of power and the presence of Israel made Syria and Egypt (sometimes unwilling) allies. Ideological competition and particularly the radicalism of the first Ba'th years, however, contributed to making the two ideological rivals, divided rather than united by the 1967 defeat. The first Ba'th regimes were hostile to Nasser's Egypt, that was perceived as an ideological rival but also as a threat to the party's newly established rule. The radical Syrian regimes 'used' the presence of Israel and the Palestinian cause as a tool to challenge Nasser and expose (what they perceived as) his lack of real commitment to the Pan-Arab cause. This inter-Arab competition led to the disastrous 1967 defeat at the hands of Israel. Despite the clear tilt of the regional balance in favour of Israel, the Syrian and Egyptian regime were unable to coordinate due to their ideological differences that led to different foreign policy priorities. It was only with the reshaping of Syrian foreign policy under Al-Assad that the two regimes enjoyed a phase of cooperation. Al-Assad's pragmatic approach and limited revisionism allowed for a quick improvement in the relationship with Egypt's new supremo Anwar Sadat.

Al-Assad and Sadat spent the early 1970s planning together for the next war on Israel. This rapprochement, however, proved to be only temporary. Egypt under Sadat was in fact transitioning from limited revisionism to a 'status quo' stance by joining the American-led camp. The long-term political trajectories of Syria and Egypt were shaped by their different geopolitical conditions. Both Egypt and Syria had to cope with Israel's expansionism and effective military machine. The strengthening of Israel's partnership with the United States, the superpower that was more influential in the Middle East, increased the pressure on both Damascus and Cairo. However, because of the differences in geopolitical situation, and most of all because of its relevance in regional politics, Egyptian leader Sadat was able to 'switch off' the rivalry with Israel in the aftermath of the 1973 conflict. As Egypt aligned itself with the United States and signed a separate peace with Israel, the Syrian President was forced to look for new allies to pursue his limited revisionist goal.

Notes

1 Raymond Hinnebusch, *Syria: Revolution from Above* (London: Routledge, 2001), 140.
2 Hair Dekmejian, *Egypt under Nassir: A Study in Political Dynamics* (Albany: State University of New York Press, 1971), 58.

70 *The alliances of Syria*

3 Malcolm H. Kerr, *The Arab Cold War: Gamel Abd Al-Nasir and his Rivals, 1958–1970* (3rd edition) (Oxford: Oxford University Press, 1971).
4 Ibid., 33.
5 Patrick Seale, *Assad of Syria: The Struggle for the Middle East* (London: I.B. Tauris, 1988), 79.
6 Kerr, *The Arab Cold War*, 75–80.
7 Seale, *Assad of Syria*, 83.
8 Kerr, *The Arab Cold War*.
9 Seale, *Assad of Syria*, 120.
10 Ibid., 124.
11 Avraham Sela and Moshe Ma'oz, *The PLO and Israel: From Armed Conflict to Political Solution, 1964–1994* (London: St Martin's Press, 1997).
12 Moshe Dayan, *Story of My Life: An Autobiography* (London: Weidenfeld and Nicholson, 1976).
13 Kerr, *The Arab Cold War*, 127.
14 Dayan, *Story of My Life*, 308.
15 Sonoko Sunayama, *Syria and Saudi Arabia: Collaboration and Conflicts in the Oil Era* (London: I.B. Tauris, 2007).
16 Yoram Meital, "The Khartoum Conference and Egyptian Policy after 1967: A Reexamination," *The Middle East Journal* 54, 1 (2000): 63–80.
17 Ibid., 71.
18 Hinnebusch, *Syria*.
19 Seale, *Assad of Syria*, 54–60.
20 Ibid., 189.
21 Mohammad Heikal, *The Road to Ramadan* (London: Collins, 1975).
22 Sunayama, *Syria and Saudi Arabia*.
23 Ibid., ch. I.
24 The issue of the timing of the attack had been widely debated between the two armies and was finally solved by the Presidents.
25 William Quandt, *Decade of Decisions: American Policy towards the Arab–Israeli Conflict, 1967–1976* (Berkley: University of California Press, 1977), 165.
26 Heikal, *The Road to Ramadan*, 218.
27 Ibid.
28 Seale, *Assad of Syria*, 213.
29 Ibid., 207–211.
30 Heikal, *The Road to Ramada*, 230–238.
31 Ibid., 233.
32 Raymond Hinnebusch, *The International Politics of the Middle East* (Manchester, Manchester University Press, 2003), 239.
33 For an extensive account of Kissinger's diplomacy in the Middle East see Edward Sheehan, *The Arabs, Israelis and Kissinger. A Secret History of American Diplomacy in the Middle East* (New York: Thomas Crowell, 1976).
34 Moshe Shemesh, "The Origins of Sadat's Strategic Volte-face," *Israel Studies* 23, 13 (2008): 28–53.
35 Seale, *Assad of Syria*.
36 Quandt, *Decade of Decisions*.
37 Seale, *Assad of Syria*.
38 Ibid., 256.

6 Syria and Jordan

This chapter looks at the relationship between the Syrian Arab Republic and the Kingdom of Jordan. It focuses particularly on the 'ideological era' before 1970 and on the rapprochement of the mid-1970s. The two modern states of Jordan and Syria were carved out of the historical Bilad Ash-Sham region. Despite these common roots, the first years of the relationship saw contrasts and divisions rather than cooperation. In the immediate aftermath of World War II, the Hashemite King Abdullah of Jordan had clear ambitions to gain power in Damascus. Throughout the 1960s, the two countries were ideological rivals, as Trans-Jordan was firmly in the pro-Western campus. The two countries were also divided by their position on the Palestinian issue. A high percentage of the Jordanian population was of Palestinian origin and (from the second half of the 1960s onwards) militias established a strong military presence in Amman. The Palestinian forces grew enough to become a direct threat to the Hashemite Kingdom. This disagreement nearly escalated into a full-blown conflict in September 1970, when the Syrians committed a division in support of the Palestinian militias battered by the Jordanian King. The military response by the Jordanians, supported by the United States and Israel, forced the Syrians into an inglorious retreat.

The relationship between the two countries improved only marginally when the new Syrian leader took over power in 1970. Jordan's intervention in the 1973 conflict warmed relations between the two Arab capitals, but it was Egypt's progress towards a peace agreement with Israel and the Palestine Liberation Oragnization's involvement in Lebanon that led the two countries to set apart their differences. The relationship between the two countries went from conflict to cooperation within a few years. This rapprochement was driven by changes at the regional level and particularly by developments in Arab–Israeli relations. Syria's switch from unlimited to limited revisionism was also one of the factors that led to an improved relationship. Despite the end of 'ideological hostility', the Kingdom did not play a central role in Syria's regional strategy. Jordan was anchored to Western powers and had developed a 'silent understanding' with Israel. The alignment between the two Arab powers was therefore mostly symbolic. The 1975–1977 alliance was motivated by a momentary overlapping in their interests. However, in the long term the diverging regional goals of Syria and Jordan led the collapse of the alignment and a return to pre-1975 dynamics.

72   *The alliances of Syria*

Syria and Jordan before 1963

Modern Syria and Jordan had historically been part of the same geographical (and often political) region, the Bilad Al-Sham or Greater Syria. The two states were born out of similar processes of state formation, both artificially carved out by colonial powers in the first part of the twentieth century. In the aftermath of World War I, the Hashemite King Faisal was briefly proclaimed King of Syria, but subsequently removed by the colonial power France. When Faisal and his brother Abdullah were put in charge of Iraq and Trans-Jordan respectively, the recovery of the lost land became one of their main policy goals. Particularly active on this front was King Abdullah of Trans-Jordan, whose relations with Israel have been well documented.[1] Alon maintains that the Kingdom considered Trans-Jordan as a 'springboard' for the recovery of Syria.[2] The military success of 1948 (with the British Legion of Trans-Jordan the only Arab force able to achieve significant success against the Haganah/ Israel Defence Forces) had left King Abdullah in control of half of Jerusalem, including the religious complex including the Holy Mount and the Dome of the Rock. This had undoubtedly raised Abdullah's status among the Arab leaders and increased his ambitions within the broader Levant region. In the aftermath of the war the King was therefore one of the protagonists of the 'Struggle for Syria' described by Patrick Seale.[3] From the 1950s onwards, the political trajectories of the two countries diverged significantly. King Abdullah maintained and worked to strengthen the historical links with the former colonial power Britain. Jordan established itself as one of the West's staunchest allies in the Arab world.

The Palestinian issue and the broader Arab–Israeli conflict were from the onset a central concern for Jordanian policy-makers. Because of the social basis supporting the Hashemite regime and its strong Palestinian population, the Trans-Jordanian leadership perceived Pan-Arabism and particularly Palestinian irredentism as a threat to its survival.[4] The rising star of Abdel Nasser was as attractive to the Jordanian masses as it was to their Syrian counterparts. However, the strength of the Hashemite control over the country meant that Jordan was able to maintain its independence when Syria joined Egypt in the ill-fated United Arab Republic. The Union was, however, undoubtedly a worrying development for the Jordanian monarchy. In the early 1960s the tide in the region seemed to favour the progressive republics and particularly Nasser's Egypt. The collapse of the Union interrupted this trend and was clearly a positive development for the leadership in Amman. Jordan (together with Saudi Arabia) was the main backer of Lieutenant Abd Al-Karim Nahwali, the officer that had led the coup against the Unionist regime.[5] In Amman, the replacement of the more Pan-Arab (and pro-Egyptian) Bajhat Talhuni with the pro-Iraqi Wasfi Al-Tall had confirmed that the King and his circle saw Jordan's place as firmly within the pro-Western camp.[6]

1963–1970

The shift in favour of conservative forces was only temporary, as confirmed by the military coup that put the Pan-Arab Ba'th Party in power in both Syria and Iraq less than two years after the collapse of the United Arab Republic. The 1963 coup d'état began a new phase in Syrian politics. The regime change did not help the relationship between Syria and Jordan. The instability and internal fragmentation of the Syrian regime complicated the relationship with external actors, but in the case of Jordan the diverging long-term foreign policy trajectories of the two countries were undoubtedly the main factor of discord. This was particularly evident as the Jordanian leadership tried to consolidate its position within the conservative camp amid the strong Pan-Arab tide in the region.[7] In this phase of great regional instability, the leadership of the Jordanian Kingdom tried to reinforce its partnership with Saudi Arabia that had been started by the signing of a joint defence agreement in 1962. It also threw its (limited) weight behind the conservative forces that were fighting the civil war in Yemen. Robins shows how the Jordanian involvement derived from the Kingdom's willingness to strengthen and solidify the 'monarchies bloc'.[8] However, the Jordanians could not prevent the creation of the Palestine Liberation Organization at the hands of Nasser and were ultimately forced to accept the presence of the militias in the country (albeit within an Arab framework that was supposed to limit their range of activities). By accepting the role of the Egyptian-created Palestine Liberation Organization, the Jordanian leadership had essentially given in to 'Pan-Arab' pressure and recognised the leadership of Cairo on the Palestinian issue.

In the mid-1960s the Kingdom of Jordan found itself in a delicate position with regard to the Palestinian issue. The matter got significantly worse after another coup d'état in Damascus saw the radical Ba'th faction led by Salah Jadid take over power in the country. The radical Ba'th regime in power in Syria was implacably hostile to the Arab monarchies. Its disagreement with the Kingdom of Jordan was ideological and shaped their opposite stances over the Palestinian issue. The Jadid regime increased its support of Palestinian militias, whilst the Jordanians did their best to limit the militias' attacks directed at Israel. Tel Aviv, however, frequently decided to punish both Syria and Jordan for the Palestinian attacks, even though the latter was in fact attempting to limit the military activities.[9] The attack on the Jordanian village of Samu in November 1966 was particularly costly for the Kingdom. On the 13 November the Israeli army mounted a quick and effective sortie against the village located in the Hebron region. The Israeli army was acting in response to an alleged Fatah operation that had taken place from Syria. The attack resulted in the death of about 15 Jordanian soldiers and an unspecified number of civilians.[10] The main effect of the attack was to shake the already unstable Jordanian political system by showing the Kingdom's inability to respond to Israel's military sorties. The attack ultimately drove the Kingdom closer to the Arab powers.

The Kingdom's policy was at odds with the one carried out by the Syrian Ba'thist regimes in the 1960s. The Jadid regime in Syria pursued a 'revolutionary'

74   *The alliances of Syria*

agenda and sought to encourage an Arab popular war versus Israel. The Jordanians on the other hand were concerned with regime survival and tried to manage the risk of conflict. Nevertheless, the strength of Pan-Arab sentiment forced the Hashemite monarchy to show at least symbolic support to the Arabs in their struggle against Israel. Jordanian involvement in the lead up to 1967 was in many ways imposed by the dynamics of inter-Arab politics in the 1960s. These allowed 'radical' countries such as Syria to pressure fellow Arab states into showing at least a degree of support to the Pan-Arab and Palestinian cause (and therefore to the fight against Israel). In the case of Jordan, this was particularly risky as the Kingdom (unlike Saudi Arabia or Iraq) shared a long border with Israel and was in control of land coveted by Israel. The Kingdom effectively had to manage the clashing goals of keeping domestic control in front of the growing Pan-Arab tide and avoiding provoking Israel. Despite the well-documented contact established between the Jordanians and the leadership in Tel Aviv, this path was an increasingly narrow one for the Jordanian King. This ambiguous policy did not spare Hussein from the 1967 defeat, which saw the Kingdom lose the whole West Bank and Jerusalem to Tsahal (Israeli army). The defeat and consequent growing influence of organised Palestinian fighters in the Kingdom led to a phase of instability in the country, with Jordanian authorities losing control over parts of the country to Palestinian militias and particularly the Palestine Liberation Organization.

King Hussein bore the highest price for the 1967 war, having lost over half of his reign and all of Jerusalem. The defeat, however, created the basis for a new relationship with Egypt.[11] The 1967 Khartoum meeting (famous for the 'three nos') showed how Nasser had abandoned his more radical stance of the previous years and now shared with the Jordanian a preference for a diplomacy first approach to the relationship with Israel. This was in stark contrast with the regime in Damascus, that initially rejected United Nations Resolution 242 and (crucially) boycotted the Khartoum meeting. The regime in Damascus needed a scapegoat to blame for its defeat and pro-Western monarchies such as Jordan provided a perfect opportunity. Relations between the two Arab capitals therefore remained negative in the aftermath. It was, however, in 1970 that Syrian–Jordanian relations took a real turn for the worse, and it was over the issue of the relationship with the Palestinians. The power and prestige of the Palestinian 'fedayeen' (guerrilla fighters) had grown so much that they represented a clear threat to the Hashemite leadership in Amman.[12] King Hussein of Jordan decided to reaffirm his authority over the country and ordered the crushing of the Palestinian militias. The events that followed, commonly remembered as Black September, were a shock for the whole region. The images of an Arab army fighting Palestinian militias sparked protests in several Arab capitals and prompted most Arab leaders to condemn Jordanian actions.[13] The crisis coincided with a transitional phase in Syria, with Hafez Al-Assad progressively establishing his control over the country. Faced with an all-out confrontation and the potential destruction of the Palestinian guerrillas, the leader *in pectore* of Syria decided to intervene and Syrian troops entered Jordan on the 20 September 1970. Met by a strong Jordanian reaction and the threat of involvement by Israel and the United States, Al-Assad decided against committing its air forces and the battered Syrian troops were forced to retire on the 22 September. This episode was a baptism of fire for Al-Assad and undoubtedly shaped relations between the two countries in the following years. The events of 1967–1970 drove Jordan firmly back into the pro-Western camp, after drifting slightly away from it because of the Pan-Arab tide.[14] The crisis also represented a turning point in the long-term trajectory of Jordanian-Israeli relations. Israel had shown its value as a guarantor against external threats and the Jordanians (despite the 1973 war) started reframing their regional security strategy in the region around an unofficial relationship with Tel Aviv through American patronage.[15]

Throughout the 'radical Ba'th' years Jordan and Syria were divided by ideological differences that translated into policy issues. The Jordanian monarchy, with its pro-Western policy and its cautious approach to the Arab–Israeli issue, was the ideal propaganda target for Ba'thist regimes eager to show their commitment to the Arab and Palestinian cause. The Kingdom was in turn particularly vulnerable to this kind of accusations because of its significant Palestinian population. The 1967 defeat increased Jordan's reliance on the West and signalled the end of Jordan's brief flirt with Pan-Arabism. The 1970 crisis exposed the centrality of the Palestinian issue to Syrian–Jordanian relations. The differences between the Al-Assad and Jadid groups over how to address the crisis also showed how national interest and commitment to Pan-Arabism were at the core of the relationship between Amman and Damascus.

The Al-Assad years

The core argument of this analysis is that the shift from unlimited to limited revisionism in Syrian foreign policy led to change in Damascus' overall approach to alliances. The case of Jordan shows both this new pragmatic approach by the Syrian leadership and the continuation of a pre-existing patterns of rivalry. As outlined in Chapter 2 of this volume, the new Syrian leader actively worked to improve Damascus' relations with fellow Arab states. The relationship with Jordan, however, remained tepid, if not openly hostile. Jordan was a status quo power aligned with the Western states. The Jordanian 'informal relationship' with Israel, based on the common fear of organised Palestinian groups,[16] was clearly at odds with the 'limited' revisionism of Hafez Al-Assad. Furthermore, Jordan did not possess Egypt's military power nor Saud Arabia's financial and economic resources, making Amman less of an asset to the Syrians.

The Syrian President spent his first years in power working to build a war coalition against Israel. His main interlocutor in this phase was Anwar Sadat. The fact that King Hussein of Jordan was not involved in the organisation was unsurprising given the lack of trust between the Presidents of Syria and Egypt and the Jordanian King. Seale shows how the Syrian leader never considered the Kingdom as a potential war partner.[17] The long history of discord between the two countries, and (even more so) Jordan's relationship with Israel, suggested

76 *The alliances of Syria*

that the Kingdom was not a viable partner. In fact, there were solid reasons to distrust Hussein. The Jordanian leader during those years was holding regular talks with the Israeli leadership and particularly with Prime Minister Golda Meir and Minister of Defence Moshe Dayan.[18] These frequent meetings were probably the basis for the rumours that the Jordanian King informed the Israeli leadership of the upcoming military attack. Whilst it is difficult to know exactly what the King told the Israelis and particularly Golda Meir, contact between Tel Aviv and Amman became more frequent before the conflict. However, Hussein was most likely not aware of the crucial details, such as when the attack was to take place.[19] Despite this mutual mistrust, immediately before the war the leaders of Egypt and Syria decided to restore relations with Jordan (that had been officially suspended after the Black September events).[20] In exchange, the Jordanian King made token gestures of support to his fellow Arabs. When the war started, however, the King remained a concerned spectator. In the delicate game of regional balance, a complete victory for any of the parties would have represented a threat for Hussein. This is the main reason that the Jordanians sent a division on the 14 October in defence of Damascus. Concerned about the prospect of a Syrian collapse, King Abdullah followed Iraq's lead in committing a limited amount of forces to help the Syrian defence against the Israeli push. This Jordanian involvement contributed to improve the relationship between the two Arab capitals. It was, however, the shift in the regional balance of power caused by Egypt's path towards realignment with the United States and Israel that led to a dramatic (albeit short lived) improvement in the Syrian–Jordanian relationship.

The 1975–1977 alignment

The temporary alignment between the Syrian Arab Republic and the Kingdom of Jordan represented a meaningful development, particularly considering that the two countries were engaged in a military confrontation less than five year earlier. What drove this temporary alignment were first the developments in Egyptian–Israeli relations. In the aftermath of the 1973 conflict both Jordan and Syria were side-lined by the Egyptian–Israeli peace process led by Kissinger.[21] It was in particular the reopening of talks between Israel and Egypt in the second half of 1975 that caused a quick improvement in the relationship between Damascus and Amman. This round of negotiations led to the Sinai II Agreement. The partial withdraw of Israel from Egyptian land and the creation of a buffer zone was one of the most important steps towards a comprehensive Egyptian–Israeli agreement. Worried by Egypt's transition towards a separate peace with Israel, the two countries managed to set apart the acrimony of previous years. Another important factor in the alignment between the two countries was the hostility towards the Palestine Liberation Organization and its leader Yassir Arafat. The Jordanian King and the Palestinian leader had been mortal foes since the Black September crisis. Despite the defeat of the Palestine Liberation Organization in Jordan, Arafat represented a significant ideological and political threat for the Kingdom. The Syrian President and the Palestinian leader on the other hand were at odds over the latter's role in the developing Lebanese Civil War. The flow of Palestinian militias from Jordan to Lebanon had threatened to destabilise the already delicate balance in the Cedar country. By the mid-1970s the situation in the country was close to breaking point. Despite Syria's traditional role as a defender of the leftist and Palestinian militias, Al-Assad was increasingly worried by the potential of a radical Lebanon led by Arafat and Druze leader Kamal Jumblatt. The Syrian President cautioned the two leaders not to attempt to take over the country, but his threats were ignored. The intervention by the Syrian leader in Lebanon put Arafat on the backfoot and created a convergence of interests between Amman and Damascus.[22]

These two factors together led to a strengthening of the Syria–Jordanian relationship, and to the establishment of a joint military command during 1975–1977. The brief alignment between the two Arab capitals started with a series of economic agreements and meetings between high-level officials.[23] In 1975 the Syrian President visited Amman: during meetings with Jordanian officials a potential merger between Syria and Jordan was discussed.[24] Despite the symbolic relevance of these actions, the practical impact of these was in fact very limited. The two countries agreed to suspend previous enmity to check Egypt's progress towards a peace agreement with Israel and undermine a common foe (Yassir Arafat and the Palestine Liberation Organization). The military coordination between the two countries did not go much further than a few small-scale military exercises (ran together with the Kingdom of Saudi Arabia). Like the case of Iraq, this was more a short-term détente than a long-term alignment, and towards the end of the 1970s the two countries were going back towards the previous pattern of competition. Egyptian foreign policy in the aftermath of the 1973 war had been one of the driving factors behind the Syrian–Jordanian alignment. The issue of how to deal with Egypt's 'defection' was the immediate cause of the break-down of this temporary alignment. Sadat's Jerusalem visit in November 1977 and the Camp David Accords the following year were met with different reactions in Damascus and Amman. Syria was vocally against the agreement, a position illustrated by the Syrian ambassador to the United Nations who claimed that 'Egypt had stabbed Syria in the back'.[25] Jordan's reaction was more careful. King Hussein did not endorse Sadat's choice, but he refused to join the chorus of accusation led by Syria and Iraq. The position of the Jordanian King can be explained by uncertainty about the consequences of the agreement as well as by its close alliance with the Western powers that had supported the Egyptian–Israeli rapprochement. The King was eventually forced to fall in line with other Arab powers, but this was mostly because the Israelis and the Americans did not really tempt him with a palatable offer.[26] By then the relationship between Damascus and Amman had returned to the previous dynamics of mistrust and disagreement. Regional developments between the end of the decade and the beginning of the 1980s further increased the hostility between the two countries. This time it was the Iranian revolution and the following events that led to new tensions between the two capitals.

78 *The alliances of Syria*

The 1980s

The Iran–Iraq war shaped the relationship between Jordan and Syria throughout most of the 1980s. The polarisation of the Arab world caused by the Gulf War appeared in all its seriousness during the November 1980 Amman Summit of the Arab League. Not only did Syria and the Steadfastness Front (Algeria, Libya and the Palestine Liberation Organization) boycott the meeting, but Al-Assad also massed his troops on the Jordanian front, causing a stand-off that effectively derailed the meeting.[27] The crisis was solved due to a Saudi mediation that prevented it from escalating into a military confrontation but the relations between Amman and Damascus remained strained. In the early 1980s the relations were also marred by Jordan's support of the Syrian Muslim Brotherhood at the time when the regime was entangled in a mortal fight with Islamist forces.[28] In the aftermath of Iran's counterattack on Iraqi territory, Jordan was part of the Arab attempts to lure Syria away from Iran, but the relation between the two countries remain rocky, with temporary rapprochements followed by sudden worsening and increases in hostile propaganda. Robins[29] indicates how during one of these rapprochements in 1985 Hussein apologised for his previous support of Syrian Islamists. Despite this and other openings, the relationship between the two Arab powers never returned to the heights of the mid-1970s. It was not until the 2000s, with the new young leaders in power, that Jordan and Syria achieved a substantial improvement in their relations.[30] This confirms that, besides the ideological hostility of the 1960s, the two countries were divided by their different regional goals and the 1975–1977 alignment was only a pause in a broader pattern of competition.

Conclusion: Syria and Jordan

The Syrian–Jordanian relationship represents a particularly interesting and telling case study for this analysis. The two Arab states emerged out of parallel state formation processes. They were, however, divided by their clashing regional goals. Jordan was a status quo and pro-Western power, Syria a revisionist (albeit from 1970 a limited one) seeking to challenge Israel and Western predominance in the region. The two countries were on different fronts of the regional divide. The relationship between the two countries changed significantly during the analysed period. The first Ba'th years were characterised by ideological enmity among the two parties. The Black September events in particular show how the Palestinian issue (the quintessential Pan-Arab cause) was central to these differences. The 1970s on the other hand showed a more pragmatic relationship between the two countries amid persisting differences. Syria and Jordan remained rivals divided over important regional issues. They were, however, able to set apart their differences at least temporarily because of regional changes that brought the two powers closer. The mid-1970s in particular saw a significant deviation from the pattern of competition that had characerised Syrian–Jordanian relations in the previous years. This is particularly remarkable considering that the two Arab powers not only had a long history of mistrust and disagreements but had also been involved in a military confrontation less than five years earlier.

During the 1975–1977 years Amman and Damascus managed to put their disagreements and contrasts behind them and align. The most obvious display of this newly-found harmony was the establishment of a joint military commission in 1976. The causes of this temporary alliance were mutual opposition to the step-by-step diplomacy that was moving Egypt towards an agreement with Israel and enmity towards the Palestine Liberation Organization and its leader Arafat as the Lebanese Civil War was escalating. After the Camp David agreements, the diverging goals of Syria and Jordan re-emerged. The Syrians strongly opposed Egypt's move and sought to punish Cairo (and take advantage of their position as the main Arab front state). The Jordanians on the other hand hesitated to condemn the Egyptian leadership and were clearly more open to follow Egypt's path towards a peace agreement with Israel. This split effectively ended the short détente between Damascus and Amman. The disagreement over the issue of Egypt's engagement with Israel and the United States reflected the different (and conflicting) goals of Syria and Jordan. The alignment between the two Arab powers was caused by a temporary overlapping of interests, not by the end of the long-term structural differences that had marred the relationship in the previous years. The Iran–Iraq war was soon to start, offering a reminder of the distance between the regional policies of Syria and Jordan. The ability to strategically align itself to the Jordanian regime, however, shows the more pragmatic approach of the new Syrian leadership to alliance policy.

Notes

1 Avi Shlaim, *Collusion across the Jordan* (Oxford: Oxford University Press, 1988).
2 Yoav Alon, *The Making of Jordan: Tribes, Colonialism and the Modern State* (London: I.B. Tauris, 2009), 37.
3 Patrick Seale, *The Struggle for Syria: A Study of Post-War Arab Politics 1945–1958* (2nd edition) (Oxford: Oxford University Press, 1965).
4 Bassel Salloukh, "State Strength, Permeability, and Foreign Policy Behavior: Jordan in Theoretical Perspective," *Arab Studies Quarterly* 18, 2 (1996): 1–24.
5 Patrick Seale, *Assad of Syria: The Struggle for the Middle East* (London: I.B. Tauris, 1988), 67.
6 Philip Robins, *A History of Jordan* (Cambridge: Cambridge University Press, 2004), 121.
7 Ibid., ch.VI.
8 Ibid., 109.
9 Seale, *Assad of Syria*, 85.
10 Avi Shlaim, *Lion of Jordan: The Life of King Hussein in War and Peace* (London: Penguin Books, 2017), 223.
11 Malcolm H. Kerr, *The Arab Cold War: Gamel Abd Al-Nasir and His Rivals, 1958–1970* (3rd edition) (Oxford: Oxford University Press, 1971), 129.
12 Shlaim, *Lion of Jordan*, 311.
13 Ibid., 326.
14 Raymond Hinnebusch and Neil Quillam, "Contrary Siblings: Syria, Jordan and the Iran Iraq War," *Cambridge Review of International Affairs* 19 (2006).

80 *The alliances of Syria*

15 Ibid., 514.
16 Ibid., 516.
17 Seale, *Assad of Syria*, 187.
18 Robins, *A History of Jordan*, 140.
19 Shlaim, *Lion of Jordan*, 362–370.
20 Ibid., 359.
21 Ibid., 375.
22 Robins, *A History of Jordan*, 146.
23 Curtis R. Ryan, *Inter-Arab Alliances: Regime Security and Jordanian Foreign Policy* (Gainesville: University of Florida, 2009).
24 Alan George, *Jordan: Living in the Crossfire* (London: Zed Books, 2005).
25 Colin Legum, *Middle East Contemporary Survey* (London: Holmes and Meier, 1978), 217.
26 Robins, *A History of Jordan*, 149.
27 Sonoko Sunayama, *Syria and Saudi Arabia: Collaboration and Conflicts in the Oil Era* (London: I.B. Tauris, 2007), 95.
28 Raphael Lefevre, *Ashes of Hama: The Muslim Brotherhood in Syria* (London: Hurst and Co., 2013).
29 Robins, *A History of Jordan*, 152.
30 Ryan, *Inter-Arab Alliances*.

7 Syria and Iraq

This chapter analyses the Syrian–Iraqi relationship. Relations between the two Arab states throughout their modern history were often marred by mistrust and contrasts. This pattern of enmity and competition between the two countries is particularly puzzling if we consider that both countries were, throughout most of the period analysed, revisionist powers led by the Ba'th party. Both Syria and Iraq were unhappy with a regional system that they perceived as disadvantageous. Yet this similar attitude towards the regional balance did not push them towards cooperation but was rather a factor of competition. In the aftermath of World War II Iraq was the West's most influential ally in the Arab world. As Syria gravitated towards Egypt and the 'progressive republics', the relationship between Baghdad and Damascus became increasingly difficult. In 1963 the Ba'th party took over power in both countries (albeit in Iraq it lost it and subsequently regained it). Despite this ideological affinity, the regimes that ruled Syria and Iraq proved to be rivals rather than allies. The Jadid regime in particular engaged in a vicious propaganda war with its Iraqi counterpart.

As predicted by this study, ideological competition diminished when the more pragmatic Al-Assad regime took over power in 1970. But whilst ideological competition became less central, differences based on geopolitics and 'status' grew because of Syria's new role in the Arab world. In the aftermath of Egypt's defection, Syria and Iraq competed for a central role in the Arab world. The 1978 détente was a temporary alignment that went very much against the broader trend of relations between the two countries. This alignment did not last long and within less than two years the two countries were back to their previous (sour) relations. By the time Saddam Hussein had decided to attack Al-Assad's newest ally, Iran, the two Arab powers were back to their old competitive ways. This long conflict was only one of the scenarios in which the Iraqi-Syrian rivalry manifested itself. The Lebanese Civil War provided the two Arab powers with further issues of disagreement.

Relations before 1963

Like Syria, Iraq emerged within its modern boundaries as a result of an agreement between the colonial powers of Britain and France. The state is composed

82 *The alliances of Syria*

of three former provinces of the Ottoman empire: Baghdad, Mosul and Basra. Iraq is a very complex ethnic and religious mix, with Shias constituting about 60 per cent of the population with significant Arab Sunni and Kurdish minorities. In the aftermath of World War I, Iraq was 'given' to King Faisal after the Hashemite had been ejected from Damascus by the French. Hashemite Iraq remained during these years one of the closest allies of the West in the region. In the late 1950s the country was the main Arab rival of Nasser's Egypt, and its prime minister Nouri As-Said the main antagonist of the Egyptian President. Syrian elites were strongly divided between those that favoured a closer relationship with Iraq and those that looked at Egypt as a model and ally. The division was also geographical: the Aleppine middle and upper class represented mainly by the People's Party had historical links to Baghdad and felt penalised by the establishment of a Syrian–Iraqi border.[1] Both Egypt and Iraq used their links with domestic actors in the attempt to extend their control over Syria. Egypt appeared to have prevailed after the 1958 union, which was perceived in Baghdad as a direct threat to Iraq's regime.[2] In the same year a coup d'état led by Brigadier Qasim had brought down the Hashemite monarchy in Iraq. Despite the initial enthusiasm of the masses throughout the Arab world, Qasim's Iraq and the United Arab Republic were soon at odds. By late 1959 a military confrontation between the two Arab powers was a concrete possibility.[3] The news of the collapse of the United Arab Republic in 1961 was welcomed positively in most Arab capitals, and particularly so in Baghdad. Iraqi President Al-Qasim quickly moved to improve his relationship with the new Syrian government and met with President Al-Qudsi of Syria as early as 1962 to discuss further cooperation.[4] Within less than a year from that meeting, however, both leaders had been ejected from power, and both at the hand of Arab nationalist forces.

The radical Ba'th years

During the years immediately after World War II, Syria and Iraq had been separated by their ideological differences. In 1963 the same party took over power in Baghdad and Damascus. In both countries, the Ba'th initially had to fight several other political forces to establish its control. In Iraq the party was ousted after a few months in power, and only returned at the helm of the country in 1968. When the Ba'th finally succeeded in establishing its control over both countries, this ideological affinity appeared to create more conflict than solidarity. The two different branches of the Ba'th competed for party dominance, and the Syrian radical Ba'th perceived the regime in Baghdad as an ideological and political threat to its rule. A brief account of the development of this inter-Ba'th rivalry will allow us to underline the complex nature of the interaction between state interest and ideology in the Arab world.

Despite the debacle represented by the collapse of the United Arab Republic, the Pan-Arab tide had been growing in both Syria and Iraq for a long time. Finally, in 1963 the Ba'th party took over power in the two countries within less than one year (8 February and 8 March, respectively). In Syria, the Ba'thists took over power together with the Nasserites and other forces. In Iraq, the Ba'th was in power on its own, but had a rather small support basis and had to face threats from the country and the army. Tripartite Union talks between Egypt and the two countries started immediately. Mufti maintains that for both Iraq and Syria the talks served domestic purposes rather than aiming to achieve a real union.[5] Given their weak positions in the country, both parties sought consensus and stability in their relationship with the main Arab power.[6] With the strong symbolism typical of Pan-Arab politics, Ba'thist founders Aflaq and Bitar were put in charge of coordinating the signing of the April 1963 agreement between the three Arab powers.[7] The unity scheme was, however, short lived. It was the in-fighting between Nasserites and Ba'thists in Syria that led to the collapse of the agreement. In the immediate aftermath of this setback, Syria and Iraq decided to go ahead and negotiate a bipartite agreement.[8] This decision clearly represented a challenge to Egypt's Pan-Arab leadership role in the Arab world. The negotiations between Damascus and Baghdad were, however, interrupted by a coup d'état that ejected the Iraqi Ba'th from power in November 1963. The change of regime in Iraq led to a significant worsening in Syrian–Iraqi relations. It also marked the end of a phase where unity projects between Cairo, Damascus and Baghdad dominated the discourse between the three countries. During these years the leaderships in Syria and Iraq had sought to strengthen their position within their countries by committing themselves to a unity project with fellow Arab states. Nasser's Egypt held a very attractive proposition, for the Egyptian leader carried an aura of prestige among the Arab masses.[9] Union projects were shelved after the two 1963 setbacks, but the relationship between the three countries during the following years was strongly shaped by this debacle.

The November 1963 coup d'état in Iraq once again changed the dynamics of Syrian–Iraqi relations. The military junta led by General Arif soon proceeded to purge the Ba'thist leadership. Party founder Michel Aflaq (that had attempted a mediation to avoid open conflict in Baghdad) was forced into a rather inglorious escape from the country.[10] Once in power, Arif quickly moved to appease Nasser and declared his commitment to the tripartite agreement. The Ba'thist axis between Syria and Iraq had threatened to become a central force in Arab politics and put Nasser's Egypt on the backfoot. Now the coup d'état in Iraq had left Ba'thist Syria isolated. Unsurprisingly, the relationship between Damascus and Baghdad turned out to be a rather sour one. The Syrian Ba'th resented the expulsion of its brother party from power, but also feared that the Arif regime could act as a catalyst for its own internal opposition. This sense of threat and isolation was undoubtedly increased by the 1964 Hama riots. The revolt was essentially domestic and part of a long-term struggle between secular and Islamist forces in the country. Taking place only a few months after the ousting of the Ba'th from Baghdad, the revolt raised the profile of a combination of internal and domestic forces scheming against the party. This sense of danger was clearly one of the main motives behind the hostility between Syria and Iraq. In a phase of relative improvement of inter-Arab relations, the relationship between Damascus and Baghdad was 'the most vicious propaganda battle in the Middle East'.[11] Despite

84 *The alliances of Syria*

General Al-Hafiz and his Iraqi counterpart Abd-al Salam Arif holding a one-to-one meeting at the 1964 Cairo conference, the relationship between Baghdad and Damascus remained negative in this phase.

1966–1970

By the mid-1960s, divisions between two main branches of the Ba'th party had been crystallised and became central to Syrian–Iraqi relations. In Syria, the old guard of the party and the left military wing (that would be named NeoBath) had coexisted during the 1963–1966 phase. The latter was, however, in the ascendance. In Iraq, the party was reorganising itself after the 1963 debacle. Party founders Michel Aflaq and Salah Al-Din Bitar were extremely influential in the Iraqi branch. As a result, the key positions in the party were occupied by men ideologically close to them such as Ahmad al Bakr (head of the military branch) and Saddam Hussein Al-Tikriti (leader of the Iraqi Regional Command).[12]

In 1966 the left wing of the Ba'th party overthrew the Syrian regime. Unlike its predecessors, Salah Jadid and his men had little sympathy for the Iraqi Ba'thists that had been expelled by General Arif. The negative relationship between the two countries could therefore only be partially ascribed to the lingering bad feelings from the 1963 events. Crucially, when the Ba'th party came back to power in Iraq in 1968 the relations between the two countries did not improve but rather deteriorated. Initially the leadership in Damascus seemed to ignore the coup d'état in Baghdad. Syrian state-controlled media hardly reported the change of regime in Iraq, and when it did it barely acknowledged the Ba'thist affiliation of the new Iraqi leaders.[13] However, within a few months this silence was replaced by growing hostile propaganda. It was at this stage mostly hostile propaganda from the Syrians towards the Iraqis, that were unwilling or unable to retaliate to the accusations coming from Damascus.[14]

This hostility was confirmed at the 1968 Congress of the Syrian Ba'th, when a proposal (put forward by Al-Assad and his circle) to open negotiations with the Iraqi Ba'th was rejected by a large majority of members.[15] The Syrian Ba'th especially feared the destabilising power of its Iraqi counterpart after it took over in Baghdad. The Iraqi Ba'th also became a safe port for all the Syrian Ba'thists that had been expelled from the party in the several coups that had taken place in Damascus. As the Ba'th party in Syria was dominated by minorities and particularly by the Alawites, the Iraqi party became an obvious alternative for disenchanted Sunni, Druze and other non-Alawite Ba'thists.[16] The Syrian regime met the ideological threat coming from the Iraqi Ba'th with very strong propaganda, accusing (in typical Ba'th language) the Iraqis of being reactionaries and agents of the West. Ideological factors undoubtedly shaped the relationship between the two countries throughout the 1960s (and particularly in the phases in which the Ba'th was in power in both countries) and the pattern of rivalry that characterised the relation between Syria and Iraq (or at least their inability to align if not briefly and as a short-term reaction to changes in the system) indicates 'structural' causes underlying the rivalry.

The Al-Assad years

Syrian–Iraqi rivalry in the late 1960s had been fuelled by ideological differences. The regime that took over power in Syria in 1970 was less ideological and more pragmatic. This shift in Syrian foreign policy resulted in a decrease in the ideological competition between the two Arab capitals. However, as Syria's status and relative power in the Arab word grew, the 'structural' competition underlying the relationship between the two Arab powers emerged fully. Despite this aspect of competition, Damascus' flexible approach to alliances allowed it a strategic opening towards Iraq in the aftermath of Camp David.

When the young Alawite Defence Minister came to power in late 1970, his political stances were largely unknown to the public. One thing that had separated him from several of his fellow Ba'thists was his more pro-Iraqi stance. As a Defence Minister, Hafez Al-Assad had supported plans of union with Iraq.[17] This, however, proved to be mostly a domestic strategy, for when he reached power the new Syrian leader quickly abandoned the idea. The first years of the Al-Assad era showed only small improvements on the Baghdad-Damascus axis. The propaganda war in which the two countries had engaged relented, and vague talks of cooperation between the two countries resurfaced. This was, however, a long way from the commitment to union with Iraq that Hafez Al-Assad had shown before taking power. However, while the leaderships in both countries were more occupied with state consolidation,[18] even a marginal improvement represented a positive development for both parties.

Despite the cold nature of the relationship between the two Arab capitals, Iraq intervened in favour of Syria during the 1973 war. The troops sent by Baghdad during the last days of fighting helped relieve the pressure on the Syrians. Al-Assad's forces were facing the Israeli army nearly on their own given Sadat's decision not to advance on the Sinai Peninsula front.[19] Despite the rivalry with the Syrians, the fall of Damascus and the triumph of Israel would have represented a threat to the Iraqi state itself. The Iraqi regime also faced significant domestic and 'Arab' pressure to intervene in favour of the Syrians. Shortly after the end of the war the frictions between the two Arab capitals resumed. Syria's acceptance of the ceasefire with Israel and the following mutual accusations regarding Iraq's initial exclusion from the war provided the latest point of disagreement between the two countries.[20] The deeper reason for this rivalry was the (relative) success of Syria in the 1973 conflict that had strengthened Al-Assad's position in the region. This newly acquired status ultimately increased regional competition with Iraq.

The 'triangle' with Iran became progressively more important, and in many ways replaced the one with Egypt after Camp David and the 1979 Iranian revolution. A worsening in Iraq's relations with Iran was mirrored by a rapprochement between Damascus and Iran from the second half of 1974 onwards. Kienle[21] shows how on the other hand the 1975 Algiers agreement between Iraq and Iran worsened the competition between the two Arab powers. The geopolitical competition between Baghdad and Damascus was evident in Lebanon. When

86   *The alliances of Syria*

Syria intervened in the Cedar country to rein in Arafat and his Lebanese ally Jumblatt, Iraq openly opposed Damascus' action and showed support to the Palestinian militias. Iraq was the only member of the Arab League to stand against the deployment of an Arab mission, really a Syrian army with the token presence of other Arab forces.[22] Iraq's main concern was in this case that Syria could impose its control over the Palestine Liberation Organization and 'use it' as a weapon in inter-Arab rivalry and particularly against Baghdad, but also that Damascus could extend its territorial control over Lebanon altogether.[23] The Lebanese crisis started nearly at the same time as a new chapter in the dispute over the waters of the Euphrates. The disagreement there was caused by a temporary reduction in the amount of water received by the Iraqis and more in general by their concerns regarding Damascus' plans to use the water for its ambitious irrigation plans.[24] These three issues (Syrian intervention in Lebanon, the relationship with Iran and the Euphrates water) dominated the 1975–1977 phase and rekindled the propaganda war between the two countries. Arguably, the single most important factor in Syrian–Iraqi relations in this phase was the peace process with Israel in the aftermath of the 1973 war. Iraq, not sharing a border with Israel, was constantly able to attack both Egypt and Syria for their soft stance vis-à-vis Tel Aviv. Damascus found itself caught between the need to slow down Egypt's pattern towards peace and the pressure exerted by Baghdad's propaganda. This dynamic continued until 1977 when Egypt's progress towards peace was accelerated by Sadat's shock visit to Jerusalem. This dramatic act of diplomacy sent shockwaves through the region and altered the pattern of Syrian–Iraqi relations.

The 1978 rapprochement

Up to 1977, Syria and Iraq had alternated periods of fierce propaganda war with periods of cold relations. Egypt's dramatic shift, however, brought about something that had not happened since the early 1960s; a real alignment between the two Arab capitals. The changes in the Syrian–Iraqi relationship that followed Sadat's Jerusalem trip were immediately noticeable. The two countries first attempted a détente in the immediate aftermath of the diplomatic initiative by the Egyptian President. Under Algerian and Libyan diplomatic action, Damascus and Baghdad tried a rapprochement in late 1977–early 1978, in many ways anticipating the one that would have happened the following year. Much more significant was the alignment that started in the aftermath of the Camp David Accords. While both attempts were a reaction to steps in the peace process, the second was much more convincing because in the aftermath of the peace treaty there was an understanding that Egypt had switched sides definitively and it could not be won back to the Arab cause. The rapprochement between the two countries therefore had a strong symbolic aspect to it.[25]

Whether this rapprochement was initiated by one of the two states or by both has been subject of much discussion. What is clear, is that it was a result of a convergence of interests. The brief alignment between Iraq and Syria in 1978 was certainly rooted in the shared concern for Egypt's separate peace with Israel. The diplomatic process engineered by Henry Kissinger had taken the main Arab power out of the strategic equation, significantly increasing the advantage enjoyed by Israel over the Arab forces. Furthermore, Israel's invasion of Lebanon in March 1978 confirmed that Israel was willing and able to exploit its strategic advantage over the Arab states. The alignment was successful in putting pressure on the Saudis, the Jordanians and the other conservative powers to maintain a harsh stance towards Egypt. Cairo was expelled from the Arab League (and the Islamic Organisation Conference) after signing the Egypt–Israel peace treaty on the 26 March 1979. Despite this success, the alignment between the two countries was tactical and short term rather than a long-term alliance. Neither Iraq nor Syria saw this as the basis for long-term alliance. Damascus saw this alliance as a reaction to its isolation in the aftermath of Egypt's defection. Baghdad was similarly isolated, but the alignment was also a way to exert its influence over the neighbouring country. These goals are confirmed by the continuation of the union talks described by Kienle. Baghdad pushed to obtain a full unification of the two party structures in order to extend its control on the weaker Syrian state, while Damascus attempted to postpone all practical steps towards unification while trying to obtain as much support as possible in the economic and military field.[26] From Al-Assad's point a view a long embrace with Iraq could have been extremely dangerous.[27]

The 1980s

By late 1979 the relationship between the two Arab states could have been defined as 'cold', if not yet one of open hostility. Damascus' position was still too weak to openly break with Baghdad despite Iraq's suspected role in the rise of violence and terrorism in Syria in early 1980s (later proven but at that time strongly assumed).[28] The Iranian revolution increased the tension between Damascus and Tehran. On 12 February 1979 Hafez Al-Assad was the first to congratulate Khomeini on the overthrow of the Shah, starting a process that would have resulted in the formation of the Damascus-Tehran axis. Iraqi officials on the other hand immediately perceived the Iranian revolution, Islamic and Shiite, as a threat.[29] The Iranian revolution did not create the divide between Baghdad and Damascus, but it increased and exacerbated a pre-existing rivalry. The Iran–Iraq war shaped the nature of the Syrian–Iraqi relationship for most of the 1980s. After months of border skirmishes and tension, the Iraqi President Saddam Hussein decided to take advantage of the perceived disarray of the Iranian forces after the revolution. Tellingly, the Iraqi President had re-opened the conflict with Tehran by publicly abrogating the agreement over the Shatt Al-Arab. In 1975, the Algiers agreement had sanctioned Iranian predominance over its neighbour. Now Saddam sought a swift military victory to confirm the new balance between the two powers.[30] Having over-estimated the strength of his own army and underestimated the Iranian resistance, the Iraqi dictator soon found himself bogged down in a long and costly conflict. The conflict forced the

88 *The alliances of Syria*

Syrian President to make a difficult decision. Abandon his newly-found ally in Tehran and side with Saddam's Iraq, or challenge the unspoken norms of Pan-Arabism by siding with Persian Iran against Arab Iraq. Chapter 8 of this volume discusses why the Syrian President opted for continuing and expanding its alliance with Iran amid Arab pressure to build bridges with Iraq. It is, however, important to stress here how the conflict between Baghdad and Tehran put the Syrian President in a difficult position within the Arab arena. Al-Assad had clearly no sympathy for the Iraqi leadership that he perceived as a threat to his position at the helm of the Syrian state. However, he considered Israel his main enemy and saw the war as a waste of resources that could have been better spent on that front. The conflict also put him in a delicate diplomatic position. He relied on the relationship with supporters of Iraq in the Gulf but feared that an Iraqi victory would leave him vulnerable to Saddam's attacks. Three weeks into the conflict, Saddam's Iraq had already broken off its relationship with Syria, accusing its neighbour of providing arms to Iran.[31]

With the start of the Iran–Iraq war, the hostile propaganda between the two states regained the venom of previous years. Particularly damaging for the credibility of the Syrian regime were the accusations coming from Baghdad of 'sectarianism' and betrayal of the Arab cause because of the support given by the (Alawite) regime of Damascus to the (Persian and Shia) Iranian government in its war against another Arab state. The pressure for a Syrian–Iraqi rapprochement grew in the aftermath of the Iranian counter-offensive in the spring of 1982. King Fahd of Saudi Arabia tried to favour reconciliation between Al-Assad and Hussein in the hope of drawing Syria away from Iranian influence. This attempt failed, as did those by different Arab actors and the Soviet Union in the following years. The Saudi–Jordanian reconciliation initiative of May 1986 seemed to have relative success. Under King Hussein's mediation the two countries appeared to be closer than ever to re-establishing a working relationship. Kienle maintains that this was due more to problems between Damascus and Tehran in Lebanon as well as concerning the supply of oil from the Persian state.[32] The threat of re-establishing relations with Saddam Hussein's Iraq was used by Syria as a diplomatic tool in the negotiations with its ally. The first meeting between Al-Assad and Hussein prompted Iran to sign a new oil agreement and to donate one million tons of crude to Syria.[33] In the aftermath of this agreement, despite another meeting between the foreign ministers of Baghdad and Damascus, the possibility of an opening between the two states faded. Once again, one of the two countries had used the relationship with the other as a tool in its dealings with a third party. This flexible diplomatic posture, accompanied by Ba'thist rhetoric, did not substantially change the conflicting nature of the relationship between Damascus and Baghdad. What had changed during the 1980s was the power relation between the two Arab capitals. Despite going through a severe economic crisis, Al-Assad's Syria had progressively established itself as a relevant actor in the region (and by the mid-1980s Al-Assad had defeated the internal threat posed first by the Islamist revolt and later by his own brother Rifat) while Iraq was locked in a deadly confrontation with Iran.

Conclusion: the Syrian–Iraqi relationship between rivalry and solidarity

The Syrian–Iraqi relationship in the years of this study was one of inter-Arab competition and conflict. Relations between Iraq and Syria between 1963 and 1970 were marred by instability in both countries, but also by strong ideological competition over the respective Pan-Arab credentials. Hostile rhetoric and propaganda wars between the two countries became the norm, interrupted by short periods of ease. In 1963 the Ba'th party took over power in Damascus and Baghdad. The ideological alignment between the two countries frequently proved to be a factor of division rather than cooperation and solidarity. Both Ba'thist regimes were in extremely vulnerable positions during their first months in power in 1963 and both sought domestic legitimacy in union plans between the two countries and Nasser's Egypt. When the Ba'th returned to power in Iraq in 1968, relations between the two Arab capitals worsened rather than improving. Ideological competition was particularly marked during the years of the radical Jadid regime. This can be (at least partially) explained by the fact that the two leaderships belonged to different Ba'thist factions. The 'leftist' Syrian regime perceived the Ba'th in Baghdad as an ideological threat to its Pan-Arab credentials.

When the more pragmatic Hafez Al-Assad took over in 1970, the ideological dimension of the competition somehow diminished. The pattern of competition between the two countries was, however, not only based on ideological rivalry. The clash of regional interests between the two powers increased as Syria gained a more central role in the Arab world. Despite Iraq's intervention in favour of the Syrians in the 1973 war, the improved status of the Syrian leader divided the two Arab capitals. Both Syria and Iraq were revisionist powers, unhappy with the regional system and seeking to alter it to their advantage. Yet the two Arab powers were competitors rather than partners because they disagreed over their respective position in the system itself. Baghdad had hegemonic ambitions in the Arab world, ambitions that increased in the aftermath of Camp David. Syria on the other hand perceived Iraq's ambitions as a threat to its own position within the region and therefore sought to limit Baghdad's influence and expansion. The 1978 détente represented a significant break in this pattern of competition, but it was brief and mostly motivated by Egypt's path towards rapprochement with Israel and the United States. The two countries were soon back to their old pattern of competition, and officially severed their relationship because of Syria's support for Iran during the Iraq–Iraq war.

Notes

1 Ebherard Kienle, *Ba'th vs Ba'th: The Conflict between Syria and Iraq 1968–1989* (London: I.B. Tauris, 1990), 13.
2 Phebe Marr, *The Modern History of Iraq* (Boulder: Westview Press, 2004), 76.
3 Malik Mufti, *Sovereign Creations: Pan-Arabism and Political Order in Syria and Iraq* (Ithaca: Cornell University Press, 1996).

90 *The alliances of Syria*

4 Malcolm H. Kerr, *The Arab Cold War: Gamel Abd Al-Nasir and His Rivals, 1958–1970* (3rd edition) (Oxford: Oxford University Press, 1971), 27–40.
5 Mufti, *Sovereign Creations*, ch. 9.
6 Ibid.
7 Kienle, *Ba'th vs Ba'th*, 15.
8 Kerr, *The Arab Cold War*, 93.
9 Kienle, *Ba'th vs Ba'th*, 15.
10 Patrick Seale, *Assad of Syria: The Struggle for the Middle East* (London: I.B. Tauris, 1988), 91.
11 Kerr, *The Arab Cold War*, 95.
12 Kienle, *Ba'th vs Ba'th*.
13 Ibid., 39.
14 Ibid., 40.
15 Nicholas Van Dam, *The Struggle for Power in Syria: Politics and Society under Asad and the Ba'th Party* (4th edition) (London: I.B. Tauris, 2011), 63.
16 Kienle, *Ba'th vs Ba'th*, 36.
17 Raymond Hinnebusch, *Syria: Revolution from Above* (London: Routledge, 2001), 142.
18 Mufti, *Sovereign Creations*.
19 Seale, *Assad of Syria*, 215.
20 Kienle, *Ba'th vs Ba'th*, 70
21 Ibid., 87–88.
22 Adeed Dawisha, *Syria and the Lebanese Crisis* (London: Macmillan Press, 1980), ch. 6.
23 Rabinovich Itamar. *The War for Lebanon: 1970–1983* (Ithaca: Cornell University Press, 1984), 52.
24 Kienle, *Ba'th vs Ba'th*, 100.
25 Ibid., 135.
26 Ibid., ch. IV.
27 Ibid., 136.
28 Raphael Lefevre, *Ashes of Hama: The Muslim Brotherhood in Syria* (London: Hurst and Co., 2013).
29 Jubin Goodarzi, *Syria and Iran: Diplomatic Alliance and Power Politics in the Middle East* (London: I.B. Tauris, 2009), 18.
30 Charles Tripp, *A History of Iraq* (Cambridge: Cambridge University Press, 2000).
31 Kienle, *Ba'th vs Ba'th*, 132.
32 Ibid., 167.
33 Goodarzi, *Syria and Iran*, 182–185.

8 Syria and Iran

The Syrian–Iranian alliance has in recent years been a central feature of Middle Eastern politics and one of the most stable and durable regional partnerships. This chapter analyses this relationship to understand how the alliance originated, what tensions it had to overcome and how it became one of the longest standing and most comprehensive alliances in the region. The alliance between Ba'thist Syria and the (Persian and Shia) Islamic republic is very much a triumph of real-politik over ideology. Its formation therefore fits well the 'realist' foreign policy shift carried out by Hafez Al-Assad. A more ideological regime would have struggled to form an alliance with Iran, and more so to maintain it whilst Iran was engaged in a war with Arab Iraq.

This chapter will provide an overview of the historical development of the relationship. It will then focus on the formation of the alliance and on the two main scenarios (the Iran–Iraq war and the Lebanese crisis) where the alliance operated. The relationship between the two countries before 1979 had oscillated between ideological hostility and indifference. The Al-Assad regime had initially tried opening towards the Shah's Iran in the hope of benefiting from its closeness to the United States and the Western powers. It was only with Egypt's defection and the Iranian revolution that the conditions for the establishment of the alliance materialised. In 1979, both Iran and Syria were isolated and threatened by other regional actors, Israel and Iraq in particular. The leadership in Damascus and Tehran were both opposed to (and felt threatened by) American–Israeli hegemony in the region. Both Iran and Syria were revisionists who opposed the American and Israeli role in the region and perceived these powers as hostile. Furthermore, the two countries did not have contrasting interests. Unlike the case of Iraq, Syria and Iran were not 'geopolitical rivals' and did not perceive each other as a threat. While both Iran and Syria were Middle Eastern powers, their main interests were in different sub-regions, the Levant for Syria, the Gulf for Iran. The alliance therefore allowed them to add a further dimension to their foreign policy.[1]

Relations before 1963

Unlike Syria, Iran had a long history as an independent political entity. The country traced its origins back to the Ancient Persian empire established as early

92   *The alliances of Syria*

as the sixth century BC. The relationship between ancient Persia and its Arab neighbours had often been one of conflict but had also been characterised by rich interactions and exchanges in the cultural, economic and political realms.[2] Because of its long history as a political entity, Persia (that became Iran in 1932) had a comparative advantage over most of its Arab neighbours in the state formation process. Ruled by the Pahlavi dynasty since 1941, the state had progressively gained more autonomy from the British but had kept itself firmly within the Western camp. Diplomatic relations between Syria and Iran were established as early as 1946. The relationship between the two countries in those years remained, however, limited and superficial. Syria was during those years a secondary regional actor, and Iran focused its foreign policy towards the Arab world on neighbouring Iraq and regional powerhouse Egypt. A relevant trend that was already evident in that phase was the influence of third parties and particularly of Iraq on the relations between the two countries. It was the state of Syrian–Iraqi and Iranian–Iraqi relations that often shaped the interactions between Damascus and Tehran. The rivalry between Iraq and Iran pre-dated the Iranian revolution and later became an important factor in the establishment of the Syrian–Iranian alliance.[3]

Throughout the late 1950s and early 1960s Syria and Iran were placed on opposite sides of the regional divide. Syria gradually moved closer to the progressive Arab republics. Under the Shah Iran was a staunch ally of the West and maintained good relations with pro-Western conservative states such as Jordan. It was, however, Iran's growing partnership with Israel that alienated the progressive Arab republics.[4] Tehran in turn observed the developments in inter-Arab politics as an external but interested (and often concerned) party. As the leader of a non-Arab country surrounded by Arab neighbours, the Shah feared any unity project that could have resulted in the creation of a 'super-Arab state'. Relations between Nasser's Egypt and the Shah's Iran were therefore extremely negative, to the extent that Nasser broke diplomatic relations with Tehran in 1960 over the latter's recognition of Israel.[5] Like several other states, Iran felt threatened by Nasser's growing influence in the region. The collapse of the United Arab Republic was therefore welcomed as a positive development in Tehran as it was in Baghdad and other Arab capitals. In the aftermath of the breakdown of the union the Shah's government was fast in reaching out to Damascus, but this short-lived improvement was interrupted by the Ba'th party taking over power in Syria in 1963.

1963–1970

In the years before the Ba'th party's takeover, relations between Tehran and Damascus had been at best cold and in some phases (such as during the United Arab Republic years) outright negative. The 1963 coup d'état led to a further worsening of relations. The Pan-Arab discourse became more central and constant in Syrian politics, and Persian Iran became the target of hostile rhetoric. From Tehran's perspective, the growing Pan-Arab tide threatened once again to leave the country isolated and encircled. These fears reached higher levels when the Ba'th party took over power in Syria, just one month after the same had happened in Iraq. The involvement of Baghdad in any unity project was particularly concerning for Iran. Tehran's worst nightmare seemed to materialise itself when tripartite talks between Egypt, Syria and Iraq kicked-off. To the Shah's relief, the talks between the three countries failed within a few months. Equally unsuccessful were the following talks between Syria and Iraq, cut short by the November 1963 coup d'état in Baghdad.[6] Given Iran's long-term rivalry with Iraq, the emergence of a pattern of competition between Baghdad and other Arab states represented a positive development for Tehran. However, this change did not result in an improvement in Syrian–Iranian relations. On the contrary, in 1965 the Syrian regime dialled up its criticism of Iran by calling for the liberation of Arabestan (Khuzestan for the Iranians), a long-term demand of Arab nationalists.[7] The diplomatic crisis that followed resulted in the withdrawal of the Iranian ambassador from Syria and in a freezing of the relationship for the following two years.

1966

Relations between the two parties were already at an historical low when the Jadid regime came into power. As an 'ideological' regime committed to Pan-Arabism, the Jadid regime had no interest in an improvement of the relationship with Iran. Relations therefore remained nearly non-existent, but the anti-Persian rhetoric of the 1965 incident diminished. The Jadid regime had other priorities and saved its worst venom for fellow Arab states. At the same time Iran clearly saw Iraq and particularly Egypt as its main Arab rivals.[8] A modest improvement in relations took place after the 1967 conflict. The Shah condemned the Israelis' occupation of the Arab land, a position that was reiterated on other occasions.[9] This slight improvement was, however, halted by the 1970 Black September crisis. During the crisis, the Shah supported his long-term ally King Hussein. Furthermore, according to some sources, the Shah went as far as mediating an informal agreement between the king and Israel.[10]

The Syrian–Iranian relationship during the first Ba'th years largely followed the trend established during the previous phase. The aggressive rhetoric coming from the Ba'th regime, together with a more assertive regional role assumed by the Shah, led to sporadic episodes of tension. These incidents were framed within the broader context of Persian–Arab rivalry. The relationship between Syria and Iran remained throughout these years one of secondary relevance, particularly if compared with the Iranian–Iraqi rivalry.

The Al-Assad years

When Al-Assad took over power, his focus was on mending the relations with fellow Arab states that had been damaged during the radical Ba'th years. Iran was initially not a priority, particularly considering that Al-Assad had previously

94 *The alliances of Syria*

emphasised the importance of his relationship with Tehran's regional rival, Iraq.[11] Accordingly, relations between the two countries did not change significantly during the first years of the Al-Assad era. The 1973 war on the other hand brought a significant improvement. Iran partially broke its traditional pro-Israeli policy in favour of a more equidistant position. Tehran went as far as offering a $150 million credit to Syria and hosting a number of Syrians that had been wounded during the war.[12] In the aftermath of the conflict diplomatic relations were upgraded to ambassadorial level and Tehran offered further loans to Syria.[13] Typically, an improvement in Syrian–Iranian relations happened at the same time as the Syrian–Iraqi ones worsened.[14] Donovan shows how Iranian policy under the Shah aimed at establishing regional dominance in the Gulf after British withdrawal from the region.[15] A prime example of this policy is the occupation of Abu Musa and the Tunbs in November 1971.[16] This policy created significant tensions with Ba'thist Iraq. In 1969/1970 the two countries were on the brink of war after Iran rejected the 1937 London Agreement.[17] Border skirmishes characterised the first part of the 1970s, but in March 1975 the Iraqis had to give in to Iranian superiority as the two countries signed the Algiers agreement. Iraq conceded the division of the Shatt-al-Arab river at the Thalweg line in exchange for Iranian commitment to stop supporting Kurdish separatists. In the aftermath of the Algiers' accord between Iran and Iraq, Al-Assad visited Tehran in the attempt to strengthen his ties with Iran that were threatened by the Iraqi-Iranian rapprochement.

In this phase the new Syrian leadership valued Iran for its close relationship with the United States. Al-Assad was concerned by the post-1973 developments of the peace process. The Syrian President felt side-lined by the Americans and hoped that the Shah could play a role in the peace process and favour a more balanced American approach. His calculation proved to be wrong in this case. The Shah threw his weight behind the Egyptian peace efforts, damaging in this way his relations with Syria.[18] Iran's uncompromising pro-United States stance was the main factor behind Al-Assad's choice to support the Iranian opposition in the late 1970s. An important link between the Syrian regime and the future leadership in Tehran was in this phase the Imam Musa Al-Sadr. The Iranian-born cleric was the charismatic leader of the Lebanese Shia and a friend of Hafez Al-Assad.[19] In October 1978 Al-Assad offered Khomeini asylum after his expulsion from Iraq. While the Ayatollah rejected the offer, he did not forget to show his appreciation for Syrian friendship once he took over power.[20]

In the pre-revolution phase, Syria and Iran[21] were placed respectively in the Western and Soviet camps. Despite this, the two countries had no specific clashing interests. Their opposition never went further than hostile propaganda (that was relatively moderate if compared with that exchanged among Arab capitals at different stages). Furthermore, the two countries had a mutual interest in containing Iraq, that was perceived as a threat by Al-Assad nearly as much as it was in Tehran. During the mid-1970s the Syrian leader already showed signs of opening towards Iran, confirming that he was ready to break with a rule of Pan-Arabism to pursue Syria's national interest. Hafez Al-Assad imposed a more pragmatic approach in the relationship with Iran. Tehran was an asset because of both its status and its resources. These considerations were behind the formation of the alliance between Damascus and Tehran in the aftermath of the 1979 Islamic revolution. Yet the Shah's Iran was firmly rooted in the pro-Western camp and was therefore of limited use regarding Al-Assad's goals. This realisation led the Syrians to support the Iranian opposition, thus creating a positive relationship with the group that was going to lead the country in the aftermath of the revolution.

Relations between Syria and Iran improved in the immediate aftermath of the revolution. The change of regime in Tehran was undoubtedly one of the factors that contributed to the formation of the alliance. On the 12 February, in the immediate aftermath of the deposition of the Shah, Hafez Al-Assad was the first leader to send a congratulatory telegram to Khomeini. Only a few days later Al-Assad's brother Rifat sent some envoys to Tehran to discuss forms of cooperation.[22] Seale describes the decision to befriend Iran as one of Al-Assad's personal intuition.[23] The regime that took over in Iran was so isolated in the region that it could not afford to discount any offer of help. By over-throwing the Shah the revolutionaries had joined the list of the enemies of the West. The furore created by the Islamic revolution also made Khomeini's Iran a danger to many Arab countries. Particularly threatened were those with significant Shiite populations like Saudi Arabia, Bahrain, and most of all, Iraq. Iran attempted to portray itself as an 'Islamic power' (and therefore downplay its Persian-ness) and even offered to reconsider the status of Abu Musa and the Tunbs Islands.[24] Despite this, by the end of 1979 most of the Arab world had regrouped against the perceived Iranian threat. This isolation made Damascus ever more valuable as an ally, as it allowed Tehran to downplay the rhetoric of Persian versus Arabs that the Iraqi leader Saddam Hussein had adopted in preparation for the war.

The 1980s: the Iran–Iraq war and the consolidation of the alliance

On the 20 September Saddam Hussein's troops launched an attack by air and land against Al-Assad's new ally. Months before the start of the conflict, Syria had started an airlift of Soviet weapons to re-arm the arsenals of the Islamic republic depleted by the end of its partnership with the United States.[25] This policy cost Syria the expulsion of its ambassadors from Baghdad and the general hostility of most Arab states.[26] When the war started, Iraq increased its propaganda war against the Syrian regime. During the first days of the conflict Al-Assad tried to cooperate with King Hussein of Jordan and King Khaled of Saudi Arabia to end 'the wrong war against the wrong enemy at the wrong time'.[27] In Al-Assad's view, the war was wasting energies that should have been spent confronting Israel. The war also presented clear risks for the Syrian leader. A swift Iraqi victory (that seemed to be predicted by all observers when the conflict started) would have left him with a triumphant Saddam Hussein on his eastern border. Iraq was one of the main sponsors of the Islamic revolt that was threatening the survival of the Syrian regime.[28] The likelihood that the Iraqi leader

96 *The alliances of Syria*

would have tried to get rid of Al-Assad's regime and extend his influence over Syria was high. On the other hand, a continuation of the conflict risked straining Al-Assad's vital relations with the Gulf monarchies.

Al-Assad flew to Moscow on the 7 October 1980 to obtain Soviet arm deliveries to Iran and to allow Syrian airlifts to Tehran.[29] By that time, it was obvious that Iran had survived the impact of Saddam's offensive and had denied the Iraqi dictator the fast victory he had dreamt of. The conflict polarised the Arab world. Algeria and Libya joined Damascus in its support of Iran.[30] Baghdad was forced to reach out to Egypt to purchase arms and ammunition. Cairo had been treated as an outcast after Camp David and the Iraqis had been particularly vocal in their criticism of the Egyptian leadership. In November 1980 tension grew between Syria and Jordan, two of the contenders' main allies. Saudi diplomatic intervention prevented the conflict from erupting, yet this incident shows the level of tension within the Arab world caused (mainly, if not only) by the Iran–Iraq war. Despite his firm support of Iran, Al-Assad still feared isolation in the Arab world and was therefore keen on showing his commitment to ending the war. The Kuwaiti diplomatic initiative of late 1981, despite failing to stop the conflict, allowed the Syrian President to re-open some channels with the Gulf countries.[31] In March 1982, however, Syria and Iran took a step further in their alliance when Syrian Vice-President Khaddam visited Iran to sign a comprehensive economic agreement that:

> included the annual export of 9 million tonnes of Iranian oil to Syria, with some 20,000 barrels a day gratis and other discounts, and a reciprocal export of Syrian phosphate to Iran. Syria first closed its borders with Iraq and then shut down the vital Iraqi–Syrian pipeline from Kirkuk to Banias and Tripoli in North Lebanon, thus reducing Iraq oil exports by half.[32]

The Spring of 1982 saw significant gains by the Iranian troops, that recovered virtually all the territory lost at the beginning of the war and now threatened to invade Iraq. While officially declaring its opposition to Iran entering Iraqi (and therefore Arab) land, Syria was instrumental to the Iranian success. The Al-Assad regime kept providing weapons for the Iranian war efforts and also deployed troops on the border with Iraq (therefore forcing Saddam to use precious units to 'cover' the Western front). Furthermore, Damascus supported the Kurdish guerrilla warfare and damaged Iraq's economic interests by closing the Kirkuk–Banias pipeline. This and other forms of economic 'warfare' proved to be extremely important for Iran.[33] When in June 1982 Israel invaded Lebanon, the Syrian–Iranian alliance was already a stable feature of Middle Eastern politics – and was about to gain one further dimension.

In the aftermath of the Iranian revolution, Al-Assad and his men decided to bet on the partnership with Iran to address the loss of Egypt. This bet proved to be an extremely risky one as Iraq and Iran soon appeared to be at odds. As Saddam Hussein's rhetoric towards Tehran grew increasingly more belligerent, the strength of Syrian commitment to his new ally was severely tested. The

Iran–Iraq war itself was central to the establishment and the consolidation of the Syrian–Iranian alliance. First, it provided the baptism of fire for this new alliance given the pressure that the Syrian leader had to withstand from his fellow Arab leaders. The fact that Al-Assad supported Iran confirms that the Syrian leader and his circle were thinking about the long-term balance and the potential of Iran as an ally. Second, the war created and reinforced mutual interests: Iran was, for most of the conflict, dependant on Syria for material and diplomatic support, and in exchange it showed its value as an ally in a variety of ways (from oil deliveries at favourable prices to leverage with Lebanon's Shia community).

The Lebanese scenario

The Lebanese scenario became central to the Syrian–Iranian alliance after the Israeli invasion of 1982. The relationship between the two allies throughout most of the 1980s was characterised by the war efforts on the Iraqi front and the engagement with Israel and the United States in Lebanon. Both countries saw their vital interests involved in one scenario (Lebanon for Syria, Iraq for Iran) but had significant interests at stake in the other. This synergy helped build a mutually beneficial partnership. Lebanon had long been a central concern for Syrian policy-makers. This was not only because of the intimate connection between the two countries but also because of the strategic competition between Syria and Israel in the Levant.[34] The Syrian leadership considered Lebanon their own backyard but were also aware that it could also have been their weak spot. An Israeli attack through Lebanon would have circumvented Syrian defences. The Civil War erupted in the country in 1975, with the Christian militias facing the Palestinians and leftist forces. Al-Assad faced a dilemma. A victory of his 'allies' led by Kamal Jumblatt, would have created a radical Lebanon difficult to control. The involvement of Palestinian militias carried the risk of an Israeli intervention. A Christian victory would have handed the country to the Israelis who were more than ready to reach out to their allies.[35] For this reason, Al-Assad and the foreign minister Khaddam frantically engaged in talks with the different factions and tried to convince Jumblatt and Arafat of the risks connected with their policy. Finally, Al-Assad felt compelled to intervene in mid-1976 to 'save' Lebanon when the leftists/Palestinians seemed to be close to overrunning the Christians.[36] The Syrian initiative appeared to succeed in pacifying the country and was 'legitimised' by the Arab states at the Riyadh meeting on the 16 October. The intervention against the Palestinians, however, was going to remain a stain on Al-Assad's Pan-Arab credentials for a long time. Even worse for the Syrian leader, while he intervened to prevent Israel from getting involved in Lebanon, his actions ended up having the opposite effect. After having reinforced its links with its Christian allies, Israel occupied Southern Lebanon in March 1978 in what was named Operation Litani. The stage was set for that strategic confrontation that Al-Assad dreaded but seemed to be unable to avoid.

Iranian involvement in Lebanon was rather different – and more recent. While the Shia community of Lebanon had historical connections with Tehran, it was

98 *The alliances of Syria*

not until the Iranian revolution that these links became an important political factor. In the aftermath of the Iranian revolution, Tehran offered to get directly involved in support of the 'anti-Zionist forces'. Iranian support for its Syrian ally was not motivated by pure generosity, as Iran hoped to gain both material but even more symbolic benefits for this involvement.[37] Hafez Al-Assad refused, wary of Iran becoming a central player in Lebanon at the expense of Syria. Agha and Khalidi maintain that offers to establish an Iranian military presence in Lebanon at the start of the war 'had been apparently blocked by Hafez Al-Assad himself'.[38]

In the aftermath of the 1982 Israeli invasion of Lebanon, the Syrians were in a much worse position and therefore acquiesced to more substantial Iranian involvement.[39] The diminishment of the role of Syria's traditional ally Amal in favour of other groups (after 1985 particularly Hezbollah) that looked directly at the Iranian model made cooperation with Tehran necessary. Iran and its proxies on the Lebanese front proved fundamental in Al-Assad's 'shield and sword' strategy. Al-Assad boosted air defences, and in the aftermath of the 1982 Syrian–Israeli clashes, the Soviet Union provided the former. The latter was represented by actions against the Israel Defense Forces, the Western forces and the Gemayel regime carried out by Syria and its allies. From mid-1983 Israel gradually abandoned the Lebanese President to fight on his own for his political survival. As pro-Syrian militias swept away the Christian forces from most of the country, Syria achieved its main goal in Lebanon. Lebanese President Gemayel rejected the 17 May agreement (that included the signing of a peace treaty with Israel) by accepting an eight-point peace plan negotiated by Saudi Arabia. Finally, Gemayel abandoned his pro-Western stance and made the 'historic pilgrimage' to Damascus'.[40] With the support of his Iranian ally, Al-Assad had denied Israel the fruits of its military victory. Al-Assad's success was a lesson in realpolitik and re-established his control over Lebanon. However, the increased role played by Iran was soon going to create tensions between the two allies.

Syrian and Iranian goals in Lebanon up to the mid-1980s coincided perfectly. Both allies were determined to stop the Americans and the Israelis from imposing their solution: a Maronite President signing a peace agreement with Israel and leading the way to a pro-Western and pro-Israeli Lebanon. Once they succeeded, significant differences emerged over the future of Lebanon and the role that Syria, Iran and their respective proxies would play in the country. Syria had long-established relations with Amal, founded by the Imam Musa Al-Sadr with Syrian backing.[41] Those relations had been consolidated further during the Lebanese Civil War.[42] Amal's influence within the Shia community had been challenged by the emergence of new radical groups and particularly Hezbollah. The latter group was closely aligned to Iran. These developments posed a dilemma to Damascus.[43] The Amal/Hezbollah differences were in many ways part of the wider divergence over the future of the country. Syria wanted a pacified Lebanon (under its control) and therefore moved to normalise the situation, attempting to re-establish some sort of understanding between the different confessional groups. Iran saw Lebanon as the forefront of the fight against imperialism and therefore favoured a more confrontational stance. Relations between Damascus and Hezbollah were also strained because of the Western hostages issue, seen by Damascus as a direct threat to its authority in Lebanon.[44] In the Spring of 1988 Syria gave the green light to Amal to mount a military attack on Hezbollah. Amal swiftly defeated Hezbollah in southern Lebanon. This was a priority for Damascus that feared that Hezbollah's attacks would have caused an Israeli reaction and entangled Syria in another military confrontation. Bolstered by his initial success, Amal moved on to attack Hezbollah's positions in southern Beirut. The attack was a direct threat to Hezbollah's survival and was met with a strong reaction by the organisation.[45] Within two days, Hezbollah (backed by fighters and Revolutionary Guards coming from Baalbek) counter-attacked and started rolling back Amal. Despite the continued calls for a halt in the fighting, Hezbollah was on the rise and several ceasefires were broken as the pro-Iranian militia took control over nearly all the southern suburbs. Finally, on the 15 May, Ghazi Ka'nan (Al-Assad's men in Beirut) announced that the Syrians had no other alternative but to intervene in Beirut.[46] Both Syria and Iran wanted to stop the clashes, but also sought to secure the best outcome for their proxies. The Syrian leader finally 'bypassed' the Iranians by holding direct talks with Hezbollah's leaders in Damascus on the 25 May. The meeting finally solved the crisis; militiamen from both parties left the streets and Syrian troops made their triumphant entry into the southern suburbs.

On the Lebanese scenario, Iran had shown its value as an ally for Damascus. The crisis also gave the Syrian leadership a possibility to 'draw some lines' on the respective spheres of influence of the two allies. The Iranians had to acknowledge Syrian supremacy in Lebanon and Syria's determination to defend its areas of primary influence. Hafez Al-Assad had shown his role as power-broker in Beirut but both Syria and Iran had confirmed that despite their different opinions on specific issues they recognised having a fundamental interest in not jeopardising the alliance. This is particularly relevant because while the two allies were fighting something close to a proxy war in Lebanon, Syria was subject to significant pressure from the other Arab states in order to abandon its support of Iran in its war against Saddam's Iraq.

Conclusion: the Syrian–Iranian alliance

The Syrian–Iranian relationship represents arguably the clearest example of the 'realist' and non-ideological alliance policy followed by Al-Assad's Syria. The alliance between Ba'thist Syria and the Persian and Shia Islamic republic went openly against the principles of Pan-Arabism. Within a few months of the formation of the alliance Iran was engaged in a bloody war with Arab and Ba'thist Iraq. Pan-Arab solidarity should have driven Al-Assad to side with Baghdad, realpolitik and the fear of Iraqi expansionism on the other hand convinced him to support his new ally.

The development of a close relationship with Tehran was not only against the norms of Pan-Arabism, it was also a new pattern in Syrian politics. Relations

100 *The alliances of Syria*

between the two countries in the aftermath of Syria's foundation had been limited and largely hostile. During the first Ba'th years, the relationship worsened significantly due to different diplomatic incidents. The hostility towards Pahlavi's Iran was mostly motivated by the Syrian regime's belligerent Pan-Arab stance. The main factor dividing the two states was, however, the fact that they belonged to the two opposite camps of regional politics. During the first years of the Al-Assad regime, the relationship between Damascus and Tehran did not change significantly. The Syrian leadership, however, saw a window of opportunity in the aftermath of the 1973 conflict, seeking to utilise the Shah's connection to the West as a diplomatic tool. Whilst this attempt failed, it indicates the flexible approach to alliance policy adopted by the new Syrian regime. This debacle also strengthened the contacts between the Iranian opposition and the Syrian regime. These links proved to be extremely important in the aftermath of the Iranian revolution, when Al-Assad and his men decided to bet on the new Iranian leadership as a regional partner. This choice was clearly motivated by regional changes that had left Syria isolated and in need of allies. The bet proved to be a successful move when Iran survived Iraq's attack and pinned Saddam Hussein forces down in a long and bloody conflict.

What allowed the Syrian–Iranian relationship to absorb external pressure and systemic changes were the overlapping interests of the two regional powers. In the aftermath of the 1979 Iranian revolution the two countries were both revisionists opposed to American–Israeli predominance in the region. The two countries were threatened by the same enemies, Iraq and Israel. Furthermore, the two regional powers had no clashes over vital interests. Their key interests lay in different sub-regions, the Levant and the Gulf respectively. This separation meant that the two powers had no geopolitical rivalry.

Notes

1 Particularly in the case of Iran, its alliance with Syria allowed Tehran to become symbolically involved in the Arab–Israeli conflict as well as projecting its power onto the Lebanese scenario.

2 Michael Axworthy, *A History of Iran: Empire of the Mind* (London: Penguin Books, 2007), ch. IV.

3 Several actors (including Saddam Hussein) painted the modern rivalry as a continuation of the historical rivalry between Arabs and Persians and later between the Ottoman and Persian empires.

4 Anoushiravan Ehteshami, "Wheels within Wheels: Iranian Foreign Policy towards the Arab World," in *Reconstruction and Regional Diplomacy in the Persian Gulf*, eds. Hooshang Amirahmadi and Nader Entessar (London: Routledge, 1995), 117–146.

5 Jubin Goodarzi, *Syria and Iran: Diplomatic Alliance and Power Politics in the Middle East* (London: I.B. Tauris, 2009), 165.

6 Malcolm H. Kerr, *The Arab Cold War: Gamel Abd Al-Nasir and His Rivals, 1958–1970* (3rd edition) (Oxford: Oxford University Press, 1971).

7 Nader Entessar, "The Lion and the Sphinx: Iranian Egyptian Relations in Perspective," in *Iran and the Arab World*, eds. Hooshang Amirahmadi and Nader Entessar (London: Macmillan, 1973), 162–163.

8 Shireen T. Hunter, "From Hostility to Limited Alliance," in *Iran and the Arab World*, eds. Hooshang Amirahmadi and Nader Entessar (London: Macmillan, 1973), 198–216.
9 Jacob Abadi, *Israel's Quest for Recognition and Acceptance in Asia: Garrison State Diplomacy* (London: Franc Cass Publisher, 2004), 44.
10 Rouallah Ramazani, *Revolutionary Iran: Challenge and Responses in the Middle East* (Baltimore: Johns Hopkins University Press, 1988), 176.
11 Raymond Hinnebusch, *Syria: Revolution from Above* (London: Routledge, 2001).
12 Hunter, "From Hostility to Limited Alliance," 206.
13 Goodarzi, *Syria and Iran*, 16.
14 Eberhard Kienle, *Ba'th vs Ba'th: The Conflict between Syria and Iraq 1968–1989* (London: I.B. Tauris, 1990).
15 Jerome Donovan, *The Iran–Iraq War: Antecedents and Conflict Escalation* (London: Routledge, 2011).
16 Ibid.
17 The 1937 London agreement established, among other things, the division of the Shatt-Al-Arab river between Persia and British controlled Iraq. This agreement had long been resented by the Iranians who considered it to have been imposed on them by the dominant colonial powers.
18 Relations never went as low as in the mid-1960s, but this is probably more due to Al-Assad's pragmatic approach as opposed to the radical Pan-Arab rhetoric of most of the Ba'thist governments in the 1960s.
19 Musa Al-Sadr disappeared in mysterious circumstances during a visit to Libya. Muhammar Ghaddafi was suspected of being responsible for his death; this poisoned the relation between Libya and Iran in the first months after the revolution.
20 Patrick Seale, *Assad of Syria: The Struggle for the Middle East* (London: I.B. Tauris, 1988), 353.
21 While Iran was undoubtedly an ally of the United States in this phase, it is hard to describe its foreign policy as the one of a status quo power given its activism in the region and particularly in the Gulf.
22 Goodarzi, *Syria and Iran*, 18.
23 Seale, *Assad of Syria*, 351.
24 Goodarzi, *Syria and Iran*, 21.
25 Ibid., 30.
26 Libya and the Palestine Liberation Organization were the notable exception, at least in the first phase.
27 Seale, *Assad of Syria*, 357.
28 Raphael Lefevre, *Ashes of Hama: The Muslim Brotherhood in Syria* (London: Hurst and Co., 2013).
29 Goodarzi, *Syria and Iran*, 31–32.
30 G.H. Jansen, "The Attitude of Arab Governments towards the Gulf War," in *The Iran–Iraq War: An Historical, Economic and Political Analysis*, ed. Muhammad S. El Azhary (London: Croom Helm, 1984), 85.
31 Ibid., 51.
32 Husayn Agha and Ahmad Khalidi, *Syria and Iran: Rivalry and Cooperation* (London: Royal Institute of International Affairs, 1995), 13.
33 Yair Hirshfeld, "The Odd Couple: Ba'thist Syria and Khomeini's Iraq," in *Syria under Assad*, eds. Moshe Ma'oz and Avner Yaniv (London: Croom Helm, 1986).
34 Seale, *Assad of Syria*, 267–269.
35 Ibid., ch. 16.
36 Adeed Dawisha, *Syria and the Lebanese Crisis* (London: Macmillan Press, 1980).
37 Ibid., 15.
38 Goodarzi, *Syria and Iran*, 15.
39 Al-Assad did nonetheless try to limit Iran's direct involvement in Lebanon as confirmed by the closure of a training camp established by the Iranian Revolutionary

102   *The alliances of Syria*

Guards in Baalbek, see John K. Cooley, "Assad Has Problems," *Middle East International*, 4 May 1984, 13.

40   Goodarzi, *Syria and Iran*, 106.
41   The relations between Syria and Amal had suffered a temporary setback when the latter seemed to assume a positive (or at least neutral) attitude towards the Israeli occupation of the south.
42   Anoushiravan Ehteshami and Raymond Hinnebusch, *Syria and Iran: Middle Powers in a Penetrated Regional System* (London: Routledge, 1997), 129–130.
43   Agha and Khalidi, *Syria and Iran*, 21.
44   Ibid., 133.
45   Goodarzi, *Syria and Iran*, 265.
46   Ibid., 268.

9 Syria and Saudi Arabia

This chapter focuses on the relationship between the Syrian Arab Republic and the Kingdom of Saudi Arabia (also referred to in this chapter as Saudi Arabia or KSA). This alliance is particularly interesting and challenging for any theoretical framework. The pattern of relations between the two countries changed significantly throughout the Ba'th years. During Syria's unlimited revisionism years relations between the two countries were overall negative. Successive Ba'thist leaderships showed strong ideological hostility towards the Gulf kingdoms and particularly towards Saudi Arabia. The Jadid regime saw the KSA as its main ideological rival. The less ideological Al-Assad regime changed this policy. Riyadh was the primary target of the new regime's diplomatic initiative aimed at improving Syria's relations with the Arab world. The opening toward the KSA was the result of a precise strategic calculation. Within the context of Syria's limited revisionism, Saudi Arabia was valued as a partner, given its resources and diplomatic weight, despite the ideological distance between the two states. The KSA in turn benefited from Damascus' contribution to regional stability, as well as gaining legitimacy at both domestic and international levels by aligning itself with a front-line Arab state.

The establishment of an 'informal alliance' between the two Arab powers shows how, during the Al-Assad years, realpolitik trumped ideology. The Ba'thist republic led by an Alawi officer and the Wahhabi Kingdom were on paper 'ideological rivals', champions of Pan-Arabism and Wahhabism respectively. Damascus was a regional client of the USSR and the closest ally of Tehran during the Iran–Iraq war. Riyadh was a staunch opponent of the Islamic republic and highly dependent on the United States for its security. Despite these differences, the constant flow of money from Riyadh to Damascus, the regular occurrence of meetings between the two countries' officials during the Iran–Iraq war, the joint effort to impose a solution on the Lebanese scenario (or rather a 'pro-Syrian solution') all indicate the presence of an informal alignment between the two countries.

Relations before 1963

Extensive relations between the Bilad Al-Sham and Gulf regions long predate the formation of the modern states. The Saudi monarchy in particular had strong

104 *The alliances of Syria*

connections with the tribes of the Syrian desert. These links had been functional to the establishment of the Al-Saud's rule over the country.[1] In the aftermath of the foundation of the Syrian state, Saudi policy-makers attempted to exploit these links to influence political developments in Damascus. The elites that led the country in the aftermath of independence were in fact aligned to the KSA. The first Syrian President Shukri Al-Quwatly hailed from a Damascene family that had strong connections to the Kingdom. Saudi Arabia was one of the key actors in the 'Struggle for Syria', the competition among different Arab states to exert their control over the country.[2] During these years the main opponents of the Kingdom were the Hashemites of Jordan and Iraq. Traditional rivals of the House of Saud, the Hashemites had briefly been in control of Syria through King Faysal in the aftermath of World War I. Saudi policy aimed at preventing them from imposing their control over the weak Syrian state that had emerged out of the decolonisation process.

With the rise of Pan-Arabism in the late 1950s and 1960s, Nasser's Egypt became the main threat to the Saudis. Riyadh's regional policy remained one of containment aimed mainly at avoiding the emergence of a regional hegemon. In 1958, with establishment of the United Arab Republic, Egypt appeared to have defeated both Iraq and the KSA by imposing his control over Damascus. Tellingly, the man that had formally 'handed in' Syria to the Egyptian President was Shukri Al-Quwatly. The formation of the United Arab Republic appeared to be a decisive step towards regional leadership for Nasser, but it soon proved to be his first setback in power. It is perhaps unsurprising that the KSA (together with Jordan) was the main sponsor of Lieutenant Colonel Nahwali, the Syrian officer that led the secessionist coup d'état in 1961.[3] The collapse of the Union led to a brief return in power of the upper class that had historical links to Iraq and the KSA. This was, however, a short interlude, as a series of coups and countercoups saw Arab nationalist forces gain power in the country. The regimes that took power in Syria in the years after the separation with Egypt were weak, their reputation tainted by the collapse of the United Arab Republic. As tensions rose between the progressive republics and the conservative monarchies, these regimes used anti-Saudi propaganda to reinforce their Pan-Arab credentials. The Syrian scenario was, however, not the only one that the progressive and conservative Arab forces were competing in. The rivalry between the KSA and Egypt (and their respective allies) reached the highest level with the outbreak of the civil war in Yemen in 1962.[4] This conflict saw Egypt and Saudi Arabia intervene in support of republicans and royalists (loyal to the deposed Imam Al-Bakr), respectively.[5] Within this context of regional competition, the March 1963 coup d'état in Syria was unlikely to go unnoticed in Riyadh.

In the phase before 1963 some features of the KSA's policy that were to affect significantly its relations with Syria were already well-defined. Being unable to aspire to the role of regional hegemony because of its small population, limited armed forces and relatively peripheral (at least in geopolitical terms) location, Saudi Arabia carried out a policy sometimes comparable with the 'balance of power' traditionally played by England, and later the United

Kingdom, in Europe. The KSA manoeuvred to prevent the formation of a potentially hostile hegemonic block within the Arab world.[6] This policy often meant trying to protect Syrian independence from the ambition of some regional power, whether Abdallah's Trans-Jordan or Nasser's Egypt.

The radical years

The regimes that led Syria during the 1963–1970 years were dominated by the Ba'th party and committed to Pan-Arab ideology. As such, they all showed a certain degree of ideological hostility towards the conservative monarchies and particularly the KSA. This was part of the broader contrasts between conservative and progressive Arab states that was prominent during the 1960s. Within this context, different Pan-Arab forces used their hostility towards the Kingdom to show their commitment to the progressive cause. The KSA was therefore the target of a hostile propaganda that started in the early 1960s and culminated with the Jadid regime between 1966 and 1970 (unsurprisingly the most radical and ideological regime in Syrian history).

The Ba'thist era started in Syria with the March 1963 coup d'état. This military putsch brought to power a heterogeneous coalition of Ba'thists, Nasserites and independent officers. These forces had little in common other than their commitment to Pan-Arabism (that they, however, interpreted in very different ways). One of the few things that they seemed to agree on was their opposition to the KSA. Radio Damascus became a constant source of anti-Saudi propaganda. Saudi Arabia's position was undoubtedly weakened by these attacks, as the Kingdom was unable to challenge the prestige of the champions of Pan-Arabism. Riyadh reacted by using the weapons at its disposal. The Saudi regime clamped down on all those who were suspected of Ba'th sympathies, particularly Syrian expats working in the country.[7] It threatened to suspend financial aids to frontline Arab states. The KSA also strengthened its partnership with its old-time foe, the Hashemite Kingdom of Jordan.[8] These measures allowed the KSA to mitigate the effects of the hostility from the progressive republics. Riyadh was, however, unable to address the gradual loss of relevance of its traditional allies in Syria. The Kingdom had used its links and money to influence developments in Damascus. The years between 1963 and 1966 saw the groups traditionally close to Saudi Arabia lose their influence in the country, replaced by young officers from minority groups that had no connections to Riyadh, and even less sympathy towards the Wahabi Kingdom. This was clearly a negative development for the KSA, that culminated in the takeover of power by the radical Jadid regime.

1966–1970

The Jadid regime has been defined here as the most radical in Syrian history. Quite predictably, it was also the most ideologically hostile towards Saudi Arabia and the conservative monarchies. Salah Jadid and most of his cabinet

106 *The alliances of Syria*

conceived foreign policy as a competition between revolutionary and conservative forces. The reactionary forces within the Middle East and the Arab world were therefore the 'front-line' enemies. Saudi Arabia, as the leader of the conservative monarchies, incarnated their main ideological opposition. Riyadh became the object of a vehement propaganda campaign from Damascus, just as the tensions with Cairo were diminishing after a Saudi–Egyptian understanding in Yemen.[9] The Jadid regime also took more drastic and unprecedented measures.[10] Trade with the KSA was limited and the Syrian regime refused to repair the Tapline (the Trans-Arabian oil pipeline running through Syria) when it became damaged. This resulted in significant income loss for the Saudis.[11] Furthermore, Syria supported and encouraged Saudi leftist groups, hosting several high profile members in the country.[12] Just as concerning for the Saudi regime was the fact that the Syrians increased their support for revolutionary groups in Yemen. The Syrian regime became progressively more involved in the Yemeni civil war, where it provided planes and pilots to the republican forces.[13] The 1967 defeat and the humbling at the hands of the Israeli army did not appear to dampen the Syrian regime's hostility towards Riyadh. In the aftermath of the conflict, the Syrian leader Jadid refused to attend the Arab League meeting in Khartoum. The Syrian foreign minister Ibrahim Makhus was initially chosen to lead his country's delegation but left in protest during the summit.[14] This was an open challenge to the Saudi role in the Arab world after the 1967 war, given the central role played by King Fahad in convening the summit.

Saudi Arabia's reaction to this hostility was twofold, and apparently contradictory. The KSA responded to Syrian hostile propaganda with its own criticism of 'un-Islamic' Ba'thism. It also adopted domestic measures to suppress potential support for Arab nationalism in the country, as well as banning the import of Syrian goods.[15] On the other hand, the KSA kept subsidising Damascus for its efforts against Israel, and at the Khartoum meeting increased its financial support to Syria.[16] The support of front Arab states clearly had domestic as well as international purposes. The 1967 defeat had been nearly as damaging for the reputation of the monarchy in Riyadh as it had been for the countries that had been defeated on the battlefield. The House of Saud had been unwilling or unable to do anything concrete to protect Muslim land and particularly the Holy City of Jerusalem. Financing the Arab resistance was a way of deflecting criticisms in the aftermath of an Arab military disaster that had resulted in the loss of the third holiest site for Islam.

The Al-Assad years

Syrian foreign policy towards the Kingdom during the radical Ba'th years was characterised by a high degree of ideological hostility. The change from unlimited to limited revisionism brought about by the new Syrian regime completely changed the dynamics of the relationship. During the Jadid years the KSA was regarded as the embodiment of conservative and pro-Western policies in the region, and was therefore the sworn enemy of the revolutionary Ba'th. Al-Assad and his men had no ideological affinity with the Wahabi Kingdom. However, they believed that the KSA could have represented an important asset for Syrian foreign policy. With its resources and diplomatic weight, the KSA could have been functional to Damascus' limited revisionist goal of narrowing the gap with its main regional rivals. As a status quo power, Riyadh sought to build positive relations with key Arab actors that could have contributed to regional stability.

Given the state of relations at the end of the 1960s, Saudi Arabia could have only expected an improvement when Hafez Al-Assad took over power in Damascus. The new Syrian leader moved rapidly to show a new, more pragmatic approach. Saudi Arabia was the first beneficiary of this change in Syrian foreign policy. The propaganda war waged by previous Ba'th regimes relented. Relations between the two powers improved quickly also thanks to Egyptian mediation. After Nasser's death, the KSA was able to play a more proactive and less defensive role.[17] King Faisal became a central figure in Arab politics.[18] His positive personal relations with Hafez Al-Assad eased the path towards reconciliation between Damascus and Riyadh. The meeting between the foreign ministers Khaddam of Syria and Umar Shaffaq of Saudi Arabia in May 1971 was the first of several high profile summits between the two leaderships.[19] In early 1972 the new alliance was 'sealed' by an offer of $200 million of aid from Riyadh to Damascus.[20]

Changes implemented by Syrian regime at a domestic level also favoured the improvement of the Syrian–Saudi relationship. Al-Assad's 'Corrective Movement' aimed at reaching out to societal groups that had been alienated by Jadid's radical policies.[21] One of the main results was the pacification of the Sunni bourgeoisie of Syria's main cities. Syrian expats and Arab businessmen benefited greatly from the Infitah (the limited liberalisation policy introduced by Al-Assad).[22] These sectors of the population typically had strong economic and personal links with the KSA. Another cornerstone of Hafez Al-Assad's rule was the relationship with Syria's most powerful tribes. The research carried out on this underlines how some of the tribal groups had close historical links to Saudi Arabia, particularly through related Saudi tribes.[23] Some particularly influential tribes had strong links and 'privileged access' to the Saudi royal family members.[24]

After several years of conflict and mutual distrust, the regimes of the KSA, Syria and Egypt appeared to be closer than ever. The 1973 war represented the zenith of the Damascus-Riyadh-Cairo axis. More than the symbolic deployment of a brigade on the Golan Heights, it was the use of the oil weapon and the generous funding of the war efforts that confirmed the KSA's closeness to Damascus and Cairo. The imposition of an oil embargo on the United States and its Western allies had great impact. The KSA openly defied its superpower ally in support of the Arab 'frontline' states. Just as important from Damascus' point of view were the generous loans and grants that Saudi Arabia (together with other Gulf States) conceded to Syria in the aftermath of the war.[25] From 1974 until early 1975 there was unprecedented cooperation between the two Arab states. The 1974 Rabat summit was the most visible sign of this partnership:

108   *The alliances of Syria*

Saudi Arabia and Syria were the driving force behind the achievement of an Arab consensus on controversial topics such as the recognition of the Palestine Liberation Organization as the sole representative of the Palestinians. Despite this show of unity, divisions between Egypt and Syria had already emerged during the conflict and grew in its immediate aftermath. Saudi Arabia attempted to keep a united Arab front by mediating between Cairo and Damascus.[26]

Arab politics in the mid-1970s had been dominated by the Cairo–Damascus–Riyadh axis. Despite Saudi attempts to prevent a break-up, the triangle was torn apart by Egypt's path towards reconciliation with Israel and the United States. Camp David effectively shattered every chance of restoring the Cairo–Damascus–Riyadh axis.[27] Predictably, the Syrians reacted furiously to the accords. Together with Iraq, they sought to punish Cairo by completely isolating Sadat from the rest of the Arab world. Saudi Arabia found itself stuck between the two former allies. Riyadh's predicament was complicated by its relationship with the United States, that had been the main sponsor of the Egyptian–Israeli agreement.[28] Saudi Arabia had previously been open to an American-sponsored solution to the Arab–Israeli conflict, and initially the KSA appeared to be inclined towards accepting the Camp David agreements.[29] However, for both domestic and external legitimacy reasons, Riyadh could hardly afford to challenge Arab consensus and throw its weight behind Egypt. The Kingdom opted instead to back Damascus and Baghdad's rejectionist stance.[30] The 1978 Baghdad summit saw Saudi Arabia and the conservative monarchies approve a ten-year funding plan to the front-line Arab states. Unsurprisingly, Syria was the main beneficiary, while the KSA was the main contributor. Damascus (together with Baghdad) had succeeded in bringing the Saudis close to the rejectionists' position. This consensus was, however, short-lived; Syria and Iraq were soon back to their familiar pattern of conflict.

Syrian–Saudi relations had survived the Camp David Accords. It was the Iranian revolution that threatened to unravel the alliance between the two Arab powers. As outlined in the previous chapter, Damascus was quick to open up to the Islamic republic, seeing the revolution as an opportunity to acquire a much-needed ally. The Saudi monarchy on the other hand saw the revolution as an existential threat. The Saudis were particularly concerned about the spreading of revolutionary ideas to their own Shia population. The Iranian revolution brought Riyadh closer to Saddam Hussein.[31] The Iraqi dictator was seen by the Saudis as the only option to keep the Iranian expansionism in check. The Saudi perception of insecurity increased when the Soviet Union decided to invade Afghanistan in December 1979. Moscow intervened to prop up the crumbling Communist government of Afghanistan. In Riyadh this was, however, perceived as a Soviet attempt to encircle the KSA. Moscow was already heavily involved in the Yemeni civil war, as well as supporting leftist groups hostile to the KSA throughout the Middle East and North Africa region.

By the end of the 1970s the KSA and Syria were at odds on virtually all key regional issues. The two Arab powers disagreed on how the Arabs should approach the Arab–Israeli conflict, on the relationship with Washington and

Saudi Arabia disliked Syria's alignment with the Soviet Union. Crucially, the two Arab powers were at odds over the Iranian revolution. Despite these contrasts, the two powers maintained a working relationship, albeit a sometimes uneasy one. The case of the Iran–Iraq war and the developments of the Lebanese scenario show the specific dynamics at play between the limited revisionism of Syria and the status quo pursued by policy-makers in Riyadh.

Iran–Iraq war

On the 22 September 1980 Iraq invaded its neighbour Iran. The role that the KSA played in encouraging and supporting Iraq has been the subject of much debate and speculation.[32] Whether it instigated the start of the conflict or not, the Saudi leadership was certainly supportive of Iraq's war effort. From the Iranian revolution onwards, the KSA considered Tehran the biggest threat in the region. At the same time the rivalry between Syria and Iraq had regained momentum after a short rapprochement between 1977 and 1978.[33] The Arab world was divided by the conflict, and Riyadh and Damascus found themselves on opposite sides of a long and gruesome war. Saddam Hussein had planned for a quick military campaign in Iran. A swift military success would have eliminated the threat of revolutionary Iran and promoted Iraq to the status of regional hegemon. This proved to be a spectacular miscalculation, as Iran was able to withstand the Iraqi attack and, by the second year of the war, appeared to be in the ascendance. The possibility of an Iranian victory rang alarm bells in most Arab capitals. It what was by then a usual pattern; Riyadh responded to the perceived threat by trying to re-create Arab unity. This meant facilitating a reconciliation between Syria and Iraq as well as re-integrating Egypt into Arab politics. Despite the good relations between Riyadh and Damascus, the KSA's attempts to lure Syria away from Iran proved to be unsuccessful. When it became obvious that the conflict between Iraq and Iran and had taken a turn in favour of the latter, Damascus found itself in a mediator role given its privileged access to Tehran.[34] Sunayama outlines how the start of the tanker war in 1984 initially enhanced Damascus' position, with Syria 'collecting rewards from both the moderate Arab states on the one hand, and Tehran on the other'.[35] Unwilling to sever its alliance with Iran, but dependant on the aid coming from the Gulf, the Syrian leadership had to juggle to keep an open channel with both. The Syrian inability to restrain Iran in this phase threatened to damage Damascus' relationship with the KSA. The Saudis had adopted a tougher anti-Iranian stance after the events of the Hajj in 1987, and at the Amman Summit that year the KSA and the Gulf states refused to discuss the renewal of the 1978 Baghdad Summit aid commitment.[36] Despite this, the Saudis (along with the Jordanians) did not halt their attempts to reconcile Damascus and Baghdad until the end of the Iran–Iraq war the following year, confirming that they still saw Syria as an important factor in the regional balance.

The case of the Iran–Iraq war illustrates the dynamics of the relationship between Damascus and Riyadh. The level of cooperation, the 'open channel' and

110   *The alliances of Syria*

the resources that Damascus was able to extract from Riyadh while the two countries were the main allies of the Tehran and Baghdad respectively are remarkable. The attempts to pacify Syria and Iraq during the conflict can be explained by the fact that Riyadh saw its own position and security threatened by divisions within the Arab world. While Riyadh looked unfavourably to Damascus' alliance with the Islamic republic, the KSA also hoped that Damascus could play a 'moderator' role with its ally. Syria was able to keep an open channel with both Tehran and the Gulf countries, managing to extract resources from both parties. Crucially, throughout the years of the Iran–Iraq war, the KSA and Syria managed to keep a working relationship on other regional topics, as shown by the developments of the Lebanese scenario.

Lebanon

The Lebanese case represents an excellent example of the dynamics at play between Syria and Saudi Arabia. When the Lebanese crisis erupted in 1975, Riyadh used its influence to mediate an end to the conflict, and initially succeeded in doing so. It is worth outlining that the Saudis focused their diplomatic approach on the regional players rather than on the local actors.[37] The KSA saw in the re-establishment of that 'Arab consensus' shattered by the Sinai II agreement the key to stability in the region. This approach was a way to avoid the occurrence (or at least limit the consequences) of potentially devastating crises such as the Lebanese one.[38] The Riyadh agreement (October 1976) recognised the Syrian role in Lebanon and gave it an Arab mantle by approving the deployment of an 'Arab Deterrence Force' composed nearly entirely of Syrians. The mission was also financed by Gulf states.[39] These generous concessions were the price Riyadh was ready to pay to rebuild the regional system around the 1973 alliance. Despite Riyadh's best efforts, the flaring up of the conflict and the 1978 Israeli invasion of southern Lebanon created exactly that scenario of regional instability that the Saudis had sought to avoid. The Lebanese crisis was particularly troublesome for Riyadh because it pitted Syria against the KSA's superpower's ally, the United States.

During the 1982 Israeli invasion of Lebanon, the KSA and other Gulf countries made a show of supporting the Syrians battered by Israel. Despite this support Riyadh and Damascus had different ideas about Lebanon's future. While Syria wanted to maintain and strengthen its control over affairs in Beirut, the KSA favoured a more independent Lebanon (one where the Saudis, with their links and economic power, could have played a central role). Regardless of this fundamental disagreement, Hafez Al-Assad was in 1983 able to prevent the Saudis from supporting the Israeli–Lebanese treaty that would have sanctioned Israeli/American supremacy over the country.[40] As his position was boosted by the Israeli retreat, Hafez Al-Assad proceeded to settle the scores with his Arab arch-rival Yassir Arafat, long time protégé of the Saudis.[41] Riyadh, despite the relevant economic help given to Syria, was not able to control Damascus' policy.

The dynamics of Saudi–Syrian relations emerged clearly with the Ta'if Agreement of 1989. This accord, brokered by Saudi Arabia, led to the end of the 15-year long civil war in Lebanon. Sunayama outlines how Damascus was struggling to impose a presidential candidate because of the opposition by Maronite forces.[42] The Syrians had to face a serious challenge by General Michel Aoun, directly backed by Saddam Hussein. The support obtained by the Saudis legitimised the Syrian military operation against the general in the eyes of the international opinion and the Arab world. The Ta'if Agreement went along with virtually all Syrian requests. The sectarian system was 'rebalanced' in favour of Al-Assad's allies, and only a loose framework for Syrian withdrawal was approved.[43] The agreement legitimised Syria's control over the Cedar country. In this instance, the KSA was central to the establishment of the Syrian supremacy in Beirut. In key phases such as 1976 and 1989, the KSA proved to be able and willing to support Syrian policy in Lebanon. Despite contrasts over specific aspects of Syrian policy, Saudi Arabia opted to back and help legitimise the Syrian position in Lebanon.

Conclusion: Syria and Saudi Arabia, the triumph of realpolitik?

The Ba'thist Syrian Arab republic and the Wahabi Kingdom of Saudi Arabia were in many ways an odd couple. Looking only at their ideological differences, it would be reasonable to expect that the two countries should be sworn enemies. The first Ba'th regimes were in fact ideologically opposed to the KSA because of their commitment to Pan-Arabism. The radical regime of Salah Jadid in particular was devoted to a revolutionary mission and considered the KSA its greatest ideological rival. Riyadh was the main target of fierce verbal attacks and other hostile diplomatic measures. These dynamics, however, changed completely when Hafez Al-Assad took over power in 1970. The new Syrian President clearly aimed at building a positive relationship with Riyadh. The KSA, with its oil wealth and diplomatic leverage, was functional to Syria's goal of opposing Israel. The Saudi leadership on the other hand not only benefited from the end of a damaging propaganda war, but also came to see Damascus as an important contributor to regional stability.

Despite their ideological differences, the two Arab powers maintained a working relationship on several key issues. Riyadh consistently financed Syrian foreign policy and supported Damascus on key issues such as the Lebanese Civil War. Notably, the relationship between the two Arab powers also survived the strains caused by their alignment to the two superpowers and the pressure of the Iran–Iraq war. The conflict between the two Gulf powers proved to be the most divisive issue in regional and inter-Arab politics throughout the 1980s. Saudi Arabia and Syria were the main supporters of Iraq and Iran respectively. The Kingdom tried throughout the conflict to 'separate' Damascus from its new ally, in an attempt to recreate an Arab balance that had been shattered by Camp David and the Iran–Iraq war itself. The ability and willingness by both parties to

112 *The alliances of Syria*

maintain a working relationship amid these differences shows that Syria and Saudi Arabia enjoyed significant rewards from this partnership. In the case of Syria, this 'rational' calculation of the benefits connected to a positive relationship with the KSA only took place with the change of regime in 1970. This confirms how ideological regimes such as the Jadid one often chose to disregard balance of power-like considerations in order to pursue wider 'extra-state' goals.

Notes

1 Madawi Al-Rasheed, *Politics in an Arabian Oasis: The Rashidis of Saudi Arabia* (London: I.B.Tauris, 1997).
2 Patrick Seale, *The Struggle for Syria: A Study of Post-war Arab Politics 1945–1958* (2nd edition) (Oxford: Oxford University Press, 1965).
3 Patrick Seale, *Assad of Syria: The Struggle for the Middle East* (London: I.B. Tauris, 1988).
4 Malcolm H. Kerr, *The Arab Cold War: Gamel Abd Al-Nasir and His Rivals, 1958–1970* (3rd edition) (Oxford: Oxford University Press, 1971), 39–40.
5 Navrad Safran, *Saudi Arabia: The Ceaseless Quest for Security* (Ithaca: Cornell University Press, 1988), 119–121.
6 Gregory Gause III, "The Foreign Policy of Saudi Arabia," in *The Foreign Policy of Middle East States*, eds. Raymond Hinnebusch and Anoushiravan Ehteshami (London: Lynne Rienner, 2002).
7 David Holden and Richard Johns, *The House of Saud* (London: Pan Books, 1991).
8 Ibid.
9 Sonoko Sunayama, *Syria and Saudi Arabia: Collaboration and Conflicts in the Oil Era* (London: I.B Tauris, 2007), 31.
10 Yaacov Bar-Siman-Tov, *Linkage Politics in the Middle East: Syria between Domestic and External Conflict, 1961–1970* (Boulder: Westview, 1983).
11 Sunayama, *Syria and Saudi Arabia*, 32.
12 Tabitha Petran, *The Struggle over Lebanon* (New York: Monthly Review Press, 1987).
13 Gregory Gause III, *Saudi–Yemeni Relations: Domestic Structures and Foreign Influence* (New York: Columbia University Press, 1990).
14 Kerr, *The Arab Cold War*.
15 Holden and Johns, *The House of Saud*.
16 Sunayama, *Syria and Saudi Arabia*, 33.
17 Ibid., 34.
18 James Piscatori, "Islamic Values and National Interest: The Foreign Policy of Saudi Arabia," in *Islam in Foreign Policy*, ed. Adeed Dawisha (Cambridge: Cambridge University Press, 1983).
19 Sunayama, *Syria and Saudi Arabia*, 37.
20 Holden and Johns, *The House of Saud*, 299.
21 Seale, *Assad of Syria*, ch. XII.
22 Volker Perthes, *The Political Economy of Syria under Asad* (London: I.B. Tauris, 1995).
23 Al-Rasheed, *Politics in an Arabian Oasis*.
24 Torsten Schoel, "The Hasna's Revenge: Syrian Tribes and Politics in their Shaykh's Story," *Nomadic People* 15, 1 (2011): 96–113.
25 Seale, *Assad of Syria*, 255.
26 Safran, *Saudi Arabia*, 241–245.
27 Ibid., 229–230.
28 Gause, "The Foreign Policy of Saudi Arabia," 207.

29 Sunayama, *Syria and Saudi Arabia*, 53.
30 This rapprochement is described in detail in Chapter 6 of this volume.
31 Safran, *Saudi Arabia*, 352.
32 For a discussion of Saudi Arabia's role see Shahram Chubin and Charles Tripp, *Iran and Iraq at War* (London: I.B. Tauris, 1988).
33 Eberhard Kienle, *Ba'th vs Ba'th: The Conflict between Syria and Iraq 1968–1989* (London: I.B. Tauris, 1990).
34 Anoushiravan Ehteshami and Raymond Hinnebusch, *Syria and Iran: Middle Powers in a Penetrated Region* (London: Routledge, 1997), 96.
35 Sunayama, *Syria and Saudi Arabia*, 176.
36 Ibid., 204.
37 Sunayama, *Syria and Saudi Arabia*, 43–47.
38 Graeme Bannerman, "Saudi Arabia," in *Lebanon in Crisis: Participants and Issues*, eds. P. Edward Haley and Lewis W. Snider (Syracuse: Syracuse University Press, 1979).
39 Adeed Dawisha, *Syria and the Lebanese Crisis* (London: Macmillan Press, 1980), ch. IX.
40 Jim Muir, "Assad Plays a Strong but Cautious Hand," *Middle East International*, 14 October 1983.
41 On this aspect see Seale, *Assad of Syria* and Robert Fisk, *Pity the Nation: Lebanon at War* (Oxford: Oxford University Press, 1990).
42 Sunayama, *Syria and Saudi Arabia*, 211.
43 Ibid., 212.

10 Syria and the USSR

This book has so far explored the regional alliances of Syria. This chapter deals with the relationship between Syria and one of the two superpowers, the USSR. The choice to include an extra-regional power in a study of regional alliances might at first seem odd, however, superpower involvement in the Middle East during the Cold War years was a central factor in regional politics. The relationship between Moscow and Damascus has been included because of its relevance to Syrian regional strategy. Syrian limited revisionism aimed at containing and challenging Israeli–American predominance in the region. The involvement and support of the USSR was crucial to the achievement of this goal.

The Syrian–Soviet alliance represents a classic example of global power patron/regional power client alliance. The USSR provided Syria with weapons, generous loans, economic help and diplomatic support. The alliance allowed the USSR to project its power in a region where its superpower rival had a comparative advantage. The relationship between the two countries was established as early as 1955, when Syria was the first Arab country to receive Soviet weapons.

During the early Ba'th years, the Syrian leadership's anti-imperialist ideology brought it closer to the USSR. This affinity allowed the relationship to overcome the tensions created by contrasts between the Ba'th and Communist parties. It was with the radical Ba'th regime of Salah Jadid that the two countries reached their strongest ideological alignment. The switch from unlimited to limited revisionism did not, however, affect the relationship between the two powers. The factors driving the alliance partially changed from ideological solidarity to power calculations under the more pragmatic Al-Assad regime. The new leader came into power with the reputation of being less sympathetic towards the USSR. Despite this, during his reign the partnership between the two countries grew. In 1980 Syria and the USSR signed a Treaty of Friendship confirming the strength of their alliance. Cooperation between the two parties grew throughout the early 1980s, when its strength manifested itself in scenarios such as Lebanon. The collapse of the USSR and its partial retreat from the region represented a big setback for Damascus.

Relations before 1963

The relationship with the Soviet Union represented a cornerstone of Syrian foreign policy during the Cold War, but it was only as recent as Soviet involvement in the region. Prior to World War II, the Levant had not been a primary region of interest for Russian and later Soviet foreign policy-makers.[1] Moscow's traditional goal in the wider Middle East region had been gaining access to the sea through the Bosporus and Dardanelles straits. In the immediate aftermath of World War II the USSR was still more interested in extending its influence on Turkey and Iran, very much at the periphery of Middle Eastern politics in that phase. The European powers' progressive decline opened a void in the region that was rapidly filled by the United States and the USSR. Syria was seen by the Soviets as a potential ally in the region since the overthrow of the pro-Western government of Shishakli in 1954.[2] The 1955 Turkish–Syrian crisis was fundamental in the establishment of the relationship. On that occasion the Soviet Union provided diplomatic support to Syria as the country was facing the risk of a Turkish (and possibly Iraqi) invasion, as well as granting Syria the first loans provided to any Arab state.[3] After the 1956 Suez Crisis, the Soviet Union progressively increased its involvement in the Middle East. The relationship with Syria was particularly promising for Soviet policy-makers, given the robust presence of anti-imperialist forces in the country. These forces were, however, extremely divided and in competition among themselves. The growing rivalry between the Ba'th and Communist parties was particularly troublesome for Moscow. Despite these contrasts, Syrian Ba'thists were strongly influenced by the Soviet ideology.[4] These links would prove to be particularly important when the Ba'th took over in the following decade.

The relationship between Syria and the USSR worsened significantly during the United Arab Republic period (1958–1961). The Soviet Union publicly recognised the new state but was extremely critical of it. The Soviets feared that Nasser's control over the country would reduce Moscow's influence;[5] Nasser was more openly anti-Communist than the Ba'th or other Arab nationalist forces in Syria. After the establishment of the Union, the Syrian Communist party found itself banned.[6] Nasser's harsh stance on the Communists was one of the key factors behind the 'diplomatic duel' between the Egyptian President and Soviet leader Khrushchev that took place in late 1959 and 1960.[7] Moscow, however, worked to keep its economic links established with Syria in place. Given its hostility to the unity project, the Soviet Union unsurprisingly welcomed the collapse of the United Arab Republic and was quick to re-establish official diplomatic relations with Damascus. Despite the conservative inclination of the 'secessionist' regime that was in power in Syria during 1961–1963, the relationship between Moscow and Damascus remained altogether positive. The Communist party remained illegal in the country, but moderate improvements took place in the fields of economic and cultural cooperation.[8]

116 *The alliances of Syria*

The radical years

1963–1966

In March 1963 a coalition of different Pan-Arabist forces took up power in Syria. Ba'thists and Nasserites, the two main forces, were both at odds with the Communist party. This ideological tension clashed with the new regime's need for external support. Immediately after taking power the new regime denounced the Syrian Communist party, causing a significant worsening in the relationship with the USSR.[9] Moscow retorted with scant attacks towards the Ba'th party, in some cases questioning the party's placement in the anti-imperialist camp.[10] Within about one year, however, the tensions had diminished as both sides showed an interest in maintaining a working relationship.

By that time, the Ba'th party had managed to exclude the other forces and gain exclusive control in Damascus. The faction of the party that took up power was the 'right wing', one that was more ideologically distant from Moscow, Despite this, Syria remained a client of the USSR and the overall relationship between the two parties remained positive. Clearly, the USSR prioritised the relationship with Syria because of its relevance to its overall regional strategy, despite its unhappiness about the treatment received by the Syrian Communist party.[11] The Syrian leadership in turn was not insensitive to the Soviet position, and regularly attempted to appease the Soviet leadership. Once the Ba'thist regime succeeded in cementing its control over the country, it relaxed its attitude towards Communist militants and it also embarked on a policy of nationalisation of key assets that won it plaudits in Moscow.[12]

1966–1970

With the 1966 coup d'état, the leftist wing of the Ba'th party reached power for the first time in Syrian history. This faction of the Ba'thists had openly drawn inspiration from the Communist bloc and the Soviet model in particular. Unsurprisingly, the new Syrian regime invested heavily in the relationship with Moscow. The first sign of this budding partnership was the inclusion of Communist members in the newly formed Syrian government. Samy Atiyah was appointed Minister of Communication, while other Soviet sympathisers were given high profile jobs.[13] Domestically, the Jadid regime embarked on an ambitious plan of economic reform and nationalisations. On the international front, the new Syrian regime aimed to boost its 'revolutionary' credentials and sought to make Damascus the centre of anti-imperialist resistance in the region.[14] Accordingly, it increased its support of Palestinian militias based in the country. As discussed in previous chapters, this support was one the factors that led to the 1967 war. The Soviet Union played an important yet unclear role in the build up to the conflict.[15] Ramet maintains that the mixed and often contrasting signals sent by the USSR to both its Arab allies and Israel depended on the domestic division among factions of the Soviet leadership.[16] Soviet reaction to the Israeli attack was rather restrained. Moscow broke diplomatic relations with Israel but was very careful to avoid an escalation that might have resulted in direct involvement of the Western powers.[17] In the aftermath of the conflict, however, the USSR committed to a significant rearmament plan with both Egypt and Syria.

The Jadid regime had chosen to strengthen its partnership with the USSR for ideological reasons. The 1967 defeat increased its dependence on Moscow. Israel's military superiority had become clear, and the only realistic hope of qualitative and quantitative improvements in this sector came from the Soviets. Furthermore, in the aftermath of the conflict the limited economic help from the West and particularly the United States virtually ceased, further increasing Damascus' dependence on the USSR.[18] This reliance on Moscow was a source of division within the already fragmented Syrian leadership. The relationship with the USSR and the Soviet bloc was at the core of the division between the radical faction led by Salah Jadid and the moderate (or nationalist) faction led by Hafez Al-Assad. The former prioritised the implementation of a Soviet-style revolution in the country, and naturally aimed at strengthening the relationship with Moscow. The latter group favoured a less radical economic model and was overall critical of the growing influence of Moscow in Syrian affairs. Moscow (unsurprisingly) sided with Jadid. This preference was reinforced by the fact that Al-Assad had publicly criticised Soviet involvement in Syrian domestic politics.[19] As the Minister of Defence gradually took up power, Moscow kept its preferences for the radical faction but made sure it did not close the door to the young Alawite officer that was imposing himself as the new strongman in Damascus.

During the first Ba'th years, ideology was clearly a strong factor shaping Saudi–Syrian relations. Syria and the USSR both belonged to the anti-imperialist and anti-Western camp, and this ideological affinity contributed to the formation of the partnership. Disagreements caused by differences between Ba'thists and Communists in Syria marred the relationship but did not alter the overall strengthening of the partnership. Given the difficult state of Syrian–Israeli relations, the leadership in Damascus also valued the positive effect of further Soviet involvement in the region.[20] During the Jadid years ideological solidarity became more relevant. The regime looked at the USSR as an important political and cultural point of reference as its sought to promote its own version of class struggle and revolution. On this there was strong disagreement from the other Ba'th faction led by Hafez Al-Assad. The latter had no sympathy for the Soviet model and was concerned about Soviet influence in Syria. With the takeover of power by Al-Assad, the element of ideological solidarity declined, but this did not cause an end to the Syrian–Soviet partnership.

The Al-Assad years

The Soviet leadership had reason to be concerned when Jadid was ousted from power. The new Syrian leader Al-Assad appeared to have no sympathy for the Soviet Union.[21] More worryingly for Moscow, Al-Assad had been critical of

118 *The alliances of Syria*

Damascus' over-reliance on the superpower. The USSR had been supportive of Jadid when the two leaders had been engaged in a confrontation, but when their man was ousted Soviet officials preferred to adopt a neutral approach towards the new Syrian leadership. At the same time many Western capitals hoped for a shift in their favour in Syrian politics.[22] During his first months in power, the Syrian leader halted the 'revolutionary' project carried out by his predecessor. His Corrective Movement was a rejection of the Soviet model pursued during the Jadid years and an opening towards the Syrian middle class alienated by his predecessor's policies. However, in foreign policy the reshaping of Syrian goals did not result in a distancing from Moscow. On the contrary, the Soviet Union was central to the planning of the 1973 war with Israel and more broadly to the goal of changing the power balance in Arab–Israeli relations. Despite being portrayed as an 'anti-Soviet' within Syria's ruling class, once he established his control over the country Hafez Al-Assad moved to solidify the alliance with Moscow rather than distancing himself from the superpower. Clearly, in the aftermath of its disastrous 1967 military performance, Syria had no alternative but to try to improve cooperation with the Soviet Union in order to obtain the state-of-the-art military technologies that Al-Assad badly needed.

Al-Assad's alignment to the USSR was based on strategic and geopolitical considerations rather than ideological ones. Syria needed weapons to counter Israeli supremacy, and the only possible source of these weapons was the Soviet Union. The help provided by the Soviets during these years was important, but rather limited, mainly because Syria was in this phase only the third focus of Soviet foreign policy in the region after Egypt and Iraq. Before the 1973 war, the new President of Egypt had started the process of dissociating himself from its Soviet patron. This pattern that would make Syria the key ally of the Soviet Union in the region within a few years. When in July 1972 Anwar Sadat expelled Soviet advisors from the military bases on Egyptian soil (officially as a reaction to the failure of an arms agreement) the Soviets tried to balance this loss by improving the relations with their other two allies in the region. Iraq was at this stage the obvious choice as the second biggest Arab power after Egypt, but Syria also benefited from this balancing act.[23]

After Sadat's 1972 decision to expel Soviet advisors, the Soviets faced a dilemma in their relations with their main Arab ally. They did not want to lose Egypt to the West and feared that denying Sadat the weapons he wanted would have pushed him further in that direction. At the same time, they wanted to avoid a war that would have risked jeopardising their détente with the United States. Ultimately, the Soviets chose to agree to Egyptian requests, while trying to avoid a military confrontation.[24] This goal proved to be elusive, as Egyptian and Syrian leaders had already decided on a military initiative. Facing the *fait accompli* of the October War the Soviets were caught in between the need to find a diplomatic solution together with the United States and support for their Arab allies. The Soviets provided Damascus with significant arms transfers in the months before as well as during the conflict. These resupplies were fundamental to Syrian (and Egyptian) war efforts.[25]

Aftermath of the 1973 war

The support obtained by the USSR had been central to Syria's 1973 war effort. The military performance from the Arab powers was a marked improvement on the 1967 one. However, in the aftermath of the conflict both Moscow and Damascus found themselves in a difficult position. The Soviet Union was one of the diplomatic losers of the war. In the aftermath of the conflict Sadat relied on Kissinger's diplomacy to find a solution to the dispute with Israel. Syria's position was equally difficult, as Damascus found itself gradually cut off from its war ally. Egypt's path towards peace with Israel (and towards the pro-Western camp) had the effect of strengthening the Syrian–Soviet alliance by making each partner more important for the other. The USSR was poised to lose its main ally in the region, and therefore relied more heavily on its remaining regional partners. Syria on the other hand was left isolated by Egypt's defection, and needed its superpower ally for protection from Tel Aviv and Washington.

By the mid-1970s it was quite clear (well before Sadat's abrogation of the 'Treaty of Friendship' in 1976) that the USSR was to 'lose' Egypt. Syria (whose status in the Arab world had increased significantly after the 1973 war) became, by Soviet calculations, a much more important ally. Karsh maintains that every step that Egypt made towards a peace agreement made Syria more important to the Soviets.[26] Nevertheless, Syria's approach to the Arab–Israeli conflict, rooted in Damascus' limited revisionism, created tensions with the USSR. The Soviet Union was adamant about finding a solution for the Arab–Israeli conflict through an international peace conference sponsored by the two superpowers. The Soviets were therefore particularly displeased at Al-Assad's refusal to participate in the Geneva conference. While Moscow defended its ally's position at the conference, Al-Assad's intransigent line in late 1973/early 1974 increasingly upset the Soviets and resulted in an arms supply cutback.[27] The contacts between Damascus and Washington in the following months worried the Soviet Union and favoured a more generous approach towards the ally. During Al-Assad's visit to Moscow in April 1974 the two parties signed several agreements including a long-term economic deal and an important arms deal, consisting mainly of T62 tanks and surface-to-air missiles.[28]

While the Soviet Union obtained less immediate benefits from the renewed partnership, Al-Assad showed Syria's importance as an asset in the longer term. It gradually became clear that behind the façade of the Geneva conference the real peace process was being orchestrated by Kissinger and was held between Egypt and Israel only. Al-Assad, together with Iraq, prevented other Arab leaders from following Egypt's example. In this way, the Syrian leader avoided the achievement of a 'Pax Americana' in the region and the loss of influence of the Soviet Union that would have followed from it.[29] Despite all the pressure applied by Syria and the Soviet Union, Egypt's march towards a peace agreement with Israel and its switch to the pro-Western camp could not be stopped. The second disengagement agreement signed by Israel and Egypt in November 1975 represented a point of no return. The loss of Egypt to the Americans

120   *The alliances of Syria*

Table 10.1 Arms transfers to Syria from the USSR and total transfers (millions of US dollars)

Year	1970	1971	1972	1973	1974	1975	1976	1977
USSR	589	562	1400	3327	3702	1254	454	855
Total	599	572	1410	3435	3702	1259	462	898

Year	1978	1979	1980	1981	1982	1983	1984	1985
USSR	810	1661	1837	1358	1865	2294	1789	1584
Total	881	2115	2012	1403	2042	2378	1889	1629

Year	1986	1987	1988	1989	Total
USSR	1160	1359	1256	623	29740
Total	1164	1359	1256	623	31087

Source: Stockholm International Peace Research Institute Arms Transfers Database.

therefore undoubtedly created a bigger coinciding of interests between the USSR and Syria, and particularly in Syria's case, created further dependence on its patron. While its position as the last remaining 'frontline Arab state' improved its status in the long term, in the short term the Syrian leader had to face a worsening of the regional balance that made him extremely reliant on the USSR for support and diplomatic 'protection'.[30]

Despite this growing reliance on the USSR, Damascus strived to keep an independent stance on what it saw as crucial issues. In cases such as Lebanon, this often meant testing the solidity of the partnership with Moscow. The Cedar country was central to Syrian strategic thinking (particularly in the frame of Damascus' geopolitical confrontation with Israel). Given this centrality, it is not surprising that Al-Assad was willing to go against his superpower ally to pursue his agenda in Lebanon. The Soviet Union initially supported Syria's attempt to solve the Lebanese Civil War, sharing Damascus' view that this was a Western and Israeli plot to divide the country. Much more problematic for the USSR was the intervention of June 1976, that pitted Syria against its former allies (and Soviet clients) the Palestine Liberation Organization and the leftist forces led by Jumblatt. According to Golan, the Soviets feared that the Syrian invasion would have created an overlapping of interests between Damascus and Washington, pushing Syria closer to the United States.[31] Faced with the Syrian military action, all the Soviets could do was to cool off their relations with Damascus and condemn the invasion. The Palestine Liberation Organization and leftist forces wrongly hoped that this diplomatic stance would be followed by a more direct Soviet intervention in the crisis.[32] The Soviets' displeasure was summed up by Brezhnev's letter to Al-Assad, in which the Soviet leader explicitly stated that a continuation of the Syrian initiative could jeopardise their alliance.[33] The Syrian leader, however, was determined to punish Arafat and Jumblatt. A series of Syrian victories in the late summer of 1976 did so, and Al-Assad's action was approved by a peace meeting in Riyadh on 16 October, where the Syrian President celebrated the bitter victory in a war that he would have rather avoided fighting.[34] In terms of the relationship with Moscow, the Lebanese crisis contained some important lessons. First, despite the importance of the alliances with the Soviet Union, Al-Assad was not ready to accept interference in what he perceived as his own backyard. Second, the Soviet Union had, at this stage, only limited leverage on its client. The temporary suspension of arms delivery had not managed to alter Syrian foreign policy. Third, the Soviet Union's refusal to take a more active part in the conflict (by delivering weapons to the battered Palestinians and leftist forces) confirms that Syria had become a strategic partner for the USSR, as the Soviets were not willing to risk their alliance with Damascus to defend the Palestine Liberation Organization (despite the symbolic value of supporting the Palestinian cause within the Arab and the Third World).

In the aftermath of the 1976 disagreements over Lebanon, it was the Soviet Union that tried to build bridges with Al-Assad. The Syrian leader's emphasis on the 'Arab front' and his opening to the United States (particularly in the aftermath of Carter's election) had clearly worried the Soviet Union. Al-Assad refused Moscow's invitation to visit in January 1977. It is, however, hard to establish whether the Syrian leader was attempting to put pressure on his ally or whether he was genuinely convinced that he could achieve an improvement in his relationship with the United States. Syrian policy paid off as during two official visits to the USSR in April and June 1977 (led respectively by Hafez Al-Assad and the Defence Minister Mustafa Tlas). A new agreement on technical and economic cooperation as well as a new arms deal were signed.[35] In the aftermath of the visit, the delivery of weapons that had been delayed or postponed during the previous months restarted regularly.[36]

The 1980s

Throughout the 1970s, the Syrian–Soviet alliance had survived the perils of the peace process and tensions over important scenarios such as Lebanon. In the early 1980s this alliance reached its zenith, before declining due to changes in Soviet domestic and foreign policy. The decade started with the signing of a Treaty of Friendship in 1980. This had been a long-term demand of the Soviet Union. Moscow had already signed a similar agreement in 1971 with Egypt (then abrogated in 1976) and in 1972 with Iraq. The reasons why Al-Assad had, up to that point, refused to sign a Treaty of Friendship were several. The Syrian leader hoped that maintaining some distance from the USSR would have allowed him to keep working on relations with the United States.[37] Furthermore Al-Assad was wary of losing his autonomy to the superpower. Up until 1978, the Soviet Union had hoped that the signing of a treaty would lead to a higher level of cooperation between Syria and Iraq.[38] These initiatives were always seen with a certain degree of concern in Damascus.

122 *The alliances of Syria*

Despite the outstanding issue of Syria's relationship with Iraq, from 1979 to 1980 the relationship between the two allies improved significantly. From the spring of that year the Soviet Union started delivering to Syria the armaments that Damascus had long asked for, as well as writing off part of the Syrian debt. Damascus reciprocated by providing the Soviet Union with much needed diplomatic support in the Arab and Muslim world in the aftermath of the invasion of Afghanistan.[39] By late 1979, Syria appeared to be the party actively seeking a treaty. This was also a consequence of the weakened domestic position of Al-Assad. Challenged domestically by the Islamic opposition and isolated in the region, the Syrian President perceived a strengthening of the relationship with the USSR as advantageous. When the Treaty of Friendship was signed in October 1980, it appeared to be the obvious conclusion of the steady progress of the cooperation over the previous couple of years.

It was not going to be long before the alliance, strengthened by the treaty, had to go through some severe tests. The lack of cooperation between Syria and Iraq had been a source of disagreement between Moscow and Damascus. The start of the Iran–Iraq war and Syria's support of Iran predictably did little to ease Soviet displeasure. Despite the USSR's initial neutrality on the conflict, the divisions between Damascus and Baghdad generated by the conflict were clearly troublesome for Moscow.

A few weeks after the signing of the Treaty of Friendship, the Syrian–Jordanian crisis erupted.[40] The Soviet Union was at the time seeking an improvement in its relations with the conservative monarchies and particularly Amman. During the crisis, Soviet officials stressed the peaceful aims of the bilateral treaty with Damascus. Moscow sought to constrain its ally and defuse the crisis. This attempt was successful in the Jordanian case largely due to Saudi mediation. Much more problematic were to be (at least from a Soviet point of view) the developments in Lebanon the following year. The delicate Syrian–Israeli balance first threatened to explode in April 1981 when Al-Assad reacted to the downing of two Syrian helicopters by moving SA-6 surface-to-missile batteries into Lebanon.[41] The crisis finally erupted on the 6 June 1982 when the frail Palestine Liberation Organization–Israeli ceasefire collapsed, and Tel Aviv launched a full-scale invasion of Lebanon. Israeli forces immediately engaged Syrian troops in the Beka'a Valley, inflicting significant damages on the Syrian surface-to-air-missile network as well as Syrian air forces.[42] Within a few days, Begin's goal of annihilating the Palestine Liberation Organization and Syrian forces in Lebanon to pave the way for a pro-Israeli regime in Beirut became evident.[43]

Despite their spirited performance, Syrian troops were unable to stop Tsahal's push towards Beirut. The Soviets were initially slow to react to the crisis, but once they fully understood the range of the Israeli initiative they attempted to defuse the threat. Their help was two-fold: first, they put diplomatic pressure on the United States to restrain Israel.[44] This did not have any immediate effect on the conflict.[45] Begin and Sharon were at that stage ready to realise their goals regardless of the Americans' opinion. Furthermore, the United States administration was hesitant and divided in the face of the crisis. More effective was the delivery of new and more advanced weapons from Moscow to Damascus.[46] The new SAM-5 were a dramatic upgrade to the Syrian air defences, and together with other armaments (as well as the deployment of Soviet advisors), provided a qualitative improvement in Syrian military capabilities.[47] While avoiding getting entangled in any mechanism that could trigger direct Soviet involvement, the USSR had definitively shown its value as an ally. Unlike the Palestine Liberation Organization, Syria manifested its appreciation for Soviet support both during and in the aftermath of the crisis through statements by several top officials.[48]

The year 1983 was the zenith of the alliance and the year in which Soviet investments in the relationship with Syria paid off. With the help of its partners, Damascus managed to turn Begin's triumphant march in Lebanon into a quagmire, denying Israel the fruits of the success it had obtained on the battle ground.[49] It was Al-Assad's diplomatic action (supported by the Soviets) that torpedoed Reagan's Middle Eastern plan and any attempt to impose a 'Pax Americana' that would exclude the Soviet Union from the region. Finally, Al-Assad was the mastermind behind the Israeli and American retreat out of Lebanon. In March 1984 President Gemayel was forced to abrogate the peace treaty signed with Israel the previous year. Despite the concerns caused in Moscow by Syrian–Palestine Liberation Organization tensions (and the attempts by Al-Assad to establish his control over the Palestinian organisation through the advancement of pro-Syrian factions), the Soviet–Syrian partnership had reached in the 1983–1984 phase its highest level of cooperation and had obtained its most important achievements.

Sunset of the alliance

The partnership that appeared to be so effective and solid in early 1984 was soon to go through significant changes. In the aftermath of the Israeli invasion of Lebanon, Syria had become deeply dependant on the Soviet Union, with the core of the Syrian air defences operated by Soviet 'advisors'. This led to a limited Syrian autonomy but had also enhanced Syrian security by tying it more closely to that of the Soviet Union. Under the leadership of Gorbachev (and Chernenk before him) Moscow moved to reorient its Middle Eastern policy, inevitably causing some strains in the relationship with Damascus. Gorbachev aimed to scale down Soviet involvement in the Middle East. Two specific developments in Soviet foreign policy were particularly dangerous for Damascus. The openings towards Israel that had intensified from 1985 onwards (and led to slow improvements in the relations) and the related new Soviet attitude towards Damascus' conflict with Israel.[50] During his first meeting with Al-Assad in June 1985, the new Soviet leader stated clearly that Syria's goal of strategic parity was unrealistic, that Syria should seek support from its fellow Arab progressive forces and that is had to pursue its goals through diplomacy rather than war.[51]

In the following years the Soviets tried to re-establish a link between weapon deliveries and increased cooperation with other pro-Soviet Arab forces. Moscow

124　*The alliances of Syria*

also attempted in several instances to convince Syria to abandon its pro-Iranian stance and build bridges with Arafat. Arms deliveries diminished significantly: Golan estimates that they 'fell from the previous average of $2.3 billion per year to no more than $1 billion per year in the period of 1985–1989'.[52] Furthermore, given the renewed tensions in Lebanon in 1986, the Soviet leadership struggled between showing support to its main regional ally and signalling to Damascus its unwillingness to get involved directly in the defence of the Syrians. Soviet foreign policy under Gorbachev was also characterised by an attempt to improve relations with several actors as a way of diminishing its dependence on its traditional allies in the region. By 1988 the improvement in Soviet–Egyptian and Soviet–Israeli relations had created significant tension with Syria (as well as with Ghaddafi's Libya).[53] Moscow's shifting policy was clearly perceived in Damascus as an 'abandonment' by its ally. In spite of their discontent, the Syrians avoided open conflict with the USSR and showed a flexible attitude aimed at maintaining a positive relationship with Moscow. This appears to confirm that the relationship between the two allies had significantly changed from the 1970s, and Syria was now extremely reliant on its superpower patron. By the late 1980s, the Soviet Union's focus had shifted away from the region because of the instability within its own borders and in the Eastern bloc. Damascus attempted to limit the damage caused by the collapse of its ally. The shift from bipolarity to unipolarity was to force more than just a few adjustments to Syrian policy.

Conclusion: the Syrian–Soviet relationship

Throughout the Cold War years, the Soviet Union represented the most likely alliance choice for revolutionary and leftist forces in different parts of the world. Ba'thist Syria, with its strongly anti-imperialist and anti-Western mix of Pan-Arabism, was ideologically close to the Soviet Union. This ideological solidarity allowed the two parties to overcome the tensions caused by the rivalry between the Ba'th and Communist parties in the country. Ideological solidarity played an important role in favouring the alignment between the radical Ba'th regime of Salah Jadid and the USSR. The Jadid regime looked at the Soviet Union as a model for its own domestic reforms. The relationship with Moscow was one of the things that the Ba'thist radicals and the realist faction led by Hafez Al-Assad disagreed on. The latter had no sympathy for the Soviet Union and had publicly denounced Syria's excessive dependence on its superpower ally.

The change from unlimited to limited revisionism did not result in the end of the relationship. The factors driving the alliance changed (from a Syrian perspective) from ideological to functional. Cooperation between Damascus and Moscow grew during the following years. Al-Assad and his men re-adjusted Syrian foreign policy, but the relationship with Moscow remained an important asset. Damascus had to reduce its gap strength with Israel and, given the growing strength of the Israeli–American links, its only realistic option was the Soviet Union. Moscow was engaged in a global competition with the United States, and the Middle East was an important battleground. The regional power and the superpower both aimed to limit the influence of the American–Israeli partnership in the region. Within the frame of different grand strategies (the containment of a stronger regional enemy for Syria, the global competition with the other existing superpower for the Soviet Union), their interests in the region largely coincided and allowed them to overcome difficulties and differences over specific policy issues.

Notes

1 Adeed Dawisha, "The Soviet Union in the Arab World," in *The Soviet Union in the Middle East: Policies and Perspectives*, eds. Adeed Dawisha and Karen Dawisha (London: Royal Institute of International Affairs, 1982).
2 Pedro Ramet, *The Soviet Syrian Relationship since 1955: A Troubled Alliance* (Boulder: Westview Press, 1990), 14.
3 Galia Golan, *Soviet Policies in the Middle East: From World War II to Gorbachev* (Cambridge: Cambridge University Press, 1990), 140.
4 John Devlin, *The Ba'th Party: A History from its Origins to 1966* (Stamford: Hoover Institution Press, 1976).
5 Golan, *Soviet Policies in the Middle East*, 54.
6 Ramet, *The Soviet Syrian Relationship since 1955*, 28.
7 George Lenczovski, *Soviet Advances in the Middle East* (Washington: American Institute for Public Policy Research, 1971).
8 Ramet, *The Soviet Syrian Relationship since 1955*, 32.
9 Lenczovski, *Soviet Advances in the Middle East*, 111.
10 Ramet, *The Soviet Syrian Relationship since 1955*, 34.
11 Cooperation increased despite gradual improvement of Soviet–Egyptian relations from 1962 onwards, that could have made Damascus less relevant in Soviet geopolitical calculations.
12 Ramet, *The Soviet Syrian Relationship since 1955*, 54.
13 Patrick Seale, *Assad of Syria: The Struggle for the Middle East* (London: I.B. Tauris, 1988), 107–109.
14 Raymond Hinnebusch, *Syria: Revolution from Above* (London: Routledge, 2001), 54.
15 Robert O. Freedman is one of the scholars claiming that the USSR gave Egypt false information on an Israeli military attack in order to bring Syria and Egypt closer together, see *Soviet Policy towards the Middle East since 1970* (New York: Praeger, 1975).
16 Ramet, *The Soviet Syrian Relationship since 1955*, 46.
17 George Breslauer, *Soviet Strategy in the Middle East* (Boston: Unwin Hyman, 1990), ch. II.
18 Efraim Karsh, *The Soviet Union and Syria: The Assad Years* (London: Royal Institute of International Affairs, 1988), 4.
19 Ramet, *The Soviet Syrian Relationship since 1955*, 54.
20 The documents reported by Abraham Ben-Tzur in *The Syrian Baath Party and Israel: Documents from the Internal Party Publications* (Tel Aviv: Sifriat Poalim, 1968) show how the Ba'th Party intended to show close affiliation to the Socialist movements also as a way to draw the Socialist movements (and the USSR) to support Syria more closely in the Arab–Israeli conflict.
21 Seale, *Assad of Syria*.
22 Karsh, *The Soviet Union and Syria*, 4–6.
23 Robert O. Freedman. *Soviet Policy towards the Middle East since 1970* (New York: Praeger, 1975), 89.

126   *The alliances of Syria*

24 Golan, *Soviet Policies in the Middle East*, ch. VI.
25 Freedman, *Soviet Policy towards the Middle East since 1970*, 128–129.
26 Karsh, *The Soviet Union and Syria*, 6.
27 Ramet, *The Soviet Syrian Relationship since 1955*, 16.
28 Ibid.
29 Karsh., *The Soviet Union and Syria*, 21.
30 Ibid., 24.
31 Golan, *Soviet Policies in the Middle East*, 151.
32 Seale, *Assad of Syria*, 286
33 Karsh, *The Soviet Union and Syria*, 36.
34 Seale, *Assad of Syria*, 288.
35 Karsh, *The Soviet Union and Syria*, 43.
36 Ramet, *The Soviet Syrian Relationship since 1955*, 132.
37 The Syrian leadership gradually became more pessimistic about the role of the United States in the region and its potential involvement in the peace process.
38 Ramet, *The Soviet Syrian Relationship since 1955*, 132.
39 Robert O. Freedman, *Moscow and the Middle East: Soviet Policy since the Invasion of Afghanistan* (Cambridge: Cambridge University Press, 1991).
40 This episode is described in more detail in Chapter 6 of this volume.
41 Like in the case of the Jordanian crisis, Hafez Al-Assad took an important strategic decision without consulting his patron, despite what was stipulated in the 1980 treaty.
42 The account of how many planes were downed in the Beka'a battle varies according to different sources, with the number 23 as indicated by Galia Golan somewhere in the middle, see *Soviet Policies in the Middle East: From World War II to Gorbachev* (Cambridge: Cambridge University Press, 1990), 128.
43 Seale, *Assad of Syria*, ch. XXII.
44 Soviet moves included the deployment of some more warships in the Mediterranean as well as a series of warnings – mainly via the Soviet press – of the potential consequences of Israeli actions.
45 Golan, *Soviet Policies in the Middle East*, 127–131.
46 Helena Cobban, *The Superpowers and the Syrian–Israeli Conflict: Behind Crisis Management* (Washington, Centre for Strategic and International Studies, 1991).
47 Golan, *Soviet Policies in the Middle East*, 137.
48 Karsh, *The Soviet Union and Syria*, 71.
49 Chapter 7 of this volume describes the events in Lebanon in detail.
50 Freedman, *Moscow and the Middle East*, 213–216.
51 Karsh, *The Soviet Union and Syria*, 89.
52 Golan, *Soviet Policies in the Middle East*, 279.
53 Freedman, *Moscow and the Middle East*, 300.

Part III
Alliances and beyond

11 Alliances and beyond

The previous chapters applied the model of this book to six alliances of Syria. The analysis has shown how domestic and international factors both influenced the foreign policy of Damascus. The use of a model based on neoclassical realism has allowed me to integrate the leadership's ideological orientation in a structure-based model. Ideological orientation proved to be an important factor behind the changes in Syria's foreign policy and alliances. The first section of this chapter will sum up the main points of the analysis. It will do so by looking at Syria's overall foreign policy and its links with the alliances analysed in this study. The second section of the chapter will look at the alliances of Damascus after 1989. Regional politics and the foreign policy of Syria changed significantly after the end of the Cold War. This section will not provide a comprehensive analysis of all the developments that took place after 1989, but rather concentrate on a few trends and how they relate to the model of this book. Finally, the last section will look at alliances and the Syrian Civil War. The conflict that has engulfed the country for the last seven years started as a domestic phenomenon, but soon saw the involvement of several regional actors.

System and ideology: the alliances of Syria

I opened this book describing the alliances of Syria as complex and often puzzling. How successful has this model been in explaining them? The answer to this question rests on two key points. The first is whether the analysis has provided a convincing interpretation of the phenomena it seeks to explain. The second is whether it kept an acceptable degree of theoretical consistency. The starting point to both questions is the alternative frameworks evaluated in this study. In Chapter 2, I showed how two dominant paradigms in the study of Middle Eastern politics, structural realism and constructivism/institutionalism, offered partial explanations for Syria's alliance pattern. Both theoretical frameworks share important similarities with the model of this book, so it is unsurprising that their account of the alliances of Syria present some overlaps with the one of this study. More specifically, structural realism focuses on short-term alliances formed as a response to external threats. These are not rare occurrences in a region such as the Middle East, where conflict is a regular feature of inter-state

130 *Alliances and beyond*

relations. Syria was often subject to external threats from neighbouring states. As predicted by the balance of threat, it often reacted by aligning itself with other states to balance against the danger. For instance, the 1978 alliance with Iraq or the 1979 alliance with the Islamic Republic of Iran were clearly formed in reaction to external threats. Not all alliances, however, follow this logic. Structural realism therefore struggles to register alliances such as the Saudi–Syrian one, an 'unorthodox' and often uneasy alliance based on mutual interests rather than mutual threats. Similarly, structural realism cannot explain the strengthening and growth of the Iranian alliance despite the relative decrease of the threat represented by Iraq. Crucially, because of its focus on the short-term nature of alliances, the balance of threat does not contribute much to explaining foreign policy shifts such as the 1970 one analysed in this work.

Constructivism/institutionalism represents the mirror image of structural realism. While structural realism relies on power, constructivism/institutionalism focuses on the role of ideology and how it affects foreign policy. Like structural realism, this framework provides an interesting and insightful analysis of regional foreign policy. Barnett's analysis of the interaction (and clash) among Arab states over the meaning of Pan-Arabism is particularly effective, and greatly contributes to explaining the dynamics at play between Syria, Iraq and Egypt throughout the 1960s.[1] This framework is, however, less well equipped to explain relationships that are based on different factors. In the case of Syria, it is for instance hard to explain the development of an alliance between Ba'thist Syria and the Islamic Republic of Iran using ideology as the key analytical factor. Similarly, the alignment between Syria and the Wahabi Kingdom of Saudi Arabia was based on the mutual benefits that the two countries obtained from the alliance rather than on ideological affinity.

The model of this analysis brings together elements from both previous frameworks. In line with neoclassical realist research, the model of this book incorporated a domestic factor 'within' structural analysis. It therefore sought to establish how the interaction between systemic incentives and threats and the ideological orientation of the foreign policy executive shaped the alliances of the country. Syria provided a fascinating and testing case for the model. The 'structural' conditions of the country were particularly stringent. Syria is a middle-sized power located in a conflict-ridden region and surrounded by several stronger and potentially threatening neighbours.[2] It is therefore reasonable to expect that external constraints would have shaped the alliance choices of Damascus. At the same time, Syria is the self-styled 'beating heart of the Arab nation', a country that has been dominated since 1963 by the Pan-Arab Ba'th Party. Significant sections of the population in the country have traditionally identified themselves with a larger Arab community rather than with the Syrian state. Syria is therefore a prime candidate for 'ideological' foreign policy and alliances, meant as choices made based on ideology- and power-based considerations.

The key contribution of this analysis is the (re)introduction of state goals. State goals represents a state's attitude towards the regional or international system. They indicate whether a state supports or opposes the status quo. State goals are determined first and foremost by systemic factors. In the case of Syria, its position within the system and its relative strength made it a revisionist. Syria's geopolitical conditions in fact were particularly unfavourable. Policy-makers in Damascus saw the regional system as hostile to them. Syria, however, was only a secondary power in the Middle East, a middleweight surrounded by regional heavyweights. Based on its relative power it could therefore aim at obtaining only relative improvements within the system rather than subverting the regional system altogether.

Structural factors made Syria a limited revisionist, concerned with its position within the system but also aware of the limitations derived from its relative power. However, during the first years of this study the foreign policy of Syria is clearly closer to unlimited revisionism. The country showed ideological rigidity in the pursuit of goals dictated by Pan-Arab ideology. Given the strong anti-imperialist connotations of Ba'th ideology, those powers that were considered conservatives and allies of the West (such as Saudi Arabia) were targets of hostile propaganda. Furthermore, in the aftermath of 1967, the Jadid regime (considered the most radical and ideological ever to rule the country) largely disregarded the balance of power that emerged after the war. Rather than seeking to build an alliance to counter the threat represented by Israel, the Syrian regime doubled its hostility towards all 'enemies'. This behaviour is explained by the factor I described as 'leadership ideological orientation'.

This 'ideological' foreign policy was one of the factors behind the split in the regime in the aftermath of the 1967 war; on one side the 'radicals' led by Salah Jadid and on the other the 'realists' (or nationalists) led by Hafez Al-Assad. The divide between the two factions was evident during the 1970 Black September crisis in Jordan. Hafez Al-Assad was at the time the Defence Minister, but very much the man in ascendance. When the conflict between the Jordanian army and Palestinian militias flared, Al-Assad order his troops to enter Jordan in defence of the Palestinians. Met with a strong Jordanian reaction (and with the threat of an Israeli intervention), the Syrian leader *in pectore* refused to commit his air forces and order his troops to retreat.[3] This episode contains, in a nutshell, the existing tensions in Syrian politics between 'realist' and Pan-Arab goals. On one side national interest suggests avoiding a confrontation with Jordan and the pro-Western forces. On the other side Pan-Arabism should have driven Al-Assad towards intervening in defence of the Palestinians. When Al-Assad took over power in 1970, the tension between these two poles was solved in favour of 'realist' foreign policy. The new regime sought to impose a more moderate foreign policy at both a domestic and international level. In the former, the 'leftist' agenda of the Jadid regime was toned down in favour of a less extreme domestic policy. This allowed Al-Assad and his men to increase regime support by opening it to sectors of society that had been alienated by Jadid's radical policies.[4] In terms of foreign policy, the radical Pan-Arab approach was replaced with a Syria-centric approach more geared towards the pursuit of national interest. A new alliance policy was the cornerstone of this foreign policy approach.

132   *Alliances and beyond*

State goals and alliances

The model of alliance formation of this study has been used to explain six key relationships of Syria. These six alignments have been chosen based on two criteria.[5] The first is that the country entered (or was already) into some sort of formal or informal alliance with Syria during the period of this analysis. The second criterion is the involvement in the region and 'level of relationship' with Syria. States that are peripheral to the politics of the sub-region, such as Algeria, have been excluded from the analysis. The six alliances selected based on these criteria are the ones with Egypt, Jordan, Iraq, Saudi Arabia, Iran and the USSR. These six relationships have offered a good test for the model. The states selected include a global superpower (the USSR), great regional powers such as Egypt and smaller powers such as Jordan. The relationships analysed vary from long-term alliances such as the Syrian–Iranian one to short-term détente such as the Syrian–Iraqi one. This variety has allowed me to analyse how the change from unlimited to limited revisionism has affected the alliance choices of Damascus.

1963–1970: unlimited revisionism and alliances

The Ba'th party took power for the first time in the country in March 1963. The coup d'état against the Al-Qudsi regime was carried out together with other Pan-Arab forces, most notably a large group of Nasserite officials. The Ba'thists, however, soon moved to eliminate their internal rivals and established their control over the country.[6] The Ba'th, the Pan-Arab force par excellence, was for the first time in power in Syria (and briefly in neighbouring Iraq). The party founded by Michel Aflaq and Salah-din Bitar is considered the 'purest' form of Pan-Arab ideology.[7] Ba'thism therefore aimed at unifying the Arabs divided by borders and called for the pursuit of 'Arab' (rather than national) interests. Its ideology is based on a strong anti-imperialist ethos, that translated into opposition to the establishment of an Israeli state in the region and a total commitment to the Palestinian cause. The tension between 'Pan-Arab' and 'national' foreign policy was particularly strong in Syria, a country with no pre-existing history as an independent state.

Did the ideological orientation of the Ba'thist leaders influence the alliances of Syria? Throughout the 1960s Syria faced a stronger and threatening power in the state of Israel. A realist/rational behaviour would have driven Syrian policy-makers to recognise the power gap with Israel and operate in order to reduce it. This would have meant balancing against the threat represented by Israel by attempting to obtain diplomatic, economic and political support from any potential ally. The alliance policy of the first Ba'thist regimes was, however, characterised by a high degree of hostility towards both conservative powers and states with a different interpretation of Pan-Arab ideology. The former is the case for Saudi Arabia and (to a lesser extent) the Kingdom of Jordan. Both powers were, throughout the radical Ba'th years, the subjects of hostility and propaganda war from Damascus. Unsurprisingly the hostility towards the conservative powers increased when the Jadid regime took over in 1966. This was by far the most radical leadership to ever rule the country. During the Jadid years, Saudi Arabia was regarded as the incarnation of conservative and regressive politics, and the main ideological rival of Syria.[8] Despite the emphasis on Arab unity, Ba'thists proved to be just as hostile towards different interpretations of Pan-Arabism. Negotiations with Egypt and Iraq over a tripartite agreement started soon after the takeover of power by the Ba'th in Damascus and Baghdad. However, relations with Egypt soon turned sour over clashes between Ba'thists and Nasserites in Syria. Throughout the following years the two countries proved themselves 'Pan-Arab rivals', with the Syrian regime challenging Egypt over its support of the Palestinian cause and its relationship with the state of Israel. This competition over the respective Pan-Arab credentials was one of the factors that led to the 1967 conflict.[9]

The 1967 defeat represented a turning point in the history of the region but also an important landmark for this analysis. With the 1967 defeat, the gulf between the foreign policy goals pursued by the Jadid regime and the geopolitical reality on the ground became much broader. The war had clearly tilted the regional balance in favour of Israel. This new balance of power did not, however, result in a readjustment of Syrian foreign policy. Rather than increasing the cooperation with potential allies such as the Kingdom of Saudi Arabia, Iraq or Egypt, the Syrian regime continued its ideologically rigid stance that had led to its isolation within the Arab world. Given the realistic and immediate threat represented by Israel and the inability to cooperate with Egypt, the power that would have been an ideal candidate to 'balance against the threat', is particularly puzzling. This aspect of Syrian foreign policy cannot be explained by structural considerations, as it has its roots in ideological rivalry between the two parties and particularly in the Ba'thist dislike of Nasser and his policies.

Relationships with non-Arab powers were similarly affected by the ideological stance of the Syrian leadership. In the case of the Soviet Union, this aspect is particularly evident during 1966–1970. The Jadid regime represented the wing of the Ba'th party ideologically closest to the Soviet model. The strengthening of the Soviet–Syrian alliance during these years was motivated by the strong identification of the Syrian regime with the anti-imperialist cause. As the Syrian leadership looked at implementing its own domestic revolution, the Soviet Union was an obvious partner as well as a model to follow.[10] In the case of Iran, the regime commitment to Pan-Arabism represented a cause of hostility despite the lack of clashing interests between the two countries. This is particularly evident in the Syrian regime's belligerent stance on the issue of the Iranian occupation of Khuzestan, a region with a largely Arab population traditionally claimed by Iraq. Different Syrian leaders throughout the 1960s expressed their support for the reclaim of the region referred to by Arabs as Arabestan, occasionally causing the outbreak of diplomatic crisis with Iran.[11]

134 *Alliances and beyond*

1970: limited revisionism and alliances

The 1970 coup d'état was an intra-Ba'th affair. Hafez Al-Assad was the Minister of Defence during the Jadid years, and a man of the party. The Ba'th remained the party in power, and its ideology remained the official one of the Syrian state. Under Al-Assad and his men, however, the foreign policy of Syria and particularly its alliance pattern changed significantly. The alignments with Egypt and Saudi Arabia were the most immediate and most obvious results of this new foreign policy. Working on an alliance with Cairo was one of the first concerns of the new Syrian President. Al-Assad and Sadat planned and together carried out the 1973 war, before their roads split over the latter's rapprochement with Israel and the United States.[12] An alliance with Cairo represented the only real possibility to achieve military success in a confrontation with Israel that the Syrian policy-makers considered inevitable. What Al-Assad and his men could not know was that Sadat considered the war with Israel as a chance to open negotiations with Tel Aviv and 'switch' to the American-led camp. Al-Assad and Sadat entered the 1973 war pursuing different regional goals. Al-Assad's limited revisionist strategy aimed at changing the balance of power in favour of the Arabs (and Syria in particular). Sadat on the other hand aimed at starting a peace process that would allow Egypt to re-align itself with the dominant American side. The 'divorce' between the two Arab powers in the aftermath of the conflict was a consequence of these diverging goals.

The changes in the Syrian–Saudi relationship after 1970 were probably even more remarkable. Within a few years the two countries went from ideological hostility to establishing an alliance, although a tacit and sometimes uneasy one. The new Syrian regime stopped the propaganda war directed at Riyadh and moved to improve its relations with Saudi Arabia. The opening towards Riyadh was based on strategic calculations. The new Syrian regime valued Saudi Arabia as a potential ally because of Riyadh's economic resources and diplomatic influence. In exchange for its bankrolling of Syria's foreign policy and its support on key diplomatic scenarios such as Lebanon, the Kingdom of Saudi Arabia benefited from the legitimacy (both at the domestic and regional level) that derived from supporting a front-line Arab state.[13] As a status quo power, Riyadh also appreciated Damascus' role as a regional stabiliser. This was a strong contrast with the previous decade during which Syria had been a factor in regional instability.

In the aftermath of Egypt's defection, Syria attempted to reduce its isolation by aligning with other Arab powers that had similarly been left out by the peace process. The 1975–1978 rapprochement with Jordan and the 1978 détente with Iraq shared significant similarities. Both were mainly a reaction to Egypt's gradual rapprochement with Israel. The rapprochement with Jordan took place in the immediate aftermath of the Sinai II agreements, when it became obvious that the American-led peace initiative had succeeded in separating Egypt from its fellow Arab states. This brief alignment represented a break in a long history of rivalry and hostility. Syria and Jordan were a revisionist and a status quo power that had clashing rather than overlapping interests, and after their brief strategic rapprochement the two countries returned to their pattern of competition.

Unlike Jordan, Iraq was a revisionist power and was led by the Ba'th party. These similarities with Syria, however, were a factor of conflict rather than cooperation. Syria and Iraq were both revisionists but also regional rivals. Both Syria and Iraq were unhappy with the system, yet they disagreed on how the system should look and crucially on who should have a central role in regional and inter-Arab politics. Their temporary rapprochement was a consequence of their isolation in the aftermath of Egypt's defection (particularly Syria's isolation) and an attempt by Iraq to extend its control over its fellow Arab state. This alliance (as well as the one with Jordan) is paradigmatic of the flexible approach to alliances adopted by the Syrian regime. Both alliances were tactical and short-term answers to external changes that occurred in Arab–Israeli relations.

It was, however, the 1979 alliance with Iran that represented the most obvious sign of the 'realist' alliance choices of Syria. This alliance was in many ways the triumph of pragmatism over ideology. The Ba'thist republic of Syria aligned itself with the Persian and theocratic Islamic Republic of Iran. This alliance was undoubtedly based on the isolation and weakness of both parties in 1979, a prime example of the 'balancing against threat' logic. It was, however, the presence of overlapping interests and (crucially) the absence of conflict over specific policies that allowed the alliance to grow and develop into a long-term partnership. It is also interesting to note how the Syrian regime had attempted an opening with the Shah's Iran in the mid-1970s, hoping that the Iranian leader could have used its good relationship with Washington to Syria's advantage. Whilst this approach failed, it does confirm the pragmatic nature of the Syrian regime post-1970.

The alliance with the USSR represented another cornerstone of the limited revisionist goals pursued by Hafez Al-Assad. In this specific case the new regime 'inherited' this alliance from the previous Ba'thist regimes. Al-Assad had previously been critical of Syria's reliance on the USSR, and at a domestic level he distanced his country from the Soviet economic model. Despite having no ideological sympathy toward the USSR, however, the Syrian leadership worked to strengthen the relationship with Moscow. Cooperation with the superpower developed throughout the 1970s and the early 1980s, declining only in the second half of the decade because of a reshaping in Soviet foreign policy (and subsequently the collapse of the USSR).

System, domestic and alliances

The use of state goals has allowed this analysis to explain the overall change in Syrian foreign policy and its effect on alliances. Realism postulates that systemic and power considerations will determine states' alliance preferences, however, in the case of Syria the pre-1970 years show a discrepancy between 'realist' behaviour and alliance choices made by policy-makers in Damascus. This analysis has explained this discrepancy by using the concept of leadership's

136 *Alliances and beyond*

ideological orientation. Ideological leadership will often pursue 'extra-state' goals that are not based on power considerations. In the case of Syria, the unlimited revisionism of the first Ba'th years (and particularly of the 1966–1970 phase) was based on the pursuit of Pan-Arab and anti-imperialist rather than 'state-centric' goals. This discrepancy is particularly evident in the aftermath of the 1967 defeat. Syria was in desperate need of allies, resources and diplomatic support to pursue its regional goals and contain the rampant Israeli–American alliance. The readjustment in Syrian foreign policy, however, did not take place after the 1967 war, but rather after the Al-Assad regime took over power. This is because, in the aftermath of the conflict, the Jadid regime followed an ideology-based unlimited revisionism goal. Hafez Al-Assad on the other hand re-aligned Syria's foreign policy with its real capabilities. In terms of this analysis, the foreign policy of the country changed in this way from unlimited to limited revisionism.

Syria after 1989

The long rule of Hafez Al-Assad guaranteed a degree of continuity in Syrian foreign policy. As the power was gradually concentrated into the hands of the President and a close circle of policy-makers, the influence of other domestic factors on foreign policy diminished significantly. Syria's goal consistently remained limited revisionism. Syrian foreign policy, however, changed dramatically in the aftermath of 1989 because of changes at the structural level. Momentous shifts in the global distribution of power had great repercussions on Middle Eastern politics and forced the Syrian leadership to reshape its regional strategy. The Middle East we described in the previous chapters was a penetrated regional system, one in which the role of external powers was extremely relevant. The collapse of one of the two superpowers and their (temporary) withdrawal from the region obviously had significant consequences for regional politics. Throughout the Cold War the United States and the USSR had competed for regional influence by seeking to build alliances with regional actors. As the Soviet Union ceased to exist, its heirs (the Community of Independent States and then Russia) withdrew from the region and focused on domestic issues. The regional powers allied with the USSR, such as Syria, suddenly found themselves without their superpower ally and were therefore forced to re-adjust their foreign policy. Under Gorbachev's lead, the USSR had progressively disengaged from the region and attempted to assume a more balanced approach to the Arab–Israeli conflict. However, the alliance still represented a key asset to countries such as Syria. The collapse of the Soviet Union represented a dramatic change for Damascus' policy-makers. The brief 'unipolar' moment in the Middle East saw different dynamics at play from the previous phase.

Syrian foreign policy in this changing region could not have remained the same, for any regional power needs to adapt to a changing environment to survive. During the 1980s Damascus had crucially obtained defensive capabilities that it would have allowed it to defend itself against an Israeli attack. In the

1990s Syria had to deal with the prospect of a widening military gap vis-à-vis Israel. Syrian participation in the Gulf War has to be interpreted as a necessity. After the collapse of the Soviet Union Al-Assad needed to appease the only remaining superpower. Furthermore, the level of acrimony between Baghdad and Damascus (and particularly between Hussein and Al-Assad) cannot be underestimated. The Syrian President saw in the United States-led coalition as an opportunity to contain his aggressive and threatening neighbour. Syrian involvement in the peace process in the 1990s is probably a more controversial issue. It is hard to establish whether Damascus entered the process genuinely thinking that it could achieve peace with Israel or if it was forced to do so by the American involvement in the region. Certainly, America's overwhelming and unchecked power pushed regional actors into displaying signs of cooperation with Washington. Most observers also appear to agree on the genuine Syrian commitment to end the state of war in exchange for the return of all the Golan Heights. At this stage Hafez Al-Assad could not commit to 'warmer' relations even if he envisaged them in the long term (and he probably did not). Ultimately, it was Israel's refusal to return the whole Golan Heights that prevented the achievement of an agreement that could have changed the Syrian foreign policy outlook.[14]

The alliances of Syria in the 1990s

The 1990s saw some changes in Syria's alliances, but also a certain degree of continuity. The Iran–Iraq war had created severe fractures within the Arab world and it facilitated the return of Egypt to the centre of regional politics after its post-Camp David isolation. It was initially Iraq and the Gulf States that opened up to Cairo in a bid to obtain as much support as possible in their struggle against Iran. The new Egyptian President Hosni Mubarak seized on the opportunity to bring his country back into inter-Arab politics. Egypt was re-integrated into the Arab League in 1989 and quickly became a close ally of the Gulf monarchies and particularly of Riyadh. Following the end of the Iran–Iraq war, this paved the way for a re-establishment of relations between Syria and Egypt that had been suspended since the Camp David Accords. Egypt's new role as a mediator and a moderate force within the Arab world also helped the improvement of the relationship with Damascus.[15] Like other regional powers, Syria had in the past often felt threatened by Egypt's hegemonic ambitions in the Arab world. The end of the Iran–Iraq war and the 'American moment' removed the main points of friction in the complex Syria–Saudi Arabia relationship described in Chapter 9 of this volume. The time seemed ripe for a revival of the 1970s Riyadh–Cairo–Damascus axis. Despite an improvement in the relationship between the three countries, however, the Arab powers never reached similar levels of cooperation as in the early 1970s. Twenty years later these three key regional actors were dealing with a profoundly different Middle East, and the Riyadh-Cairo-Damascus triangle was not as pivotal as it had been in the past.

138   *Alliances and beyond*

The alliance between Syria and Iran had been tested and strengthened during the 1980s by the Iran–Iraq war. During the following decade the American-led peace process offered a further test. By the calculations of Syrian policy-makers, however, peace negotiations with Israel (and even a potential peace deal) did not mean breaking off their relationship with Tehran.[16] The threat represented by Iraq remained a factor in bringing together Iran and Syria. Predictably, the resurgence of Iraqi power during the last years of the Iran–Iraq war had brought Damascus and Tehran closer together. The developments of the alliance in the 1990s, however, showed that while Iraq might have represented one factor bringing Syria and Iran together, the two countries had progressively developed an alliance that went far further than balancing against the Iraqi (or Israeli) threat. The American-led war on Iraq crippled the country's economic and military structure and significantly reduced Baghdad's ambitions (and therefore the threat posed by the country to both Iran and Syria). Despite this, during the 1990s the alliance between Syria and Iran thrived rather than declined. In many ways it was the need to check American power in the region that took the place of the Iraqi threat and reinforced the Syrian–Iranian alliance towards the end of the decade.[17] The Lebanese scenario and particularly the role of Hezbollah remained central in the relationship throughout the 1990s. The Ta'if agreement and its aftermath signalled the start of a new Syrian-dominated era in Lebanon. Iran had accepted Syria's predominant role in the country and the Levant. The lack of weaponry suppliers that both countries suffered in the 1990s pushed Tehran and Damascus to cooperate in this sector by acquiring and sharing technologies and weapons from third parties (such as China and North Korea) but also by developing joint weapon producers.[18] By the 1990s the Syrian–Iranian alliance had therefore assumed a multidimensional and structural nature. It is no surprise then that the American attempts to isolate Tehran by convincing and/or coercing Damascus into breaking the alliance failed, despite (or probably because of) the American predominance in the region.

A concerning development for Damascus' policy-makers in the 1990s was the tension with its northern neighbour Turkey and the parallel burgeoning Israeli–Turkish relations. Even though both states were aligned to the West, during the Cold War the relationship between Ankara and Tel Aviv had never flourished. This changed in the early 1990s. Because of both systemic and domestic developments, the relationship between the two countries became progressively closer. Worryingly for Damascus, the key dimension of this alliance was military cooperation. By the mid-1990s Turkey and Israel were regularly running joint military training in the Mediterranean and exchanging military advisors and technology. These developments occurred while relations between Ankara and Damascus were very tense. The issue of the distribution of the water of the Tigris and Euphrates rivers had created tension between the two countries since the early 1960s, but it was Syrian support of the Kurdistan Workers' Party (or PKK) that led to a crisis between the two countries. Syria's military cooperation agreement with Greece was mainly a consequence of the perceived Turkish threat, and in turn it reinforced the need for closer Turkish–Israeli relations.[19] In 1998 Turkey went as far as amassing troops on the Syrian border because of Syria's hosting of the PKK leader Abdullah Ocalan; Syria was forced to give in to Turkish requests and expelled the Kurdish leader. This decision was going to be a determinant factor in the Syrian–Turkish rapprochement of the 2000s.

Damascus' relations with Russia were difficult throughout the 1990s. The issue of the Syrian inability to repay its debt to Russia was very sensitive due to Moscow's difficult economic situation. Syria lamented Russian disengagement from the region and its inability to provide state-of-art weapons and technologies. But the biggest source of disagreement between the two countries was probably Russia's opening to Israel and its new attitude towards the Arab–Israeli conflict. This trend, which had started during the Gorbachev years, gained strength under the Yeltsin presidency. The presence of a strong Russian-speaking community in Israel and its strong cultural and economic links with Moscow was a key factor in the relationship.[20] Furthermore, the Chechen issue and the 'Islamist threat' led Russian public opinion and policy-makers to assume a more sympathetic stance towards Israel, seen as facing a similar 'Islamist threat' in the shape of Hamas. While not abandoning completely the support of the Palestinian cause, Russia assumed in the 1990s a more equidistant approach to the Arab–Israeli conflict. Syria, Russia's closest ally during the 1980s, was undoubtedly damaged by Moscow's new Middle East foreign policy. The tension in the relationship in the 1990s was very much a consequence of these differences.

Ultimately, a regional power cannot ignore structural changes in the system where it operates. The 1990s in the Middle East saw some dramatic changes that undermined Syria's position in the region. The collapse of its superpower ally and the consequential American moment in the region forced Damascus to reshape its foreign policy. One of the main consequences of this new approach was the opening of serious negotiations with Israel, which came very close to an agreement. The achievement of 'cold peace' with Israel could have opened the way for improved relations with the United States and its allies, but the collapse of the negotiations meant facing a deteriorating regional environment during the following decade. This was the hard task entrusted on the new and inexperienced President Bashar Al-Assad.

The 2000s

Hafez Al-Assad died of a heart attack on the 10 June 2000. A hugely controversial and divisive figure, the man had ruled the country for 30 years, and left power in the hands of his third-born son, Bashar. This Western-educated ophthalmologist became President because of the car accident that had killed his older brother and leader *in pectore* of the country, Basel. The leadership change did not lead to a reshaping in Syrian goals. Syrian foreign policy in the early 2000s in fact appeared to be largely a reaction to a deteriorating regional environment. During the first year of Bashar's rule, the Al-Aqsa intifada buried any hope of progress in Arab–Israeli negotiations (including Syrian–Israeli

140 *Alliances and beyond*

ones). The Bush junior presidency and the 11 September attacks on the Twin Towers started a new chapter in American foreign policy in the region. This new muscular strategy openly aimed at shaping a 'New Middle East'. The war on Afghanistan in 2001 and more importantly on Iraq in 2003 were to be fundamental steps in this direction. The 2003 invasion of Iraq was combined with very aggressive rhetoric versus the other 'rogue states', with Syria and Iran ranking very high in the American administration's target list.

Bashar was initially inexperienced and scarcely known by the country's military and party elite. Hinnebusch marks the years 2000–2005 as a transition phase between the two presidencies.[21] In this phase Bashar had to share power with members of the old guard that had been close to his father. Syrian foreign policy therefore lacked a clear direction as the policies chosen were often a result of compromises between different centres of powers within the country. Influential representatives of the old guard such as Vice-President Khaddam enjoyed their own support within the army and the party and were able, through personal contacts established during decades in power, to influence the foreign policy process. This was particularly true in some very sensitive areas: the aforementioned Abdul Halim Khaddam for example had been in charge of the Lebanese file for a long time. Only after his resignation in the aftermath of the Cedar Revolution could the new President and his men develop 'their' Lebanon policy. The progressive dismissal of members of the old guard was followed by the coming into power of a new generation of leaders, most of them close to Bashar and in several cases related to him by blood or marriage.

The alliance of Syria in the 2000s

During the first years of the Bashar presidency, Syria had faced a significant threat from the United States. In the aftermath of the 2003 invasion of Iraq, the regime in Damascus was openly spoken of by personalities close to the American administration as 'next on the list'. An American military attack appeared to be entirely possible. Quite predictably, the reaction to the threat coming from the United States was a strengthening of the alliance with Iran. Together with Hamas and Hezbollah the two countries were labelled the 'axis of resistance' to American/Israeli hegemony. The first scenario where this resistance manifested itself was precisely Iraq; both Syria and Iran condemned the American military operation and supported the resistance against the American presence. The opposition to American presence in the region was also based on concerns for the destabilisation of the region.

In the previous chapters of this volume it has emerged how developments in the Iran–Iraq war and in Lebanon were frequently closely related. Once again in the 2000s there appeared to be a close relationship between two such scenarios, and the second round of the Damascus–Washington match took place in Lebanon again. In the aftermath of Lebanese Prime Minister Rafiq Hariri's assassination in February 2005, Washington and its allies seized on the spontaneous popular protests against the Syrian military presence and passed a

Alliances and beyond 141

United Nations resolution calling for the withdrawal of Syrian troops from Lebanon.[22] Syria was forced to oblige and had to swallow the establishment of a special tribunal on the assassination of Hariri. The withdrawal of Syrian troops represented a loss of influence in a country that had long been considered the Syrian backyard. It was also a humiliation for the young President in Damascus. Ironically, redemption for Syria and its allies came the following year again from Lebanon, in the form of an ill-advised Israeli military adventure. The 'casus belli' were border skirmishes that resulted in the kidnapping of two Israeli soldiers and the death of another six. Israel decided to mount a full-scale attack on Lebanon. The military initiative lasted over a month, but it largely failed to eliminate Hezbollah's military capabilities and resulted in a public relations fiasco for Israel.[23] Quite predictably, the popularity of Hezbollah's leader Hassan Nasrallah in the region sky-rocketed. Syria and Iran also benefited as Hezbollah's closer allies, particularly given the support they had provided to Hezbollah in the lead up to the war.[24]

The 2000s saw an improvement in Russian–Syrian relations after the tensions of the previous decade. This improvement coincided with the start of the Putin presidency (that partially redirected Russian foreign policy back towards the Middle East) but was driven by several factors.[25] The American war on Iraq undoubtedly brought the two countries closer. Damascus saw a return of Russia in the region as an opportunity to combat the aggressive American role in the Middle East. Furthermore, the two countries shared concerns over the instability caused by Washington's policies in the region. Around the same time, Moscow agreed to forgive outstanding Syrian debt from the Cold War era in exchange for new arms purchases.[26] This agreement 'unlocked' the relationship by eliminating one of the most controversial issues of the previous decade, but also crucially restarted the military delivery (and the consequent military cooperation) that had stagnated during the 1990s.[27] It was in this context that Syria agreed to Russia's request to upgrade its port facilities in Tartous, an important strategic asset to Moscow in the region and the only Russian port in the Mediterranean. By the second half of the 2000s the relationship between Russia and Syria, while not as structured as at the zenith of relations in the early 1980s, had reacquired several of the features of Soviet–Syrian relations during the Cold War.

Relations with the moderate Arab states allied with the West suffered greatly because of the differences between Syria and the United States. Saudi Arabia was reluctant to condemn American adventurism in Iraq, and this divergence inevitably created tensions between Damascus and Riyadh. In Lebanon, Rafiq Hariri had been the man representing the Syrian–Saudi compromise. His assassination (whether the Syrian leadership was responsible or not) was clear indication of a new divide, with Syria on the side of Hezbollah and Iran and Saudi Arabia aligned with the pro-Western forces. Despite these issues, the relation between the Kingdom of Saudi Arabia and Syria never deteriorated into open hostility till the start of the Syrian Civil War in 2011. A significant exception to this trend was the relationship with the Kingdom of Jordan. Relations between Damascus and Amman had remained rather cold throughout the 1990s

142 *Alliances and beyond*

but had started improving towards the end of the decade. The real change, however, took place in the 2000s when under the guide of their new young leaders, relations between the two countries improved significantly. As Ryan stresses, relations under Bashar and King Abdullah were the best they had been since the rapprochement in 1970s.[28] While these positive relations never evolved into a full alliance, they overcame the tension created by the aggressive American foreign policy in the region.

The most striking development in Syrian foreign policy in the 2000s was probably its relationship with Turkey. The two countries had a long history of uneasy relations and had been on the brink of war in 1998 over Syrian support for the PKK. In the early 2000s the tensions of the previous decades seemed to vanish and give way for a close alliance. As I mentioned in the previous section (p. 139), Damascus' expulsion of the PKK leader Abdullah Ocalan was a precondition for the improvement of the relationship. The main factors driving this improvement were the new Turkish foreign policy of 'Zero Problems with Neighbours' engineered by the Justice and Development Party (the AKP) and the rise of common threats (such as Kurdish separatism after the American invasion of Iraq). The American invasion of Iraq represented a shock for the newly installed AKP government. Ankara feared the disintegration of Iraq and the formation of a Kurdish state in the north as well as more regional instability. Turkish refusal to allow the United States military to use its territory in its military campaign poisoned the relation between Washington and Ankara. From 2003 onwards, Turkey sought to carry out a more independent policy from the superpower and on several occasions took the opportunity to distance itself from Washington's policies in the region. While not representing a complete break in the relationship with Washington (still Ankara's main military partner), this new stance was clearly appreciated in Damascus. Change in Turkish foreign policy was driven by the coming into power of Erdogan and the AKP. This shift was put into practice gradually, partially because of fears of upsetting the Turkish army. But it was nonetheless significant, and the relationship with Syria was the main beneficiary of it. Damascus soon became the 'poster child' for Erdogan's new foreign policy. Syria, a central power in inter-Arab politics, was seen by policy-makers in Turkey as a gateway into the Arab world. Noticeably, this improvement of relations between Turkey and Syria started when the relationship between Ankara and Tel Aviv was still positive. It was President Erdogan's initiative that led to several rounds of indirect peace talks between Syria and Israel. According to several observers, these negotiations are the closest that the two countries have ever been to achieving peace.[29] The start of the 2008 Gaza War caused the end of the negotiations between Damascus and Tel Aviv but also strained Turkish–Israeli relations.

The Arab Spring and the alliances of Syria

The so called 'Arab Spring' reached Syria late, and when it did it took many by surprise. The story of how the death of a Tunisian street vendor started the protests that led to the oust of President Ben Ali is surely familiar to the reader. Those interested in the region and particularly in Syria will also recall how Syria was initially unaffected by protests in the region. In a (in)famous interview given to the *Wall Street Journal* in late January 2011, the Syrian President criticised his fellow Arab leaders for not putting into place any reform. Al-Assad also stated that the protests could have not happened in Syria where the leadership was 'closely linked to the beliefs of the people'.[30] Despite this display of self-confidence, the regime seemed to understand that the same factors that had led to the ousting of Ben Ali in Tunisia and Mubarak in Egypt were present in Syria. The first reaction to the protests in North Africa was an increase in public salaries and social benefits.[31] During the following month and a half, no major protests were registered in Syria. It was only on the 15 March that the country saw its first big demonstrations in the southern city of Dera'a. Following the arrest of some local boys accused of writing antigovernment graffiti, the regime decided to clamp down on the peaceful protesters asking for the release of the teenagers. This disproportionate reaction by the security apparatus (opening fire on mourners at the funeral of the first victims) caused a snowball effect, with protests registered in most Syrian provinces by late April. In the first weeks of the uprising most protesters did not go as far as calling for Bashar's removal, in most cases aiming their protests at the Syrian security apparatus or particularly unpopular individuals such as the President's cousin, tycoon Rami Makhlouf.[32]

Whether at this stage there still was a way for Al-Assad to build bridges with the protesters is a much-debated issue, but what appears to be clear is that the Syrian President had no intentions of doing so. Al-Assad's speech to the Syrian Parliament as early as the 30 March 2011, during which he blamed foreign conspirators for the unrest in the country, clearly indicated the regime's uncompromising attitude towards the protesters. The opening to some specific groups (such as the Kurdish population) was an attempt to shore up the regime's position rather than any sort of real opening towards the opposition. By the second half of 2011 it was obvious that the regime had opted for a strategy based on violent repression. Furthermore, Syrian officials started quite early on to use the rhetoric of 'Islamist terrorists' and 'sectarian divide', obtaining the rather obvious result of polarising the country further. The first signs of the formation of an armed opposition emerged amid largely peaceful protests.[33] Despite the growing isolation in the region and international condemnations of the breakdown, by 2012 the regime had nearly succeeded in eradicating peaceful demonstrations. However, it faced a growing military opposition that threatened to overrun it. The Syrian uprising had turned into a war.

The alliances of Syria

The external relationships of Syria played a fundamental role in the development of the crisis. Phillips' work shows how regional powers meddled in the Syrian conflict from its early days.[34]

144 *Alliances and beyond*

Syria's newest alliance, the one with Turkey, was immediately tested by the civil war.[35] Presidents Erdogan and Al-Assad had developed a strong personal link. A few weeks before the start of the civil war, Erdogan had shown his emotional side by crying when talking about Syria and its leader at a public rally.[36] When the Syrian regime started its brutal repression of peaceful protesters, Erdogan and his government faced a tough choice between supporting or abandoning their new ally. During the first few months, the Turkish government avoided taking a position on the developments in Syria. In August 2011, Foreign Minister Davotoglu was dispatched to Damascus to broker the start of negotiations between the regime and its opposition. Bashar's refusal to take part spelled the end of the alliance between the two countries. It was also an unprecedented blow to Erdogan's personal prestige. Relations between the two leaderships quickly turned sour, with Turkey becoming one of the main supporters of the opposition to the Syrian regime. Turkey soon became the hub for different Syrian opposition groups, including the Syrian National Council. Ankara officially supported 'moderate' rebel groups engaged in fighting both the regime and ISIS. Yet several reports and studies have contributed to cast more than a shadow on Turkey's role in its neighbouring country. While Turkey's support of groups such as Ahrar Al-Asham were well known, a growing amount of evidence showed links between the country and the Nusra Front and ISIS.[37]

Seen from Ankara, the Syrian crisis represented and still represents a huge security and stability issue. First, Turkey shares a long border with Syria and has been, since the beginning of the conflict, the main recipient of Syrian refugees. The United Nations refugee agency estimates that around 3.5 million Syrian refugees are currently in Turkey.[38] The sheer scale of this migration has changed the landscape of the regions bordering Syria. The most worrying development from Ankara's point of view is the emergence of a de facto Kurdish autonomous region bordering Turkey after the regime withdrawal from most Kurdish areas in mid-2012. Turkey maintains that the Democratic Union Party (or PYD) and its military wing (the YPG) is the Syrian wing of the outlawed Kurdish Communist Party (or the PKK). In order to prevent the establishment of a Kurdish state, Turkey started an airstrike campaign in July 2015. In January 2018 Ankara invaded and occupied the Kurdish controlled region of Afrin.

The Gulf monarchies also played an important role in the development of the civil war. Saudi Arabia and Qatar have been, since the early days of the conflict, among the main sponsors of the opposition groups. The case of Qatar is particularly striking. Many observers have noted how Doha's support of the opposition represents an unprecedented level of activism. In the first phase of the civil war, Qatar went as far as challenging the traditional predominance of the Saudis in external affairs. Relations between Doha and Riyadh reached an all-time low in early 2014 over the issue of Qatar's support of Islamist groups hostile to Saudi Arabia (such as the Muslim Brotherhood). The Saudi–Qatari rapprochement of late 2014 resulted in more cooperation among the different supporters of the Syrian opposition. The opposition's military advances between March and June 2015 were mainly spurred on by more coordination between different groups, undoubtedly favoured by the militias' regional sponsors. The progressive disengagement of these powers from the Syrian scenario, coupled with divisions among Gulf countries (that later led to a blockade being imposed on Qatar) are two of the factors that tilted the balance in favour of the Syrian regime. What led the Gulf countries and particularly the Kingdom of Saudi Arabia to support Syria's opposition? In Chapter 9 I defined the relationship between Syria and Saudi Arabia as an uneasy alliance, one based on mutual benefits rather than ideological solidarity or other aspects. Damascus, I argued, was functional to the Kingdom's stability-seeking regional policy as well as to the Saudi regime's legitimacy. For this reason, Riyadh bankrolled Syrian foreign policy and provided diplomatic support in crucial scenarios such as Lebanon. How can we explain that two decades later the Kingdom was one of the main sponsors of the opposition attempting to remove President Al-Assad? The key reason is the Saudi–Iranian competition in the Gulf sub-region. Riyadh and Tehran had been regional rivals for a long time. This competition was exacerbated by the collapse of Iraqi power in the region. Baghdad had traditionally represented a third pole of power in the Gulf. Saudi Arabia and the Gulf monarchies felt threatened by a resurge of Iranian power from the 1990s onwards. The civil war in Syria had therefore been perceived in the Gulf capitals as a chance to wrestle Syria away from Iran. This had been a goal of Saudi foreign policy at different stages, and particularly during the Iran–Iraq war. The Gulf countries therefore seized upon the initially peaceful protests against the Ba'th regime in order to attempt to change the Al-Assad regime for a less pro-Iranian one.

Syria's long-term allies Iran and Russia played a fundamental role in the conflict. Their intervention on the side of the regime prevented a very likely collapse of the Syrian army and allowed Al-Assad to gradually recover most of the territory he had lost. Chapter 8 of this volume discussed how external threats and isolation were the factors behind the formation of the Syrian–Iranian alliance, but it was the presence of overlapping interests that allowed the alliance to flourish and reach high levels of cooperation. The Iranian regime has vital interests at stake in Syria that are geopolitical and 'historical'. The Syrian regime had proved to be a key asset in crucial scenarios such as the Iran–Iraq war. Damascus is Iran's gateway to the Levant, the Arab world and the Mediterranean. The role played by the Syrian regime in facilitating the delivery of goods from Tehran to Hezbollah is just an example of this centrality. It is therefore rather unsurprising that Iran supported the Syrian regime throughout the crisis and stepped up its support for Al-Assad when the regime seemed to be threatened by significant opposition gains. The role of Iran, Hezbollah and other Shia militias has been central in boosting the capabilities of the battered Syrian regime. Hezbollah was initially mainly involved in providing training and assistance to the Syrian-Arab Army. In the second half of 2012 the number of public funerals of Hezbollah members was one of the key indicators of the increasing involvement of the Shia militia in the Syrian conflict, but it was not until 2013 that it escalated its role in the neighbouring country.[39] In April 2013 Hezbollah led the military offensive that resulted in the capture of Al-Qusayir (a town located

146   *Alliances and beyond*

close to the Syrian–Lebanese border); this was the first instance in which the Syrian army played an ancillary role to its allies in the conflict. In the following two years, most military offensives carried out by the regime saw the significant presence of Hezbollah together with other (mainly Shia) pro-Iranian militias.

Russian involvement in favour of the regime proved to be just as important as Iran's. In the previous sections I described Russian disengagement from the region in the 1990s and the rebuilding of the alliance with Damascus in the 2000s. Russian involvement in the conflict therefore has to be analysed in the context of the re-establishment of Moscow's power in the region. By the end of the Cold War, Syria had become the key ally of Moscow in the region. With the loss of Egypt and Iraq, Damascus was (and is) the only reliable Russian partner in the Middle East. Syria is a big buyer of Russian weapons as well as hosting the Tartous naval base, the only Russian naval facility in the Mediterranean. Furthermore, Putin's Russia has showed throughout the last 15 years opposition to American and Western 'regime change' practices. The recent case of Libya, where the Russians abstained from vetoing the United Nations mission that resulted in Gadhafi's removal, undoubtedly increased Russian fears over Western interventionism. Russian support of the Syrian regime in Damascus is rooted in a long-established relationship and in the presence of tangible Russian interests. Moscow's support to the regime has so far been crucial for the Al-Assad regime. Russian involvement in the country up to September 2015 has been perhaps less visible on the ground than Iran's, but very relevant at two levels. The first is diplomatic support, particularly at the United Nations. Russia has used its veto power to block several United Nations resolutions condemning Syria. A second, less publicised but vital form of support, is the provision of weapons and (crucially) of spare components to replace the losses of the struggling Syrian army. All military observers agree that without this support the army would have stopped functioning a long time ago. These two assets are the same that the USSR brought to Syria during the Cold War years, again indicating a high degree of continuity in the relationship despite the 'break' during the 1990s. The Russian air campaign in Syria started in September 2015, and signalled Moscow's commitment to support its ally which was coming under increasing pressure from resurging rebel forces. Direct Russian involvement completely changed the tide of the conflict, with the Syrian regime soon able to gain the front foot and recover key parts of the country (such as Aleppo in December 2016).

The position of the other Arab states has varied significantly. Jordan's geopolitical location forced the country to take an active role in the conflict. The Syrian–Jordanian border was one of the hot spots of the conflict during the first years of the Syrian Civil War. Dera'a itself is located a few kilometres away from the Jordanian border. As a staunch ally of the West, King Abdullah's country played an important role in supporting and training moderate rebels and particularly the Southern Front, a coalition of moderate and secular insurgent factions. Initially committed to the goal of regime change in Syria, Jordan's attention has progressively moved to the fight against ISIS, whose growth was perceived as a threat to the monarchy.[40] As southern Syria became a secondary scenario in the conflict, the Jordanian regime contented itself with a less active posture. This 'defensivist' stance resulted in the signing of a ceasefire agreement between Russia, the United States and Jordan in September 2017.[41] The Southern Front is, however, likely to regain its relevance as the Syrian regime re-establishes its authority over opposition-controlled areas. A flare up between the regime and opposition forces close to its border undoubtedly has the potential to destabilise the Jordanian Kingdom.

Egypt on the other hand has taken a more neutral and distant approach to the conflict. This approach is in line with Cairo's policy in the last two decades. Egypt has sought to play the role of a 'responsible' status quo power, a friend of the West entertaining good relations with most regional powers. This role was rather different from the Nasser era one, when the Egyptian President was the 'leader of the Arab world' and the other Arab capitals feared his power and influence. Egypt's reaction to the developments in Syria was also clearly influenced by its own domestic crisis. Caught in the revolutionary turmoil that led to the ousting of President Mubarak, Egyptian policy-makers were forced to focus on domestic developments. The presidency of Mohammed Morsi was too short-lived to lead to real foreign policy changes. Furthermore, the President and his men appeared to be far from exercising a degree of control on Egyptian foreign policy that would have allowed them significant changes on an issue as sensitive as the Syrian Civil War. The overthrow of President Morsi and the subsequent take-over of General Al-Sisi placed Egyptian foreign policy firmly on the path of the Sadat and Mubarak presidencies. The consolidation of power in the hands of the General led to an Egyptian attempt to kick-start a peace process to end the Syrian Civil War. The Egyptian regime has been particularly careful to balance its dislike of Islamist forces fighting in the country with the need to keep positive relations with Saudi Arabia and other Gulf countries, whose help is fundamental to Egypt's struggling economy.

The relationship between Syria and Iraq has often been one of competition and mutual mistrust. The regional developments that followed the Arab Spring led to parallel developments in the two countries. Both Iraq and Syria became battlefields for the Saudi–Iranian regional rivalry, and both saw the growth and spread of an Al-Qaeda offshoot group, ISIS. At the start of the Syrian uprising the Maliki government in Baghdad, previously very critical of Damascus for its alleged support of Iraqi Ba'th members, assumed a more neutral position.[42] The fear of a victory for Islamist forces in Damascus changed perceptions in Baghdad. Given this specific threat, the Iraqi government improved its relations with Damascus while most Arab states distanced themselves from the Al-Assad regime. Dramatic improvements in the Iraq–Russia relationship also favoured this rapprochement. The 'trans-border' control established by ISIS in both countries favoured a further re-alignment between the two regimes that now share a set of mutual interests, including the containment of Kurdish irredentism that represents a threat to both states' integrity. As a result, the two Arab powers have often coordinated their military actions, most recently in the case of Iraqi airstrikes on ISIS positions in Syrian territory.[43]

Notes

1 Michael Barnett, *Dialogues in Inter-Arab Politics: Negotiations in Regional Order* (New York: Columbia University Press, 1998).
2 Raymond Hinnebusch, *Syria: Revolution from Above* (London: Routledge, 2001).
3 Patrick Seale, *Assad of Syria: The Struggle for the Middle East* (London: I.B. Tauris, 1988).
4 Hinnebusch, *Syria*, 63.
5 Smaller states such as Lebanon and North Yemen have also been excluded. For a more detailed description of the case studies selection process see Chapter 1 of this volume.
6 Malcolm H. Kerr, *The Arab Cold War: Gamel Abd Al-Nasir and His Rivals, 1958–1970* (3rd edition) (Oxford: Oxford University Press, 1971).
7 John F. Devlin, "The Baath Party: Rise and Metamorphosis," *The American Historical Review* 96, 5 (December 1991): 1396–1407.
8 Sonoko Sunayama, *Syria and Saudi Arabia: Collaboration and Conflicts in the Oil Era* (London: I.B. Tauris, 2007), 32–33.
9 Kerr, *The Arab Cold War*.
10 Pedro Ramet, *The Soviet Syrian Relationship since 1955: A Troubled Alliance* (Boulder: Westview Press, 1990).
11 Nader Entessar, "The Lion and the Sphinx: Iranian Egyptian Relations in Perspective," in *Iran and the Arab World*, eds. Hooshang Amirahmadi and Nader Entessar (London: Macmillan, 1973), 162–163.
12 Mohammad Heikal, *The Road to Ramadan* (London: Collins, 1975).
13 Sunayama, *Syria and Saudi Arabia*.
14 See Marwa Daoudy, "A Missed Chance for Peace: Israel and Syria's Negotiations over the Golan Heights," *Journal of International Affairs* 61, 2 (Spring/Summer 2008): 215–234 for an explanation of how the Golan Heights' water resources played an important role in Israel's final decision.
15 Raymond Hinnebusch and Nael Shama, "The Foreign Policy of Egypt," in *The Foreign Policy of Middle East States* (2nd edition), eds. Raymond Hinnebusch and Anoushiravan Eteshami (London: Lynne Rienner, 2014).
16 Isolating Iran had often appeared to be one of the main goals of American policy in the region in the aftermath of the Iranian revolution.
17 Jubin Goodarzi, *Syria and Iran: Diplomatic Alliance and Power Politics in the Middle East* (London: I.B. Tauris, 2009).
18 Ibid., 292.
19 Berna Suer, "Ripeness Theory and Coercive Diplomacy as a Road to Conflict Resolution: The Case of the Turkey–Syria Showdown in 1998," in *Turkey–Syria Relations: Between Enmity and Amity*, eds. Raymond Hinnebusch and Özlem Tür (London: Ashgate, 2013).
20 Nicholas Gvosdev and Christopher Marsch, *Russian Foreign Policy: Interests, Vectors, and Sectors* (Los Angeles: CQ Press, 2014), 16.
21 Hinnebusch and Shama, "The Foreign Policy of Syria."
22 Ersun Kurtulus, "The Cedar Revolution: Lebanese Independence and the Question of Collective Self Determination," *British Journal of Middle Eastern Studies* 36, 2 (2009): 195–214.
23 For an Israeli perspective on why the 2006 war failed, see Efraim Inbar, "How Israel Bungled the Second Lebanon War," *Middle East Quarterly* 14, 2 (2007).
24 William Sami Abbas, "A Stable Structure on Shifting Sands: Assessing the Hizbullah–Iran–Syria Relationship," *The Middle East Journal* 62, 1 (Winter 2008): 32–53.
25 Gvosdev and Marsch, *Russian Foreign Policy*, 375.
26 Mark Katz, "Putin's Foreign Policy towards Syria," *Middle East Review of International Affairs* 10, 1 (2006).

27 Ibid.
28 Curtis R. Ryan, *Inter-Arab Alliances: Regime Security and Jordanian Foreign Policy* (Gainesville: University of Florida, 2009).
29 Daoudy, "A Missed Chance for Peace."
30 Jay Solomon and Bill Spindle, "Interview with Syrian President Al-Assad," *Wall Street Journal*, 31 January 2011, http://online.wsj.com/articles.
31 Cartsen Wieland, "Asad's Decade of Lost Chances," in *The Syrian Uprising: Dynamics of an Insurgency*, eds. Raymond Hinnebusch and Tina Zintl (St Andrews: Centre for Syrian Studies Series, 2013), 32.
32 The businessman owner of Syrian a telecom company was for the protesters a symbol of the corrupted elite of the country.
33 Nidaa Hassan, "Syria Vows to Retaliate after Attack on Police and Security Forces," *Guardian*, 6 June 2011, www.theguardian.com/world/2011/jun/06/syria-retaliate-attack-on-troops.
34 Christopher Phillips, *The Battle for Syria: International Rivalry in the New Middle East* (Yale: Yale University Press, 2016).
35 Raymond Hinnebusch and Özlem Tür, eds., *Turkey–Syria Relations: Between Enmity and Amity* (London: Ashgate, 2013).
36 Lamentably, this video has now been removed from YouTube.
37 These have been collected by David L. Phillips, Director of the Program on Peace-building and Rights at Columbia University and can be found at www.huffingtonpost.com/david-l-phillips/research-paper-isis-turke_b_6128950.html.
38 "Syria Refugee Response," UNHCR, accessed 15 June 2017, https://data2.unhcr.org/en/situations/syria#_ga=2.72390736.239392497.1529842219–1637111199.1529842219.
39 For a detailed account see Marisa Sullivan's report "Hezbollah in Syria" (April 2014) for the Institute for the Study of War, www.understandingwar.org/sites/default/files/Hezbollah_Sullivan_FINAL.pdf.
40 Aron Lundt "Defense in Depth: Jordan Eyes Increased Involvement as Borders Crumble," *Carnegie Middle East Center*, 20 April 2015, http://carnegieendowment.org/syriaincrisis/?fa=59840.
41 Gardiner Harris, "U.S., Russia and Jordan Reach Deal for Cease-Fire in Part of Syria," *New York Times*, 7 July 2017, www.nytimes.com/2017/07/07/us/politics/syria-ceasefire-agreement.html.
42 Raymond Hinnebusch, *Syria–Iraq Relations: State Construction and Deconstruction and the MENA States System* (London: LSE Middle East Centre Paper Series, 2014).
43 "Iraqi Air Strike Targets ISIS Position in Syria, Abadi Says," *The National*, 06 May 2018, www.thenational.ae/world/mena/iraqi-air-strike-targets-isis-position-in-syria-abadi-says-1.727603.

12 Conclusion

In the introduction, I stated that this book would be of relevance to two different audiences: those interested in International Relations (and particularly in foreign policy and alliances) and those interested in Syria and the Middle East. The reader will be in a better position to judge whether I was up to this task. But in line with what was promised, I will divide this conclusion chapter into two parts. The first contains some reflections on the theoretical contribution of the book. It also discusses the potential for further research in this area. The second includes some final considerations on Syria, its foreign policy and the tragic events that have taken place in the last few years in this beautiful country.

Realism, realisms and foreign policy

> The children of light must be armed with the wisdom of the children of darkness but remain free from their malice. They must know the power of self-interest in human society without giving it moral justification. They must have this wisdom in order that they may beguile, deflect, harness and restrain self-interest, individual and collective, for the sake of the community.[1]

Reinhold Niebuhr's famous quote reflects one of the core aspects of classical realism. The argument of this book has been based on the research tradition of realism. During the last few decades, realism's position as a central paradigm in International Relations has been challenged by several competing theories. These criticisms have been among the factors that had led several realist scholars to challenge the dominant realist paradigm: structural realism. Starting from the late 1990s, a series of authors have worked to update and expand the realist framework. In many cases, these new trends were more of a 'return to the past', an attempt to re-introduce some of the topics and analytical features of classical realism that had been left out from the realist mainstream with the structural revolution. Because of this, these authors have been described as neoclassical realists.[2] The model of this book represents a modest contribution to this rediscovery of classical realist themes. It can be considered as neoclassical realist inasmuch as it incorporates a domestic factor within a realist- (and structural-)

Conclusion 151

based analysis. The inclusion of domestic factors in a realist framework arguably represents the greatest contribution of neoclassical realist research. In terms of theory design, it represents a trade-off: the analysis inevitably loses some of the parsimony of structural analysis but gains explanatory power. However, this inclusion appears to be fundamental in the case of works (such as this research) that seek to analyse at the foreign policy level rather than the International Relations level. In other terms, when the subject of the study is state behaviour rather than systemic outcomes, the inclusion of domestic level factors significantly increases the usefulness of realism as a theory of foreign policy.

The key classical realist concept that has been integrated by this analysis is a state's 'goals'. State goals are ideal-types that represent a state's attitude towards the regional system. State goals were included (albeit with often different names) in the work of classical realist authors. These scholars in fact differentiated states based on the goals they were pursuing in the system using categories such as status quo and revisionist. This work has used three ideal-types: status quo, limited and unlimited revisionist. The goal that a state is pursuing will determine its alliance preferences. States will seek to establish alliances that will allow them to reach their goals within the system. State goals is also the theoretical concept used here to connect the international and domestic levels. Whether a state is a revisionist or a status quo power will depend first on systemic considerations such as its position and relative strength within the system. Domestic factors will, however, under some circumstances, also affect what goals states pursue in the system.

Several domestic parameters have been included by neoclassical realist authors in their analysis. This versatility and adaptability has been one of the strongest features of neoclassical realism but has also led to the accusation of introducing variables ad hoc.[3] In order to address this particular criticism, neoclassical realist authors Ripsman *et al.* have divided the factors used by scholars into four subcategories: images and perception of state leaders; strategic culture; state society relations; and domestic institutional arrangements.[4] The domestic factor included in this analysis, 'leadership ideological orientation', falls into the first category. This set of variables concerns 'the beliefs or images of individual decision makers that sit at the helm of the state'.[5] This factor indicates that leaders that are more 'ideological' will seek to implement policies that are based on their specific set of beliefs rather than on a more 'realist-like' idea of state interest. The inclusion of this factor has allowed the author to explain Syria's foreign policy during the early Ba'th years and the discontinuity of the foreign policy of Syria after 1970. Despite the fact that the Ba'th power remained in power during the whole time studied here, the foreign policy of Damascus (and its alliances) changed radically.

The inclusion of 'ideology' in a realist analysis confirms the flexibility and adaptability of neoclassical realism as a theoretical tool. The inclusion of this parameter can also be seen as a way of bridging the gap between realism and other theories of International Relations (in this case theories such as constructivism, that traditionally emphasise the role of ideology). As Ripsman, Lobell

152 *Alliances and beyond*

and Taliaferro stress, what makes this approach consistent with realist research is that the international system remains the primary determinant of state behaviour, and domestic variables are integrated within a 'realist framework.'[6] With this in mind, different domestic level variables can and have been integrated by neoclassical realist scholars.

In recent years scholars have expanded the scope and the topics of neoclassical realist research. This book has also shown how there is room for further application of neoclassical realist theories to the foreign policy of different states. Most contemporary neoclassical realist research has focused on the foreign policy of democratic states and great powers. However, this analysis confirms that this framework has a lot to say about the behaviour of smaller regional powers and non-democratic regimes. Smaller powers behave differently from great powers in several ways: as they are less powerful, they are more constrained by the system in which they are placed and have less to do with shaping it. However, the interaction between external and domestic factors is not necessarily different from the one that happens in bigger states. Thus, the same analytical tools that have been applied to global powers should apply in the case of smaller states. As for non-democratic states, the applicability of neoclassical realism rests on the choice of the correct intervening variables among the different ones used by neoclassical realist scholars. Ultimately, the flexibility of this framework allows the research to integrate different variables that are relevant to the specific phenomenon or phenomena that is being analysed. It is this feature that makes this theoretical framework full of potential for researchers willing to build on it and 'test its limits'.

Syria

Syria, its foreign policy and its alliances provided the case study for this analysis. The external relations of Damascus during the years of this study are complex and full of twists and changes, therefore providing an excellent test for the model of the book. Furthermore, Syria's foreign policy and goals changed throughout the time of this analysis, allowing the author to test the explanatory power of this model. The alliances of Damascus are, however, more than an interesting case study with which to test theories of International Relations. Syria has been a central player in Middle Eastern and inter-Arab politics. Former United States Secretary of State Henry Kissinger is credited with stating that 'you can't make war in the Middle East without Egypt and you can't make peace without Syria'.[7] This sentence more than any other captures how central Syria has been in the politics of the Middle East region.

All scholars, regardless of their theoretical inclinations and personal preferences, end up convincing themselves that the subject of their study is special and unique. Middle East specialists usually base their case for uniqueness on one or more of the following aspects: the role of transnational ideologies such as Pan-Arabism or Islamism; the long and rich history of the region; the presence of countless religious or ethnic groups; or the diversity in political systems. If the

Middle East is a 'unique region', then Syria is a unique state within the system. Syria has in fact a solid claim to the title of the 'cradle of civilisation' and the birthplace of Pan-Arabism. Syria is one of the most diverse countries in the region, and one where different ideologies and the men and women that represent them have engaged in fierce battles for political supremacy. For those that are less interested in politics, Syria was commonly associated with a rich cultural and historical heritage, its warm and welcoming people and (inevitably) its delicious food. However, today most people associate Syria with something more dramatic and gruesome. In the last seven years Syria has in fact witnessed one of the most violent civil wars in recent history. This conflict has already caused casualties in excess of 500,000 and displaced approximatively half of the country's population.

This book has not dealt directly with the development of the Syrian Civil War. It has not engaged in a systemic analysis of the factors that transformed the peaceful protests that started in March 2011 into a war. The previous chapter has, however, provided a broad account of the alliances of Syria throughout the civil war. Syria's relevance in Middle Eastern politics and particularly its centrality in the complex web of regional alliances are the key factors behind the involvement of regional actors in the Syrian Civil War. As Christopher Philipps shows, external actors played an important role in transforming what started as peaceful protests against a repressive regime into one of the bloodiest conflicts in recent history.[8] Syria's network of alliances has undoubtedly been one of the factors as to why several regional actors decided to get involved in the conflict in the Levantine country. Powers such as Saudi Arabia saw the conflict as an opportunity to dethrone the Syrian leadership and break the Syrian–Iranian alliance. At the same time, the strength of its alliances has been a key factor behind the regime's survival. Battered and suffering severe manpower shortages, the Syrian regime has had to rely on its allies to survive the battle against opposition forces.

At the time of writing, the Syrian regime has regained great chunks of the territory it had lost and is planning the next step military initiatives aimed at winning back control of those regions still controlled by opposition forces. This process is unlikely to be simple and will surely require a lot of time. Furthermore, the regime will have to negotiate (or clash) with the different foreign powers that control part of its territory or have some sort of military presence in Syria. Crucially for Al-Assad, the regime is in control of what has been defined as 'useful Syria'. Unless something dramatic takes place (never an option to exclude completely in the Syrian Civil War), the Al-Assad regime appears to have survived. This victory, however, has had incredibly high human and material costs. The staggering number of casualties and the equally shocking number of internally and externally displaced Syrians have been already recalled. Entire regions of the country are in ruins, the economic system has been dramatically damaged and significant parts of a whole generation of Syrians have had scarce or no access to education. The Ba'thist regime led by Bashar Al-Assad bears moral and practical responsibilities for what has happened. The protests

154 *Alliances and beyond*

that started in Syria were initially peaceful and spontaneous. The people that took to the streets of Dera'a, Homs, Hama and several other Syrian cities had perfectly legitimate claims and initially expressed them in a remarkably peaceful fashion. A few months after the start of the protests the revolution was hijacked by internal and particularly external actors. The regime did all that was in its power to take the confrontation onto military grounds, and sadly achieved its goal.

The Syrian regime might ultimately win the civil war but in the process it will have lost the country's autonomy from external actors. Patrick Seale's 1965 classic *The Struggle for Syria* described an era when Syria was a playground for different regional actors competing for regional supremacy.[9] Today's struggle for Syria shares several similarities with the situation described by Seale but the one we are witnessing today is unfortunately a much more violent struggle. When and how this war will finish, and what the country will look like when it does, is anybody's guess. Eight years after the start of the civil war, it appears that the same regime that is largely responsible for beginning it will remain in power after its conclusion. The international community has largely accepted the fact that the regime has won the war, or it has simply decided to forget about what is happening in Syria. I have no faith in the regime's ability to reform itself and lead the country into a better and more stable political phase. I do have, however, a lot of faith in the Syrian people's resilience, strength and ability to rebuild the country after the dramatic events of the last few years. All these qualities are surely going to be needed in the coming years.

Notes

1 Reinhold Niebuhr, *The Children of Light and the Children of Darkness: A Vindication of Democracy and Critique of its Traditional Defence* (Chicago: University of Chicago Press, 1944), 41.
2 Gideon Rose, "Neoclassical Realism and Theories of Foreign Policy," *World Politics* 51, 1 (October 1998): 144–172.
3 See for example Stephen Walt "The Enduring Relevance of Realist Tradition," in *Political Science: State of the Discipline III*, eds. Ira Katznelson and Helen V. Milner (New York: W.W. Norton, 2002).
4 Norrin M. Ripsman, Jeffrey W. Taliaferro and Steven E. Lobell *Neoclassical Realist Theory of International Politics* (Oxford: Oxford University Press, 2016).
5 Ibid., 61.
6 Ibid., 165.
7 Quoted in several studies including Patrick Seale, *Assad of Syria: The Struggle for the Middle East* (London: I.B. Tauris, 1988).
8 Christopher Philipps, *The Battle for Syria: International Rivalry in the New Middle East* (Yale: Yale University Press, 2016).
9 Patrick Seale, *The Struggle for Syria: A Study of Post-war Arab Politics 1945–1958* (2nd edition) (Oxford: Oxford University Press, 1965).

Bibliography

Abadi, Jacob. *Israel's Quest for Recognition and Acceptance in Asia: Garrison State Diplomacy.* London: Franc Cass Publisher, 2004.

Abbas, William Sami. "A Stable Structure on Shifting Sands: Assessing the Hizbullah-Iran–Syria Relationship." *The Middle East Journal* 62, 1 (Winter 2008): 32–53.

Adamec, Jan. "Czechoslovakian–Syrian Relations." In *Syria during the Cold War: The Eastern European Connection,* edited by Przemysław Gasztold-Seń, Massimiliano Trentin, and Jan Adamec. St Andrews: Centre for Syrian Studies Publisher, 2014.

Agha, Husayn and Ahmad Khalidi. *Syria and Iran: Rivalry and Cooperation.* London: Royal Institute of International Affairs, 1995.

Ajami, Fuad. *The Vanished Imam: Musa Al-Sadr and the Shia of Lebanon.* London: I.B. Tauris, 1986.

Al-Rasheed, Madawi. *Politics in an Arabian Oasis: The Rashidis of Saudi Arabia.* London: I.B. Tauris, 1997.

Alon, Yoav. *The Making of Jordan: Tribes, Colonialism and the Modern State.* London: I.B. Tauris, 2009.

Aron, Raymond. *Peace and War: A Theory of International Relations.* New York: Garden City, 1966.

Axelgard, Fred. "The Superpowers and the Gulf." *Middle East International,* 29 June 1984, 12.

Axworthy, Michael. *A History of Iran: Empire of the Mind.* London: Penguin Books, 2007.

Ayoob, Mohammad. "From Regional System to Regional Society: Exploring Key Variables in the Construction of Regional Order." *Australian Journal of International Affairs* 53, 3 (1999): 247–260.

Ayubi, Nazih. *Over-stating the Arab State: Politics and Society in the Middle East.* London: I.B. Tauris, 2001.

Bannerman, Graeme. "Saudi Arabia." In *Lebanon in Crisis: Participants and Issues,* edited by P. Edward Haley and Lewis W. Snider. Syracuse: Syracuse University Press, 1979.

Bar-Siman-Tov, Yaacov. *Linkage Politics in the Middle East: Syria between Domestic and External Conflict, 1961–1970.* Boulder: Westview, 1983.

Barnett, Michael N. "Institutions, Roles, and Disorder: The Case of the Arab States System." *International Studies Quarterly* 37, 3 (September 1993): 271–296.

Barnett, Michael N. "Sovereignty, Nationalism, and Regional Order in the Arab States System." *International Organization* 49, 3 (Summer 1995): 479–510.

Barnett, Michael N. *Dialogues in Inter-Arab Politics: Negotiations in Regional Order.* New York: Columbia University Press, 1998.

156   Bibliography

Barnett, Michael N. and Jack Levy. "Alliance Formation, Domestic Political Economy, and Third World Security." *Jerusalem Journal of International Relations* 14, 4 (1992).

Batatu, Hannah. "Some Observations on the Social Roots of Syria's Ruling Military Group and the Causes for its Dominance." *The Middle East Journal* 35, 3 (Summer 1981): 331–344.

Beasley, Ryan and Michael Snarr. "Domestic and International Influences on Foreign Policy: A Comparative Perspective." In *Foreign Policy in Comparative Perspective*, edited by Ryan K. Beasley, Juliette Karboo, Jeffrey S. Lantis and Michael T. Snarr. Washington: CQ Press, 2002.

Beattie, Kirk. *Egypt during the Sadat Years.* Basingstoke: Palgrave, 2000.

Beeson, Mark. "Rethinking Regionalism: Europe and East Asia in Comparative Historical Perspective." *Journal of European Public Policy* 12 (2005).

Bennet, Andrew and Colin Elman. "Qualitative Research: Recent Developments in Case Studies Methods." *Annual Review of Political Science* 9 (2005): 455–476.

Ben-Tzur, Abraham. *The Syrian Baath Party and Israel: Documents from the Internal Party Publications.* Tel Aviv: Sifriat Poalim, 1968.

Brand, Laurie A. *Jordan's Inter-Arab Relations: The Political Economy of Alliance Making.* New York: Columbia University Press, 1994.

Breslauer, George. *Soviet Strategy in the Middle East.* Boston: Unwin Hyman, 1990.

Bull, Hedley. *The Anarchical Society: A Study of Order in World Politics.* London: Macmillan, 1977.

Buzan, Barry. "The Middle East through English School Theory." In *International Society and the Middle East: English School Theory at the Regional Level,* edited by Barry Buzan and Ana Gonzalez-Pelaez. Basingstoke: Palgrave Macmillan, 2009.

Buzan, Barry and Ana Gonzalez-Pelaez. *International Society and the Middle East: English School Theory at the Regional Level.* Basingstoke: Palgrave Macmillan, 2004.

Buzan, Barry and Ole Wæver. *Regions and Powers: The Structure of International Security.* Cambridge: Cambridge University Press, 2003.

Buzan, Barry and Ole Wæver. "The Middle East: A Perennial Conflict Formation." In *Regions and Powers: The Structure of International Security,* edited by Barry Buzan and Ole Wæver. Cambridge: Cambridge University Press, 2003.

Carr, E. H. *The Twenty Years Crisis 1919–1939.* London: Macmillan, 1939.

Chalala, Elie. "Syria's Support of Iran in the Gulf War: The Role of Structural Change and the Emergence of a Relatively Strong State." *Journal of Arab Affairs* 7, 2 (1988).

Christensen, Thomas and Jack Snyder. "Chain Gangs and Passed Bucks: Predicting Alliance Pattern in Multipolarity." *International Organization* 44 (1990): 137–168.

Chubin, Shahram. "Soviet Policy in the Middle East." In *Security in the Middle East: Regional Change and Great Powers Strategies,* edited by Samuel F. Wells and Mark Bruzonsky. London: Westview Press, 1987.

Chubin, Shahram and Charles Tripp. *Iraq and Iran at War.* London: I.B. Tauris, 1988.

Cobban, Helena. *The Superpowers and the Syrian–Israeli Conflict: Behind Crisis Management.* Washington: Centre for Strategic and International Studies, 1991.

Cooley, John K. "Assad Has Problems." *Middle East International*, 4 May 1984, 13.

Curtis, Ryan R. *Inter-Arab Alliances: Regime Security and Jordanian Foreign Policy.* Gainesville: University of Florida Press, 2009.

Daoudy, Marwa. "A Missed Chance for Peace: Israel and Syria's Negotiations over the Golan Heights." *Journal of International Affairs* 61, 2 (Spring/Summer 2008): 215–234.

Bibliography 157

David, Stephen. "Explaining Third World Alignment." *World Politics* 43, 2 (January 1991): 233–256.

Davidson, Jason W. "The Roots of Revisionism: Fascist Italy, 1922–39." *Security Studies* 11, 4 (1999): 125.

Davidson, Jason W. *The Origins of Revisionists and Status Quo States.* New York: Palgrave Macmillan, 2006.

Dawisha, Adeed. *Egypt in the Arab World: The Elements of Foreign Policy.* London: Macmillan, 1976.

Dawisha, Adeed. *Syria and the Lebanese Crisis.* London: Macmillan Press, 1980.

Dawisha, Adeed. "The Soviet Union in the Arab World." In *The Soviet Union in the Middle East: Policies and Perspectives*, edited by Adeed Dawisha and Karen Dawisha. London: Royal Institute of International Affairs, 1982.

Dayan, Moshe. *Story of My Life: An Autobiography.* London: Weidenfeld and Nicholson, 1976.

Dekmejian, Hair. *Egypt under Nassir: A Study in Political Dynamics.* Albany: State University of New York Press, 1971.

Dessouki, Ali. "The Foreign Policy of Egypt." In *The Foreign Policy of Arab States*, edited by Bahgat Korany and Ali E. Dessouki. London: Lynne Rienner , 2002.

Devlin, John F. *The Ba'th Party: A History from its Origins to 1966.* Stamford: Hoover Institution Press, 1976.

Devlin, John F. "The Baath Party: Rise and Metamorphosis." *The American Historical Review* 96, 5 (December 1991): 1396–1407.

Donovan, Jerome. *The Iran–Iraq War: Antecedents and Conflict Escalation.* London: Routledge, 2011.

Drysdale, Alisdair and Raymond Hinnebusch. *Syria and the Middle East Process.* New York: Council on Foreign Relations Press, 1991.

Dukhan, Haian. *State and Tribes in Syria: Informal Alliances and Conflict Patterns.* London: Routledge (Syrian Studies Series), 2018.

Ehteshami, Anoushiravan. "Wheels within Wheels: Iranian Foreign Policy towards the Arab World." In *Reconstruction and Regional Diplomacy in the Persian Gulf*, edited by Hooshang Amirahmadi and Nader Entessar. London: Routledge, 1995, 117–146.

Ehteshami, Anoushiravan and Raymond Hinnebusch. *Syria and Iran: Middle Powers in a Penetrated Regional System.* London: Routledge, 1997.

Entessar, Nader. "The Lion and the Sphinx: Iranian Egyptian Relations in Perspective." In *Iran and the Arab World*, edited by Hooshang Amirahmadi and Nader Entessar. London: Macmillan, 1973, 161–178.

Evron, Yair. *War and Intervention in Lebanon: The Syrian–Israeli Deterrence Dialogue.* Beckenham, Kent: Croom Helm, 1987.

Fawcett, Louise. "Exploring Regional Domains: A Comparative History of Regionalism." *International Affairs* 80 (2004).

Fawcett, Louise. "Alliances and Regionalism in the Middle East." In *International Relations of the Middle East*, edited by Louise Fawcett. Oxford: Oxford University Press, 2005.

Fawcett, Louise. "Alliances and Regionalism in the Middle East." In *International Relations of the Middle East* (3rd edition), edited by Louise Fawcett. Oxford: Oxford University Press, 2013.

Fawn, Rick. "Regions and Their Studies: Where from, What for and Where to?" *Review of International Studies* 35 (2009): 5–34.

158 *Bibliography*

Fierke, Karin M. "Constructivism." In *International Relations Theories: Discipline and Diversity*, edited by Tim Dunne, Steve Smith and Milja Kurki. Oxford: Oxford University Press, 2013.

Fisk, Robert. *Pity the Nation: Lebanon at War.* Oxford: Oxford University Press, 1990.

Flemes, Daniel, ed. *Regional Leadership in the Global System: Ideas, Interests and Strategies of Regional Powers.* Farnham: Ashgate Publishing, 2010.

Freedman, Robert O. *Soviet Policy towards the Middle East since 1970.* New York: Praeger, 1975.

Freedman, Robert O. *Moscow and the Middle East: Soviet Policy since the Invasion of Afghanistan.* Cambridge: Cambridge University Press, 1991.

Gani, Jasmine. *The Role of Ideology in Syrian–US Relations: Conflict and Cooperation.* London: Palgrave-Macmillan, 2014.

Gause III, Gregory. *Saudi–Yemeni Relations: Domestic Structures and Foreign Influence.* New York: Columbia University Press, 1990.

Gause III, Gregory. "The Foreign Policy of Saudi Arabia." In *The Foreign Policy of Middle East States*, edited by Raymond Hinnebusch and Anoushiravan Ehteshami. London: Lynne Rienner, 2002.

Gause III, Gregory "Balancing What? Threat Perception and Alliance Choice in the Gulf." *Security Studies* 13, 2 (2003): 273–305.

George, Alan. *Jordan: Living in the Crossfire.* London: Zed Books, 2005.

Gilpin, Robert G. *War and Change in World Politics.* Cambridge: Cambridge University Press, 1981.

Gilpin, Robert G. "The Richness of the Tradition of Political Realism." *International Organization* 38, 2 (Spring 1984).

Gilpin, Robert G. "No One Loves a Political Realist." *Security Studies* 5, 3 (1996).

Ginat, Rami. "The Soviet Union and the Ba'th Regime: From Hesitation to Rapprochement." *Middle Eastern Studies* 36, 2 (April 2000): 150–171.

Golan, Galia. *Soviet Policies in the Middle East: From World War II to Gorbachev.* Cambridge: Cambridge University Press, 1990.

Golan, Galia and Itamar Rabinovich. "The Soviet Union and Syria: The Limits of Cooperation." In *The Limits of Power: Soviet Policy in the Middle East*, edited by Roi Yaakov. London: Croom Helm, 1979.

Goldschmidt, Arthur. *A Concise History of the Middle East.* Boulder: Westview Press, 1999.

Goodarzi, Jubin. *Syria and Iran: Diplomatic Alliance and Power Politics in the Middle East.* London: I.B. Tauris, 2009.

Gvosdev, Nicholas and Christopher Marsch. *Russian Foreign Policy: Interests, Vectors, and Sectors.* Los Angeles: CQ Press, 2014.

Haas, Michael. *The Clash of Ideologies: Middle Eastern Politics and American Security.* Oxford: Oxford University Press, 2012.

Hansen, Birthe. *Unipolarity in the Middle East.* New York: St Martin's Press, 2001.

Hawatmeh, George. "Hussein and Assad: Not Yet Eye to Eye". *Middle East International*, 10 January 1986, 8.

Heikal, Mohammad. *The Road to Ramadan.* London: Collins, 1975.

Hermann, Margaret H. "Explaining Foreign Policy Behavior Using the Personal Characteristics of Political Leaders." *International Studies Quarterly* 24, 1 (March 1980): 7–46.

Hermann, Margaret H. "Syria's Hafez Al-Assad." In *Leadership and Negotiation in the Middle East*, edited by Barbara Kellerman and Jeffrey Z. Rubin. Westview: Preager Publishing, 1988.

Bibliography 159

Herrmann, Richard. "The Role of Iran in Soviet Perceptions of Policy." In *Neither East nor West: Iran, the Soviet Union and the United States*, edited by Nicky R. Keddie and Mark Gasiorovski. New Haven: Yale University Press, 1990.

Hinnebusch, Raymond. "Revisionist Dreams, Realist Strategies: The Foreign Policy of Syria." In *The Foreign Policy of Arab States: The Challenge of Change* (2nd edition), edited by Barbara Korany and Ali E. Hillal Dessouki. London: Routledge 1991.

Hinnebusch, Raymond. *Syria: Revolution from Above*. London: Routledge, 2001.

Hinnebusch, Raymond. "The Foreign Policy of Syria." In *The Foreign Policy of Middle Eastern States*, edited by Raymond Hinnebusch and Anoushiravan Ehteshami. London: Lynne Rienner, 2003.

Hinnebusch, Raymond. *The International Politics of the Middle East*. Manchester: Manchester University Press, 2003.

Hinnebusch, Raymond. *Syria–Iraq Relations: State Construction and Deconstruction and the MENA States System*. London: LSE Middle East Centre Papers, 2014.

Hinnebusch, Raymond. "The Middle East Regional System." In *The Foreign Policy of Middle Eastern States* (2nd edition), edited by Raymond Hinnebusch and Anoushiravan Ehteshami. London: Lynne Rienner, 2014.

Hinnebusch, Raymond and Anoushiravan Ehteshami. "The Foreign Policy of Syria." In *The Foreign Policy of Middle Eastern States*, edited by Raymond Hinnebusch and Anoushiravan Ehteshami. Manchester: Lynne Rienner, 2003.

Hinnebusch, Raymond and Neil Quillam. "Contrary Siblings: Syria, Jordan and the Iran Iraq War." *Cambridge Review of International Affairs* 19 (2006).

Hinnebusch, Raymond and Nael Shama. "The Foreign Policy of Egypt." In *The Foreign Policy of Middle Eastern States* (2nd edition), edited by Raymond Hinnebusch and Anoushiravan Ehteshami. London: Lynne Rienner, 2014.

Hinnebusch, Raymond and Özlem Tür, eds. *Turkish–Syrian Relations: Between Enmity and Amity*. London: Ashgate, 2013.

Hiro, Dilip. *The Longest War: The Iran–Iraq Military Conflict*. New York: Routledge, 1991.

Hirshfeld, Yair. "The Odd Couple: Ba'thist Syria and Khomeini's Iran." In *Syria under Assad*, edited by Moshe Ma'oz and Avner Yaniv. London: Croom Helm, 1986.

Hirst, David and Irene Besson. *Sadat*. London: Faber and Faber, 1981.

Hitti, Philip K. *A History of Syria including Lebanon and Palestine*. London: Macmillan, 1951.

Hoffmann, Stanley. *The State of War: Essays on the Theory and Practice of International Politics*. Santa Barbara: Praeger, 1965.

Holden, David and Richard Johns. *The House of Saud*. London: Pan Books, 1991.

Hunter, Shireen T. "From Hostility to Limited Alliance." In *Iran and the Arab World*, edited by Hooshang Amirahmadi and Nader Entessar. London: Macmillan, 1973, 198–216.

Hurrel, Andrew. "Regional Powers and the Global System from an Historical Perspective." In *Regional Leadership in the Global System: Ideas, Interests and Strategies of Regional Powers*, edited by Daniel Flemes. Farnham: Ashgate Publishing, 2010.

Inbar, Efraim. "How Israel Bungled the Second Lebanon War." *Middle East Quarterly* 14, 2 (2007).

International Institute for Strategic Studies. *Military Balance 1970–1971*. London: IISS, 1970.

Itamar, Rabinovich. *The War for Lebanon: 1970–1983*. Ithaca: Cornell University Press, 1984.

160 *Bibliography*

Jansen, G. H. "Iraq and Iran: Exploiting the Hajj." *Middle East International*, 17 September 1982, 9.

Jansen, G. H. "The Attitude of Arab Governments towards the Gulf War." In *The Iran–Iraq War: An Historical, Economic and Political Analysis*, edited by Muhammad S. El Azhary. London: Croom Helm, 1984.

Jervis, Robert. *Perception and Misperception in Foreign Policy.* Princeton, Princeton University Press, 1976.

Jouejati, Murhaf. "Water Politics as High Politics: The Case of Turkey and Syria." In *Reluctant Neighbor: Turkey's Role in the Middle East*, edited by Henri J. Barkey. Washington: United States Institute of Peace, 1996.

Jouejati, Murhaf. "Syrian Foreign Policy: An Institutional Perspective on Why Assad Did Not Emulate Sadat." PhD diss., University of Utah, 1998.

Jureidini, Paul and R. D. McLauren. *Beyond Camp David: Emerging Alignments and Leaders in the Middle East.* Syracuse: Syracuse University Press, 1981.

Karsh, Efraim. *The Soviet Union and Syria: The Assad Years*. London: Royal Institute of International Affairs, 1988.

Kass, Ilana. *Soviet Involvement in the Middle East: Policy Formulation 1966–1973.* Boulder: Westview Press, 1978.

Katz, Mark. "Putin's Foreign Policy towards Syria." *Middle East Review of International Affairs* 10, 1 (2006).

Katzenstein, Peter. *A World of Regions: Asia and Europe in the American Imperium.* Ithaca: Cornell University Press, 2005.

Kennedy, Paul. *The Rise and Fall of Great Powers: Economic Change and Military Conflict from 1500 to 2000.* New York: Random House, 1987.

Kennedy, Paul. *Grand Strategy in War and Peace.* New Haven: Yale University Press, 1991.

Kerr, Malcom H. *The Arab Cold War: Gamal Abd Al-Nasir and his Rivals, 1958–1970* (3rd edition). Oxford: Oxford University Press, 1971.

Kienle, Eberhard. *Ba'th vs Ba'th: The Conflict between Syria and Iraq 1968–1989.* London: I.B. Tauris, 1990.

Kienle, Eberhard, ed. *Contemporary Syria: Liberalization between Cold War and Cold Peace.* London: British Academic Press, 1994.

Kissinger, Henry. *The White House Years.* Boston: Little Brown, 1979.

Kissinger, Henry. *Diplomacy.* New York: Simon and Schuster, 1995.

Kitchen, Nicholas. "Systemic Pressures and Domestic Ideas: A Neoclassical Realist Model of Grand Strategy Formation." *Review of International Studies* 36, 1 (2010): 117–143.

Korany, Baghat and Ali E. Dessouki. *The Foreign Policies of Arab States: The Challenge of Change.* Boulder: Westview Press, 1991.

Kurtulus, Ersun. "The Cedar Revolution: Lebanese Independence and the Question of Collective Self Determination." *British Journal of Middle Eastern Studies* 36, 2 (2009): 195–214.

Lawson, Fred. *Why Syria Goes to War: Thirty Years of Confrontation.* Ithaca: Cornell University Press, 1996.

Lawson, Fred. "International Relations Theory and the Middle East." In *International Relations of the Middle East* (4th edition), edited by Louise Fawcett. Oxford: Oxford University Press, 2016.

Lay, David. "Will Asad's Ambition Be Foiled?" *Middle East International*, 6 April 1984, 12.

Bibliography 161

Lefevre, Raphael. *Ashes of Hama: The Muslim Brotherhood in Syria.* London: Hurst and Co., 2013.

Lenczovski, George. *Soviet Advances in the Middle East.* Washington: American Institute for Public Policy Research, 1971.

Legro, Jeffrey and Andrew Moravcsik. "Is Anybody Still a Realist?" *International Security* 24, 2 (1999): 5–55.

Legum, Colin. *Middle East Contemporary Survey.* London: Holmes and Meier, 1978.

Levron, Aharon. "Syria's Military Strength and Capability." *Middle East Review* 19 (Spring 1987): 5–15.

Lobell, Stephen E., Norrin M. Ripsman and Jeffrey W. Taliaferro, eds. *Neoclassical Realism, the State, and Foreign Policy.* Cambridge: Cambridge University Press, 2009.

Lustik, Ian. "The Absence of Middle Eastern Great Powers." *International Organization* 51, 4 (1997): 653–683.

Lynch, Marc. *State Interests in Public Spheres: The International Politics of Jordan's Identity.* New York: Columbia University Press, 1999.

Ma'oz, Moshe. *Assad: The Sphinx of Damascus.* London: Westfield and Nicholson, 1988.

Ma'oz, Moshe and Anver Yaniv. *Syria under Asad: Domestic Constraints and Regional Risks.* London: Croon Helm, 1986.

Marr, Phebe. *The Modern History of Iraq.* Boulder: Westview Press, 2004.

McLaurin, Ronald De. *Foreign Policy Making in the Middle East: Domestic Influences on Policy in Egypt, Iraq, Israel and Syria.* London: Praeger, 1977.

Mearsheimer, John J. *The Tragedy of Great Powers Politics.* New York: W.W. Norton & Co., 2001.

Meital, Yoram. "The Khartoum Conference and Egyptian Policy after 1967: A Re-examination." *The Middle East Journal* 54, 1 (2000): 63–80.

Morgenthau, Hans J. *Scientific Man Vs Power Politics.* Chicago: Chicago University Press, 1946.

Morgenthau, Hans J. *Politics Among Nations: The Struggle for Power and Peace.* New York: Knopf, 1948.

Mufti, Malik. *Sovereign Creations: Pan-Arabism and Political Order in Syria and Iraq.* Ithaca: Cornell University Press, 1996.

Muir, Jim. "Assad Plays a Strong but Cautious Hand." *Middle East International*, 14 October 1983.

Mundell, Robert and Alexander Swoboda. *Monetary Problems of the International Economy.* Chicago: University of Chicago Press, 1969.

Niebuhr, Reinhold. *The Children of Light and the Children of Darkness: A Vindication of Democracy and Critique of its Traditional Defence.* Chicago: University of Chicago Press, 1944.

Noble, Paul. "Systemic Factors Do Matter: Reflection on the Use and Limitations of Systemic Analysis." In *Persistent Permeability: Regionalism, Localism and Globalization in the Middle East*, edited by Bassel Salloukh and Rex Brynen. Aldershot: Ashgate Publishing, 2004, 34.

Noble, Paul. "From Arab System to Middle Eastern System? Regional Pressures and Constraints." In *The Foreign Policies of Arab States: The Challenge of Globalization*, edited by Bahgat Korany and Ali E. Hillal Dessouki. Cairo: American University Press, 2008, 67–166.

Owen, Roger. "The View from Syria." *Middle East International*, 24 October 1980, 3.

Perlmutter, Amos. "The Comparative Analysis of Military Regimes: Formation, Aspirations, and Achievements." *World Politics* 33, 1 (October 1980).

162 Bibliography

Perthes, Volker. *The Political Economy of Syria under Assad.* London: I.B. Tauris, 1995.

Petran, Tabitha. *The Struggle over Lebanon.* New York: Monthly Review Press, 1987.

Philipps, Christopher. *The Battle for Syria: International Rivalry in the New Middle East.* Yale: Yale University Press, 2016.

Pipes, Daniel. *Greater Syria: The History of an Ambition.* Oxford: Oxford University Press, 1990.

Piscatori, James. "Islamic Values and National Interest: The Foreign Policy of Saudi Arabia." In *Islam in Foreign Policy*, edited by Adeed Dawisha. Cambridge: Cambridge University Press, 1983.

Posen, Barry R. *The Sources of Military Doctrine: France, Britain and Germany between the World Wars.* Ithaca: Cornell University Press, 1984.

Quandt, William. *Decade of Decisions: American Policy towards the Arab–Israeli Conflict, 1967–1976.* Berkeley: University of California Press, 1977.

Quandt, William. *American Diplomacy and the Arab–Israeli Conflict since 1967.* Washington: Brooking Institutions, 1993.

Quinn, Adam. "Kenneth Waltz, Adam Smith and the Limits of Science: Hard Choices for Neoclassical Realism." *International Politics* 50, 2 (2011): 159–182.

Rabinovich, Itamar. *Syria under the Ba'th, 1963–66: The Army–Party Symbiosis.* Jerusalem: Israel Universities Press, 1972.

Rabinovich, Itamar. *The War for Lebanon: 1970–1983.* Ithaca: Cornell University Press, 1984.

Rabinovich, Itamar. *Waging Peace: Israel and the Arabs, 1948–2003.* Princeton: Princeton University Press, 2004.

Rabinovich, Itamar. *The View from Damascus.* Portland: Vallentine Mitchell, 2008.

Ramazani, Rouallah. *Revolutionary Iran: Challenge and Responses in the Middle East.* Baltimore: Johns Hopkins University Press, 1988.

Ramet, Pedro. *The Soviet Syrian Relationship since 1955: A Troubled Alliance.* Boulder: Westview Press, 1990.

Rathbun, Brian. "A Rose by Any Other Name: Neoclassical Realism as the Logical and Necessary Extension of Structural Realism." *Security Studies* 17, 2 (2008): 294–321.

Rengger, Nicholas. "Realism Tamed or Liberalism Betrayed? Dystopic Liberalism and International Order." In *After Liberalism: The Future of Liberalism in International Relations (Palgrave Studies in International Relations)*, edited by Rebekka Friedman, Kevork Oskanian and Ramon Pacheco Pardo. London: Palgrave, 2013.

Renning, Sten and Jens Ringsmose. "Why are Revisionist States Revisionist? Reviving Classical Realism as an Approach to Understanding International Change." *International Politics* 45 (2008): 22–45.

Ripsman, Norrin M. "Threat Assessment, the State, and Foreign Policy: A Neoclassical Realist Model." In *Neoclassical Realism, the State and Foreign Policy*, edited by Steve E. Lobell, Norrin M. Ripsman and Jeffrey W. Taliaferro. Cambridge: Cambridge University Press, 2009.

Ripsman, Norrin M., Jeffery W. Taliaferro and Steven E. Lobell. *Neoclassical Realist Theory of International Politics.* Oxford: Oxford University Press, 2016.

Robins, Phillip. *A History of Jordan.* Cambridge: Cambridge University Press, 2004.

Rogan, Eugene. *The Arabs: A History.* London: Penguin Books, 2012.

Rose, Gideon. "Neoclassical Realism and Theories of Foreign Policy." *World Politics* 51, 1 (October 1998): 144–172.

Rubin, Lawrence. *Islam in the Balance: Ideational Threats in Arab Politics.* Stanford: Stanford University Press, 2014.

Bibliography 163

Ryan, Curtis R. *Inter-Arab Alliances: Regime Security and Jordanian Foreign Policy.* Gainesville: University of Florida, 2009.

Rynning, Jens and Sten Ringsmose. "Why are Revisionist States Revisionist? Reviving Classical Realism as an Approach to Understanding International Change." *International Politics* 45 (2008): 19–39.

Safran, Nadav. *Saudi Arabia: The Ceaseless Quest for Security.* Ithaca: Cornell University Press, 1988.

Salloukh, Bassel. "State Strength, Permeability, and Foreign Policy Behavior: Jordan in Theoretical Perspective." *Arab Studies Quarterly* 18, 2 (1996): 1–24.

Salloukh, Bassel. "Regime Autonomy in Regional Foreign Policy Choices in the Middle East: A Theoretical Exploration." In *Persistent Permeability?: Regionalism, Localism, and Globalization in the Middle East,* edited by Bassel Salloukh. London: Routledge, 2004, 81–103.

Salloukh, Bassel. "The Art of the Impossible: The Foreign Policy of Lebanon." In *The Foreign Policies of Arab States: The Challenge of Globalization,* edited by Bahgat Korany and Ali E. Dessouki. Cairo: American University in Cairo Press, 2009, 283–317.

Saouli, Adham. *The Arab State: Dilemmas of Late Formation.* London: Routledge, 2012.

Sartori, Giovanni. "Politics, Ideology, and Belief Systems." *American Journal of Political Science* 63 (June 1969): 358–415.

Schoel, Torsten. "The Hasna's Revenge: Syrian Tribes and Politics in Their Shaykh's Story." *Nomadic People* 15, 1 (2011): 96–113.

Schweller, Randall. "The Richness of the Tradition of Political Realism." In *Realism and its Critics,* edited by Robert O. Keohane. New York: Columbia University Press, 1986.

Schweller, Randall. "Bandwagoning for Profit: Bringing the Revisionist State Back in." *International Security* 19, 1 (Summer 1994): 72–107.

Schweller, Randall. "Neorealism's Status-Quo Bias: What Security Dilemma?" *Security Studies* 5, 3 (1996): 90–121.

Schweller, Randall. "New Realist Research on Alliances: Refining, not Refuting, Waltz's Balancing Proposition." *American Political Science Review* 91, 4 (December 1997).

Schweller, Randall. *Deadly Imbalances: Tripolarity and Hitler's Strategy of World Conquest.* New York: Columbia University Press, 1998.

Schweller, Randall. "Realism and the Present Great Powers System: Growth and Positional Conflict over Scarce Resources." In *Unipolar Politics: Realism and State Strategies after the Cold War,* edited by Ethan B. Kapstein and Michael Mastanduno. New York: Columbia University Press, 1999.

Schweller, Randall. "Unanswered Threats: A Neoclassical Realist Theory of Underbalancing." *International Security* 29, 2 (Fall 2004).

Schweller, Randall and David Priess. "A Tale of Two Realisms: Expanding the Institutions Debate." *Mershon International Studies Review* 41, 1 (May 1997): 1–32.

Seale, Patrick. *The Struggle for Syria: A Study of Post-War Arab Politics 1945–1958* (2nd edition). Oxford: Oxford University Press, 1965.

Seale, Patrick. *Assad of Syria: The Struggle for the Middle East.* London: I.B. Tauris, 1988.

Seale, Patrick. *The Struggle for Arab Independence: Riad El-Solh and the Makers of the Modern Middle East.* Cambridge: Cambridge University Press, 2010.

Sela, Avraham and Moshe Ma'oz. *The PLO and Israel: From Armed Conflict to Political Solution, 1964–1994.* London: St Martin's Press, 1997.

Sheehan, Edward. *The Arabs, Israelis and Kissinger: A Secret History of American Diplomacy in the Middle East.* New York: Thomas Cromwell, 1976.

164 Bibliography

Shemesh, Moshe. "The Origins of Sadat's Strategic Volte-face." *Israel Studies* 23, 13 (2008).

Shlaim, Avi. *Collusion across the Jordan.* Oxford: Oxford University Press, 1988.

Shlaim, Avi. *Lion of Jordan: The Life of King Hussein in War and Peace.* London: Penguin Books, 2017.

Smith, Steve. "Foreign Policy Analysis and International Relations." *Millennium Journal of International Studies* 12, 1 (1986).

Snyder, Glenn H. *Alliance Politics.* Ithaca: Cornell University Press, 1997.

Sterling-Folker, Jennifer. "Neoclassical Realism and Identity: Peril Despite Profit across the Taiwan Straits." In *Neoclassical Realism, the State, and Foreign Policy*, edited by Steven Lobell, Norrin M. Ripsman and Jeffrey W. Taliaferro. Cambridge: Cambridge University Press, 2009.

Suer, Berna. "Ripeness Theory and Coercive Diplomacy as a Road to Conflict Resolution: The Case of the Turkey–Syria Showdown in 1998." In *Turkey–Syria Relations: Between Enmity and Amity*, edited by Raymond Hinnebusch and Özlem Tür. London: Ashgate, 2013.

Sunayama, Sonoko. *Syria and Saudi Arabia: Collaboration and Conflicts in the Oil Era.* London: I.B. Tauris, 2007.

Taliaferro, Jeffrey W. "State Building for Future Wars: Neoclassical Realism and the Resource-Extractive State." *Security Studies* 15, 3 (July–September 2006): 464–495.

Taliaferro, Jeffrey W., Steven E. Lobell and Norrin M. Ripsman. "Introduction: Neoclassical Realism, the State, and Foreign Policy." In *Neoclassical Realism, the State, and Foreign Policy*, edited by Steven E. Lobell, Norrin M. Ripsman and Jeffrey W. Taliaferro. Cambridge: Cambridge University Press, 2009.

Telhami, Shibley. *Power and Leadership in International Bargaining: The Path to the Camp David Accords.* New York: Columbia University Press, 1990.

Telhami, Shibley. "Power and Legitimacy in Arab Alliances: The New Arabism." In *Ethnic Conflict and International Politics in the Middle East*, edited by Leonard Binder. Miami: University Press of Florida, 1999.

Tibawi, Abdul Latif. *A Modern History of Syria, including Lebanon and Palestine.* London: Macmillan-St. Martin Press, 1969.

Tripp, Charles. *A History of Iraq.* Cambridge: Cambridge University Press, 2000.

Van Dam, Nicholas. *The Struggle for Power in Syria: Politics and Society under Asad and the Ba'th Party* (4th edition). London: I.B. Tauris, 2011.

Walt, Stephen M. *The Origins of Alliances.* Ithaca: Cornell University Press, 1987.

Walt, Stephen M. "Testing Theories of Alliance Formation: The Case of Southwest Asia." *International Organization* 42, 2 (Spring 1988): 275–316.

Walt, Stephen M. "The Progressive Power of Realism." *American Political Science Review* 91, 4 (1997).

Walt, Stephen M. "Why Alliances Endure or Collapse." *Survival: Global Politics and Strategy* 39, 1 (1997): 156–179.

Walt, Stephen M. "The Enduring Relevance of the Realist Tradition." In *Political Science: State of the Discipline III*, edited by Ira Katznelson and Helen V. Milner. New York: W.W. Norton and Co., 2002.

Waltz, Kenneth N. *Man, State and War.* New York: Columbia University Press, 1959.

Waltz, Kenneth N. *Theory of International Politics.* New York: McGraw Hill, 1979.

Weber, Max. "Objectivity in Social Science and Social Policy." In *The Methodology of Social Sciences*, Max Weber. Glencoe: Free Press, 1949.

Weeks, Jessica. *Dictators at War and Peace.* Ithaca: Cornell University Press, 2014.

Wendt, Alexander. "Anarchy Is What States Make of It: The Social Construction of Power Politics." *International Organization* 46, 2 (Spring 1992): 391–425.

Wendt, Alexander. *Social Theory of International Politics*. Cambridge: Cambridge University Press, 1999.

Wieland, Carsten. "Asad's Decade of Lost Chances." In *The Syrian Uprising. Dynamics of an Insurgency*, edited by Raymond Hinnebusch and Tina Zintl. St Andrews: Centre for Syrian Studies Series, 2013.

Wolfers, Arnold. *Discord and Collaboration: Essays on International Politics*. Baltimore: Johns Hopkins University Press, 1962.

Yergin, Daniel. *The Prize: The Epic Quest for Oil, Money and Power*. London: Simon & Schuster, 1993.

Web sources

CIA. "CIA World Factbook." www.cia.gov/library/publications/the-world-factbook/geos/ir.html.

CIA. "CIA World Factbook-Iraq." www.cia.gov/library/publications/the-world-factbook/geos/iz.html.

CIA. "CIA World Factbook-Syria." www.cia.gov/library/publications/the-world-factbook/geos/sy.html.

Harris, Gardiner. "U.S., Russia and Jordan Reach Deal for Cease-Fire in Part of Syria." *New York Times*. 7 July 2017. www.nytimes.com/2017/07/07/us/politics/syria-ceasefire-agreement.html.

Hassan, Nidaa. "Syria Vows to Retaliate after Attack on Police and Security Forces." *Guardian*. 6 June 2011. www.theguardian.com/world/2011/jun/06/syria-retaliate-attack-on-troops.

Lundt, Aron. "Defense in Depth: Jordan Eyes Increased Involvement as Borders Crumble." *Carnegie Middle East Center*. 20 April 2015. http://carnegieendowment.org/syriaincrisis/?fa=59840.

The National. "Iraqi Air Strike Targets ISIS Position in Syria, Abadi Says." *The National*. 6 May 2018. www.thenational.ae/world/mena/iraqi-air-strike-targets-isis-position-in-syria-abadi-says-1.727603.

Oxford Business Group. "The Report. Emerging Jordan 2007." *Oxford Business Group*. 2007. http://books.google.co.uk/books?id=YuSY8llhkPQC&printsec=frontcover&source=gbs_ge_summary_r&cad=0#v=onepage&q&f=false.

Phillips, David L. "Program on Peace-building and Rights at Columbia University." *Huffington Post*. 11 September 2009. www.huffingtonpost.com/david-l-phillips/research-paper-isis-turke_b_6128950.html.

Solomon, Jay and Bill Spindle. "Interview with Syrian President Al-Assad." *Wall Street Journal*. 31 January 2011. http://online.wsj.com/articles.

Stockholm International Peace Research Institute. "SIPRI Arms Transfers Database." 12 March 2018. https://sipri.org/databases/armstransfers.

Sullivan, Marisa. "Hezbollah in Syria." *Institute for the Study of War*. April 2014. www.understandingwar.org/sites/default/files/Hezbollah_Sullivan_FINAL.pdf.

UNHCR. "UNHCR Syria Refugee response data." Accessed 15 June 2017. https://data2.unhcr.org/en/situations/syria.

The World Bank. "World Bank Open Data." Accessed 9 September 2017. https://data.worldbank.org/.

Index

Page numbers in **bold** denote tables, those in *italics* denote figures.

1967 Arab-Israeli war; aftermath of 136; and Egypt 35, 40, 62–64; and Israel 22, 62–63; and Jordan 74; as turning point 26, 29, 36, 52–53, 57, 133; and USSR 116–117

1973 Arab-Israeli war: aftermath of 28, 54–55, 66–69, 119–121; alliances 36, 37, 40, 107; and Al-Assad, Hafez 22, 54–55, 65–69, 134; and Egypt 36, 40, 54–55, 65–69, 107, 134; and Iran 94; and Iraq 85; and Israel 65–69; and Jordan 67, 71, 76; and Saudi Arabia 36, 37, 107; and USSR 66, 118, 119–121

Abdullah of Jordan, King 71, 72, 76, 142, 146

Abu Musa, occupation of 94, 95

Afghanistan 108, 140

Aflaq, Michel 24, 25, 83, 84

aggregate power 8, 33

aggressive intentions 8, 33–34

Agha, Husayn 98

AKP (Justice and Development Party) (Turkey) 142

Algiers agreement (1975) 85, 87, 94

alliances (theory) 3–4, 13–31; and balance of threat theory 32, 33–34, 104–105, 130; choice of 19–20, 28–29, 151; classical realism 9, 13–15, 42, 150–152; and constructivism 4, 32–33, 38–42, 130; definition of 6; and domestic factors 16–20; and ideology 16–18, *18*, 24, 26, 34, 38–42; models of 4–5, 13–20; neoclassical realism 4–5, 9–10, 16–17, 38, 39, 150–152; and revisionism 28–29, 131, 151; and state goals 13–20, *16*, *18*; structural realism

4, 32, 33–37, 42, 129–130, 150–152; and transnational penetration 34; *see also* Syrian alliances (general)

Alon, Yoav 72

Amal 98–99

Aoun, Michel 111

Arab League 78, 87, 106, 137

Arab Spring 142–147

Arafat, Yassir 76–77, 79, 86, 97, 110, 121, 124

Arif, Abd Al-Salam 50, 51–52, 83, 84

Al-Assad, Bashar 139–140, 142; and Arab Spring 143; and Syrian civil war 144–147, 153–154; and Turkey 144

Al-Assad, Hafez: and 1967 war 26; and 1973 war 22, 54–55, 65–69, 134; after 1989 136–137; and Arafat, Yassir 76–77; background of 27; Black September crisis (1970) 131; death of 139; and Egypt 54–55, 64–69, 134; foreign policy of 26, 27, 28, 29, 47, 53–56, 57, 131, 134; and Hezbollah 98–99; and Hussein, Saddam 87–88; and Iran 87–88, 91, 93–99, 100; and Iran-Iraq war 41, 55–56, 95–97; and Iraq 84–88, 95–97; and Israel 53–54, 56, 64–69, 97–98, 110, 137; and Jordan 74–78, 131; and Lebanon 55, 77, 97–99, 111–112, 120–121, 122; and Palestine 26, 27, 53, 55, 68, 76–77, 97, 131; and Pan-Arabism 27, 40–41, 53; rebuilding army 54; and Sadat, Anwar 54–55, 64, 65–69; and Saudi Arabia 103, 106–112; stability of 24; strengthens grip on country 28; takes power 26–27; and United States 68, 121; and USSR/Russia 54, 56, 114, 117–125; and view of society 27–28

Index 167

Al-Assad, Rifat 55, 95
Ayubi, Nazih 10

al-Badr, Muhammad 51
balance of interests theory 14
balance of power theory 33
balance of threat theory 32, 33–34,
    104–105, 130; and Syrian alliances
    34–37, 42
bandwagoning 32, 34, 36
Barnett, Michael 8, 32, 38, 39–40, 41, 42,
    130
Ba'th party: and alliances 24–28, 132–135;
    foreign policies of Hafez Al-Assad
    53–57, 134–135; foreign policies of
    Salah Jadid 50–53, 56–57, 132–133;
    ideological years 47, 50–53, 56–57,
    132–133; inter-Ba'th competition 40;
    inter-Ba'th rivalry with Iraq 82–84;
    leadership fragmentation (1963–6)
    50–51; limited revisionism (1970–89)
    26–28, 47, 53–56, 134–135; Neo-Ba'th
    25, 35, 84; radical regime (1963–70)
    25–26, 50–53, 132–133; threats and
    consolidation 55–56; *see also individual
    countries*
Beeson, Mark 10
Bilad Al-Sham 48, 72, 103–104
bipolarity 8, 15, 16
Bitar, Salah Al-Din 24, 25, 84
Black September crisis (1970) 26, 27,
    74–75, 78, 93, 131
Brand, Laurie A. 9
Brezhnev, Leonid 120
Buzan, Barry 7, 8, 10

Camp David Accords 36, 68, 77, 85, 86,
    108
civil war (Syrian) 144–147, 153–154
classical realism 9, 13–15, 42, 150–152
Communist Party of Syria 115, 116
constructivism 32–33, 38–42, 130; and
    Syrian alliances 39–41
Corrective Movement 27, 107, 118

David, Stephen 8
Dayan, Moshe 63, 76
Democratic Union Party (PYD) (Syria)
    144
Donovan, Jerome 94

Egypt and Syria 59–69; 1967 war 35, 40,
    62–64; 1970 new era 64–69; 1973 war
    36, 40, 54–55, 65–69, 107, 134; before

1963 59–60; during 1963–1970 60–64;
    during 1966–1970 62–64; and
    Al-Assad, Hafez 54–55, 64–69, 134;
    and Al-Qudsi, Nazim 61; and balance
    of threat 35, 36; Ba'th party vs
    Nasserites 61; bilateral defence pact
    62–63; and constructivism 39–40, 41;
    diverging foreign policies 38–39;
    diverging goals 67; growing distance
    between 64; ideological rivalry 69;
    importance of alliance 64; and Iran 92;
    and Iraq 35, 37, 60, 82, 83, 86–87, 96,
    137; and Israel 35, 37, 52, 54–55,
    62–63, 64, 65–69, 76, 87, 134; and
    Jadid, Salah 62, 63–64; and Jordan 74,
    76, 77; Nasserites 50; nature of
    relationship 59–69, 134, 137, 147; and
    Palestine 52, 62, 68; Pan-Arabism 35,
    39–40, 41, 61, 69; power of 21; power
    sharing 61; rivalry for Arab supremacy
    61; and Saudi Arabia 65, 104, 107–108,
    137; and Syrian civil war 147;
    Tripartite Union negotiations 50, 61,
    83; and United Arab republic 25, 49,
    60, 61; and United States 66, 67–68;
    and USSR 68, 115, 118, 119–120, 124;
    Yemeni civil war 51, 65, 104
Erdoğan, Recep Tayyip 142, 144
Etheshami, Anoushiravan 10
Euphrates, river 86
Evron, Yair 56

Fahd of Saudi Arabia, King 88
Faisal, King 48, 72, 107
Fawcett, Louise 10, 22
Fawn, Rick 10
Fierke, Karin M. 38
foreign policy executive (FPE) 17–18, 24

Gause III, Gregory 8
Gemayel, President 98, 123
Geneva Conference (1973) 67, 68, 119
Gilpin, Robert G. 7, 9, 14, 22
global power patron/regional power client
    alliance 114
Golan, Galia 120, 124
Golan Heights 22, 53, 54, 56, 66, 67, 68,
    137
Gorbachev, Mikhail 123, 124, 136, 139
Great Britain 48, 72
Greece 138–139

Haas, Mark 8, 32
Al-Hafiz, Amin 25, 84

168   *Index*

Hansen, Birthe 8
Hariri, Rafiq 140–141
Hashemites 48, 49, 71, 72, 74, 82, 104,
    105
Heikal, Mohammad 65, 66
Hezbollah 98–99, 138, 141, 145–146
Hinnebusch, Raymond 10, 22, 28, 48, 67,
    140
Hussein, King of Jordan 26, 36, 63, 74,
    75–76, 77, 78, 88
Hussein, Saddam 55–56, 87–88, 95–96,
    108, 109, 111

ideal types 14, 151
ideology: and choice of alliance 19–20,
    129–136, 151–152; concept of 7; and
    constructivism 38–42; and model of
    alliances 16–18, *18*, 19, 34; of Syrian
    leadership 24, 26, 51; *see also* Pan-
    Arabism
institutionalism 32–33, 38–42, 130
Iran and Syria 91–100; before 1963 91–92;
    during 1963–1970 92–93; 1973 war 94;
    1990s 138; and Al-Assad, Hafez 87–88,
    91, 93–99, 100; and balance of threat
    37; Black September crisis (1970) 93;
    and constructivism 40–41; economic
    agreement 96; and Egypt 92; importance
    of Syria to 145; and Iraq 40–41, 55–56,
    78, 85, 87–88, 92, 93, 94, 95–97,
    109–110, 137–138; and Israel 92, 93,
    94; and Jadid, Salah 93; and Khuzestan
    133; and Lebanon 97–99; nature of
    relationship 91, 92, 93–95, 98–100, 135,
    138, 145; and oil 88; and Pan-Arabism
    92–93, 99–100; power of 21; revolution
    in 87, 95, 108, 109; and Saudi Arabia
    95, 108, 109–110, 145; and Syrian civil
    war 145; and United Arab republic 92;
    and United States 94, 95, 138; and the
    West 92
Iran-Iraq war 78, 87–88, 95–97, 109–110,
    137–138
Iraq and Syria 81–89; before 1963 81–82;
    during 1966–1970 84; 1973 war 67, 85;
    1980s 87–88; 1990s 138; after 1989
    137; and Al-Assad, Hafez 84–88,
    95–97; and balance of threat 35, 36, 37;
    and competition 81, 82, 85; complex
    ethnic and religious mix 82; and
    constructivism 39– 41; coup d'état
    (1963) 83; and Egypt 35, 37, 60, 82, 83,
    86–87, 96, 137; and Euphrates 86;
    Hama riots 83; hostility from Syria 84;

ideological issues 81, 84, 85; inter-Ba'th
    rivalry 82–84; invasion of (2003) 140;
    and Iran 40–41, 55–56, 78, 85, 87–88,
    92, 93, 94, 95–97, 109–110, 137–138;
    and Israel 85, 86; and Jadid, Salah
    51–52, 84; and Jordan 78, 88, 95; and
    Lebanon 85–86; nature of relationship
    81, 83–89, 135, 137, 147; and Palestine
    86; and Pan-Arabism 35, 39–41, 82–83;
    power of 21, 60; radical Ba'th years
    82–84; rapprochement of 1978 86–87;
    and Saudi Arabia 88, 95, 108, 109–110;
    and Syrian civil war 147; and Syrian
    domestic unrest 55; temporary
    alignment 81; as threat to Syria 22, 24,
    138; Tripartite Union negotiations 50,
    61, 83; and United Arab republic 82;
    and United States 138, 140, 141; and
    USSR/Russia 122, 147
ISIS 146–147
Israel 1967 war 22, 62–63; 1973 war
    65–69; after 1989 136–137; and
    Al-Assad, Hafez 53–54, 56, 64–69,
    97–98, 110, 137; and balance of threat
    35, 36; demilitarised zones (DMZs) 51,
    62; and Egypt 35, 37, 52, 54–55, 62–63,
    64, 65–69, 76, 87, 134; first Arab-Israeli
    war (1948) 49; and Iran 92, 93, 94; and
    Iraq 85, 86; and Jadid, Salah 52, 62; and
    Jordan 71, 73–74, 75–76, 77; and
    Lebanon 87, 97, 98, 110, 122, 123, 141;
    nature of relationship with Syria 22,
    132; and Palestine; and Pan-Arabism 24,
    52; peace process 137, 138, 139, 142;
    power of 21–22, 29, 53; and relations
    with other Arab states 54; and Saudi
    Arabia 106, 110; as threat to Syria 22;
    and Turkey 138–139; and United
    Nations 64, 67; and United States
    67–68, 137; and USSR/Russia 54, 68,
    116–117, 119, 122, 123, 124, 139;
    withdrawal to pre-1967 lines 64; *see
    also* 1967 Arab-Israeli war; 1973 Arab-
    Israeli war
Italy, and choice of alliance 20

Jadid, Salah: and 1967 war 26, 63–64;
    Black September crisis (1970) 26, 131;
    and coup d'état 26–27, 51; and Egypt
    62, 63–64; foreign policy of 26, 27, 29,
    47, 51–53, 56–57, 131, 133; and Gulf
    monarchies 29; and Iran 93; and Iraq
    51–52, 84; and Jordan 73–74; and
    Palestine 26, 28–29, 51, 52–53, 62,

63–64, 116; and Pan-Arabism 24–25, 26, 51–52, 63–64; radical nature of 24, 25, 26, 47, 25–26, 50–53, 132–133; and Saudi Arabia 51, 63, 103, 105–106, 111; and USSR/Russia 114, 116–117, 124, 133

Jordan and Syria 8–9, 26, 71–79; before 1963 72; during 1963–1970 73–75; 1967 war 74; 1973 war 67, 71, 76; 1975–1977 alignment 76–77, 134–135; 1980s 78, 96; 2000s 141–142; and Al-Assad, Hafez 74–78, 131; and balance of threat 36, 37; Black September crisis (1970) 74–75; Camp David agreements 77; common foe 77; diverging foreign policies 73; and Egypt 74, 76, 77; ideological issues 71, 73, 75; Iran-Iraq war 78, 95; and Iraq 78, 88, 95; and Israel 71, 73–74, 75–76, 77; and Jadid, Salah 73–74; joint military command 77; and Lebanon 77; monarchies bloc 73; Muslim Brotherhood 78; nature of relationship 71, 74–79, 134–135, 141–142; and Palestine 71, 72, 73, 74, 75, 76–77; and Pan-Arabism 72, 74, 75; pro-Western 75; and Saudi Arabia 73, 105; as status quo power 75; and Syrian civil war 146–147; Syrian troops in 74–75; and United Arab republic 72; and USSR 122

Jouejati, Murhaf 32, 38–39, 40–41
Jumblatt, Kamal 77, 86, 97, 120, 121
Justice and Development Party (AKP) (Turkey) 142

Karsh, Efraim 119
Khaddam, Abdul Halim 28, 96, 97, 107, 140
Khalidi, Ahmad 98
Khomeini, Ayatollah 87, 94, 95
Khrushchev, Nikita 115
Kienle, Eberhard 85, 87, 88
Kissinger, Henry 28, 67–68, 76, 87, 119, 152
KSA see Saudi Arabia
Kurdistan Workers' Party (PKK) 138–139, 142, 144

Lawson, Fred 9
leadership ideology 16–18, 18, 19, 24, 131, 135–136, 151
Lebanon 9; in 1990s 138; in 2000s 140, 141; and Al-Assad, Hafez 55, 77, 97–99, 111–112, 120–121, 122; Civil

War in 55, 77, 97–99, 120; Hezbollah 98–99; and Iran 97–99; and Iraq 85–86; and Israel 87, 97, 98, 110, 122, 123, 141; and Jordan 77; and Palestine 77, 97; and Saudi Arabia 110–111; and United States 123, 140–141; and USSR 120–121, 122, 123; withdrawal of Syrian troops 140–141
Lefevre, Raphael 55
limited revisionism 14, 19, 20, 28, 124, 131, 134–135, 136, 151; Syrian foreign policy (1970–89) 53–56
literature review 8–10
Lobell, Steven 10, 16–17, 19, 151–152
Lynch, Marc 8

Meir, Golda 76
Morgenthau, Hans J. 13
Mubarak, Hosni 137, 147
Mufti, Malik 83
multipolarity 15, 21–22, 28
Mundell, Robert 7
Muslim Brotherhood 78

Nahwali, Abd Al-Karim 72, 104
Nasrallah, Hassan 141
Nasser, Gamal Abdel: and 1967 war 35, 40; and Al-Qudsi 61; bilateral defence agreement 52; death of 36, 65; and Egyptian supremacy 35; influence of 50; and Iran 92; and Iraq 35; and Israel 52, 62–63; and Jordan 72; and Palestine 63; and Pan-Arabism 26, 36, 40; popularity of 49, 60; support for in Syria 61; United Arab republic 25, 60, 104, 115; and Yemeni civil war 51; see also Egypt and Syria
Neo-Ba'th 25, 35, 84
neoclassical realism 4–5, 9–10, 16–17, 38, 39, 150–152
neorealism see structural realism
Niebuhr, Reinhold 150
Noble, Paul 8, 13

Ocalan, Abdullah 139, 142
October War see 1973 Arab-Israeli war
offensive intentions 33–34
offensive power 33
oil exports 88, 96, 107
'Omnibalancing Theory' 8
Ottomans 48

Palestine: and 1967 war 63–64; and Al-Assad, Hafez 27, 53, 55, 68, 76–77,

170   *Index*

Palestine *continued*
    97, 131; and Egypt 52, 62, 68; and Iraq
    86; and Israel 26, 28–29, 53; and Jadid,
    Salah 26, 28–29, 51, 52–53, 62, 63–64,
    116; and Jordan 71, 72, 73, 74, 75,
    76–77; and Lebanon 77, 97; and Saudi
    Arabia 108; support from Syria 24, 26,
    28–29, 51, 52–53, 62; and USSR/Russia
    120–121, 139
Palestine Liberation Organization 62, 73,
    74, 76, 86, 108, 120, 121, 122, 123
Pan-Arabism 4, 17; and Al-Assad, Hafez
    27, 40–41, 53; and choice of alliance
    132–133; declining importance 36; and
    Egypt 35, 39–40, 41, 60–61, 69; and
    Iran 92–93, 99–100; and Iraq 35, 39–41,
    82–83; Jadid, Salah 24–25, 26, 51–52,
    63–64; and Jordan 72, 74, 75; and Saudi
    Arabia 105–106; and shaping of policy
    38–42; and state goals 131; and United
    Arab republic 60–61
Perez, Ana Gonzalez 8
Persia 91–92
Perthes, Volker 10
Philipps, Christopher 10, 143, 153
Pipes, Daniel 49
PKK (Kurdistan Workers' Party) 138–139,
    142, 144
power: aggregate power 33; distribution of
    15–16, 21–22, 28; and geographical
    proximity 33; offensive power 33; and
    smaller states 152
Priess, David 9
Putin, Vladimir 141, 146

Al-Qasim, President 82
Qatar 144–145
Quandt, William 65, 68
Al-Qudsi, Nazim 49–50, 60, 61, 82
Al-Quwatli, Shukri 49, 104

Ramet, Pedro 116
rationalist ontology 38
rationalist/realist approach 8, 38
refugees 144
regions: bipolarity 8, 15, 16; and choice of
    alliance 19–20; and conflicts 22;
    definition of 7; as determinant of foreign
    policy 21–24; dynamics of 21–24;
    literature review 10; map of Middle East
    23; multipolarity 15, 21–22, 28; power
    distribution 15–16, 21–22; and state
    goals 14–16; unipolarity 6, 8, 15, 124,
    136

Renning, Sten 14
research methodology 4–6
revisionism 28–29, 131, 151
Ringsmose, Jens 14
Ripsman, Norrin M. 16–17, 151–152
Robins, Phillip 73, 78
Russia *see* USSR/Russia
Ryan, Curtis R. 8–9, 142

Sadat, Anwar: and 1973 war 28, 54–55,
    65–67, 134; and Al-Assad, Hafez
    54–55, 64, 65–69; and Israel 36, 40,
    54–55, 65–68, 86, 134; as new leader
    65; and United States 66, 67–68; and
    USSR 118
Al-Sadr, Musa 94, 98
Salloukh, Bassel 8, 9
Saouli, Adham 10
Sartori, Giovanni 7
Saudi Arabia and Syria 103–112; before
    1963 103–105; 1973 war 36, 37, 107;
    2000s 141; and Al-Assad, Hafez 103,
    106–112; and constructivism 41; and
    Egypt 65, 104, 107–108, 137; as
    ideological nemesis 63; and Iran 95,
    108, 109–110, 145; and Iraq 88, 95, 108,
    109–110; and Israel 106, 110; and Jadid,
    Salah 51, 63, 103, 105–106, 111; and
    Jordan 73, 105; and Lebanon 110–111;
    nature of relationship 103, 105–112,
    134, 141, 145; and oil 107; and Palestine
    108; and Pan-Arabism 105–106; power
    of 21, 104–105; and Qatar 144–145;
    shared identities 41; as status quo power
    107; and Syrian civil war 144–145, 153;
    and United Arab republic 104; and
    United States 107, 108; and USSR 108;
    Yemeni civil war 51, 65, 104
Schweller, Randall 9, 14
Seale, Patrick 25, 67, 72, 75, 95, 154
Shah of Iran 92, 93, 94, 95
Shatt Al-Arab, river 87, 94
Sinai II agreement 36, 76, 110, 134
Sinai Peninsula 52, 53, 63, 65, 66, 67
Al-Sisi, General 147
Six Day War *see* 1967 Arab-Israel war
sovereignty 38–39, 40
Soviet Union *see* USSR
state goals 13–20, *16, 18*, 130–132, 151
state sovereignty 38–39, 40
status quo powers 9, 13, 14, 15, 19–20, 28,
    69, 75, 134, 147, 151
Steadfastness Front 36, 78
Sterling-Folker, Jennifer 42

Index 171

structural realism 4, 32, 33–37, 42, 129–130, 150–152
Suez Crisis (1956) 49, 60, 115
Sunayama, Sonoko 41, 109, 111
Swoboda, Alexander 7
Syria: characteristics of 152–153; establishment of the state 47–50; power of 22, 24, 28–29, 131
Syrian alliances (general) 21–29, 129–136, 152–154; during 1963–1970 132–133; 1970 134–135; 1990s 137–139; 2000s 139–142; after 1989 136–142; and Arab Spring 142–147; and balance of threat 34–37, 42, 130; and constructivism 38–41, 130; factors shaping choice 21–29, 129–136; and ideological orientation 129–136; leadership ideology 135–136; limited revisionism 53–56, 134–135, 136; and state goals 130–131, 132; structural realism 33–37, 42, 129–130; and Syrian civil war 153–154; system and ideology 129–136; and unlimited revisionism 132–133, 136; *see also* alliances (theory); *individual countries*
Syrian Civil War 144–147, 153–154
Syrian foreign policy 47–58, 129–136, 152–154; during 1963–1970 50–53; during 1970–1989 53–56; after 1989 136–142; aftermath of 1973 war 54–55; and domestic factors 151–152; domestic unrest 55; establishment of the state 47–50; shaping of 21–29; threats and consolidation 55–56; *see also* Syrian alliances (general); *individual countries*
system: and choice of alliance 19–20, 28–29; concept of 7; as determinant of foreign policy 21–24; and state goals 14–16, *16*, 28–29; structural and domestic dimensions 18–19; *see also* alliances (theory)
systemic wars 14

Ta'if Agreement (1989) 111, 138
Taliaferro, Jeffery W. 16–17, 152
Al-Tall, Wasfi 72
terminology 6–7
threat evaluation 33–34
threat perception 33–34
Trans-Jordan 48, 49, 71, 72
transnational penetration 34
Tripartite Union negotiations 50, 61, 83, 93
Tripartite United Arab Republic 50, 61
Tsahal 65, 66, 74, 122

Tunbs Islands 94, 95
Turkey 21, 24, 115, 138–139, 142, 144

unipolarity 6, 8, 15, 124, 136
United Arab republic 25, 49, 50, 56, 60, 61, 64, 104; and Iran 92; and Iraq 82; and Jordan 72; and USSR 115
United Nations 52, 62–63, 64, 67, 146
United States 1973 war 66, 67–68; in 2000s 140, 141; and Al-Assad, Hafez 68, 121; and Egypt 66, 67–68; Gulf War 137; and Iran 94, 95, 138; and Iraq 137, 138, 140, 141; and Israel 67–68, 137; and Lebanon 123, 140–141; muscular strategy of 140; and Saudi Arabia 107, 108; as threat to Syria 140–141; and Turkey 142; and USSR 120, 121, 123
unlimited revisionism 3, 14, 19–20, 28, 56, 124, 131, 132–133, 136
USSR/Russia and Syria 114–125; before 1963 115; 1967 war 116–117; during 1963–1970 116–117; 1973 war 66, 118, 119–121; 1980s 121–124; 1990s 139; 2000s 141; and Al-Assad, Hafez 54, 56, 114, 117–125; collapse of 136; deterrent capability of 56; and Egypt 68, 115, 118, 119–120, 124; ideological issues 114, 115, 116, 117, 124, 133; invasion of Afghanistan 108; and Iraq 122, 147; and Israel 54, 68, 116–117, 119, 122, 123, 124, 139; and Jadid, Salah 114, 116–117, 124, 133; and Jordan 122; and Lebanon 120–121, 122, 123; nature of relationship 114–115, 135, 139, 141, 146; and Palestine 120–121, 139; and Saudi Arabia 108; and Syrian civil war 145, 146; Syrian debt 141; Syrian dependency on 123; Treaty of Friendship (1980) 114, 121, 122; and United Arab republic 115; and United States 120, 121, 123; weapons from 95, 96, 118, **120**, 123, 123–124, 146; withdrawal of 136

Wæver, Ole 7, 10
Walt, Stephen 6, 8, 32, 33–37, 42
Waltz, Kenneth 32, 33
Weber, Max 14
Weeks, Jessica 8
Wendt, Alexander 38
Wolfers, Arnold 9, 13

Yeltsin, Boris 139
Yemeni civil war 1962–1970 50–51, 65, 104, 106